GREAT INNINGS

GREAT INNINGS

PETER ROEBUCK

GUILD PUBLISHING
LONDON · NEW YORK · SYDNEY · TORONTO

This edition published 1990 by
Guild Publishing by arrangement with Anaya Publishers Ltd.

Editor: Peter Arnold
Picture Researcher: Caroline Mitchell
Designer: Richard Johnson

FRONTISPIECE *Peter Roebuck*
batting for Somerset

CN 6579

Typeset by Tradespools, Frome, Somerset
Colour reproduction by R.C.S., Leeds
Printed by William Collins, Glasgow.

CONTENTS

I wanted innings which, though exceptional, were not beyond imagining once the man was taken into account. From the innings I sought not gasps of disbelief so much as shouts of admiration.

INTRODUCTION

The task of picking 50 from cricket's bountiful supply of great innings was not easy. Final selections had to be made by an early publishing deadline, and selecting in haste, I have since been repenting in leisure. I find that Greg Chappell, Kim Hughes, Geoff Boycott (whose 180 for Yorkshire against Warwickshire in 1968 was a strong contender), Martin Donnelly, Merchant, Ponsford, Dudley Nourse, Barrington, Turner, Walcott, Woolley and lots of other noble batsmen have been omitted. Conversations with Australians on this matter invariably brought mention of Bill Lawry's resolute 100 on the Lord's ridge in 1961 and yet no room could be found for this either. Profoundly regretted is the absence of Doug Walters' century between tea and the close of play in Perth, a 100 he reached at the last gasp with a six off Bob Willis, not least because Doug is dear to the heart of all my Australian friends, all of whom say they will never speak to me again.

Regretted, too, are the omissions of personal favourites such as Gundappa, Vishwanath, C. K. Nayudu, Majid Khan and Rohan Kanhai, great players who have illuminated the scene with their brilliance. Having ignored them I may never speak to myself again which will bring to my Australian sojourns many of the characteristics of a Trappist monastery.

To be honest I could have picked 50 extraordinary innings played before my eyes. Last November Mark Greatbatch constructed a wonderfully obstinate effort surviving eleven hours of trenchant defence to deny Australia an apparently inevitable victory. Only deadlines prevented this late runner being included. Innings by David Boon against Hadlee in Brisbane, and by Desmond Haynes on a turning track in Sydney also banged loudly at the door.

At Somerset, Viv Richards hit a triple hundred, Ian Botham played sundry violent hands, while in 1980 Sunil Gavaskar hit as dazzling a one-day ton as can ever have been played. Martin Crowe and Steve Waugh have, arguably,

played their best cricket for Somerset, and Crowe's 190 against Leicestershire in 1984 and Waugh's astounding ton at The Oval in 1987 certainly merit acknowledgement, and probably owe their absence to the author's determination to show no favour to innings played by cricketers he cherishes. Finally Jimmy Cook twice batted through the innings for Somerset at Trent Bridge, efforts which combined rare discipline and technical accomplishment. Perhaps I will write of these innings at some other time, for I have been fortunate to witness so many at first hand and, occasionally, from the bowler's end.

Nevertheless this selection, I submit, bears the closest scrutiny. As is plain much weight has been given to triumph over adversity and to performances on an epic scale. Here is to be found a dictionary of good batsmen playing their outstanding innings with a sprinkling of good players rising to a challenge. Throughout I have tried to look inside the man and to find strength. By and large freak innings have been ignored as, for the most part, have dramatic contributions from tail-enders. This quest has not been for impossible triumphs, rather to the contrary. I wanted innings which, though exceptional, were not beyond imagining once the man was taken into account. From the innings I sought not gasps of disbelief so much as shouts of admiration. They are, accordingly, innings about which I wanted to write and, in truth, this is their common commodity.

Naturally the innings fall into separate if occasionally overlapping categories. Sometimes the innings were of intense importance to a nation's cricket, innings played at a time when national pride was at stake. Often these contributions are timely rather than masterly, as with the efforts of Pataudi, Constantine, Chappell, May, Worrell, Hanif and Congdon. Pride and dignity are at the heart of these heroic deeds.

Naturally, too, the greatest batsmen have usually been included, for such a book would appear empty without them. In their cases I have chosen innings of an epic character, innings which are in themselves statements of individuality and authority. Harsh critics might suggest that these vast creatons were more flawed than others yet, sometimes, it is size which defines. Many men can dazzle for a time; few can sustain command for a long period. Bradman, Hammond, Hutton, Headley Hanif and Macartney fit into this department.

Plainly courage is another sort of greatness. To stand up to a fast bowler on a dangerous pitch demands a character of the highest order. By scoring hundreds in the West Indies Border and Gooch won universal respect. By defying bodyline McCabe won his right to immortality, while Bert Sutcliffe and Compton both ignored painful injury to fight back against ferocious attacks.

No less plainly innings of rare skill have their part in cricket's illustrious history. To this day people talk of Hutton and Herbert Sutcliffe batting on a wet pitch, of Harvey stroking a hundred on a spinning wicket in South Africa, of Sobers conquering an impossible surface in Jamaica, of Javed hitting 200 on a spiteful track in Colchester. Nor is it necessary to disguise enjoyment of the hundreds of Ranji, Jardine and D'Oliveira, not least because they were so damnably inconvenient to certain people in high places.

But cricket is a game of excitement too and some batsmen have captured public imagination with exhilarating efforts which turn a game upon its head. No one in England will forget Jessop and Botham rescuing the national side, while Learie Constantine, Clive Lloyd, Kapil Dev and Graeme Pollock have inspired youngsters with their great deeds of derring-do with the bat.

Cricket is, too, a game which like life is touched by tragedy and in which, therefore, sentiment has its part to play. Archie Jackson, Trumper and Colin Milburn did wondrous things in their various ways before, too early, being lost to the game. Two were great batsmen, and one at least a wonderful entertainer, and they could not be excluded.

What else? A terrible weakness is here revealed for innings played by people with stinking headaches or some other infirmity. Tony Greig thought his sickness helped as it made him concentrate, while Dean Jones was eager to talk about his various ailments. Eddie Paynter's rise from a hospital bed is the stuff of romance, the sort of thing lapped up by Hollywood, and it did help to win the Ashes. Besides which Paynter is obviously too lovely a fellow to omit.

Other selections include Cowdrey's brilliant debut and Sunil Gavaskar's careful hundred on a damp pitch in Manchester, his own choice in preference to several more famous efforts, a choice made because it was the turning point of his career. Lawrence Rowe is here too, a star which slid across the firmament. His best moments will shine forever bright. Charlie Macartney's de-struction of Nottingham at Trent Bridge won a place, as did Derek Randall's valiant performance in the Centenary Test match. Destructive efforts by Hick, Fredericks, Greenidge and Viv Richards demanded a position and frankly Barry Richards was simply too good to neglect.

A few others owe their presence here to my interest in them as players. I wanted to write about Shrewsbury, W. G. Grace, Gower and Hill, and to pay tribute to them by picking an innings which most accurately captured their stature.

Despite this defence of my choice there will, of course, be any number of arguments about the selection. Beyond doubt another 50 could just as easily have been chosen. Anyhow I have laid down my hat and there I must live. Final thanks must go to the variety of ladies at Anaya and in the *Sydney Morning Herald* copytaking department who have assisted in producing this work on time, and to Mandy and Caroline, who have patiently endeavoured to decipher my hieroglyphics. Upon reflection my only true regret is that I did not think to include an innings by Lindsay Reeler, the champion woman batsman of the era.

BRILLIANT BATSMANSHIP

IAN BOTHAM

England v Australia, Headingley, 1981
SCORECARD ON PAGE 148

SCORECARD ON PAGE 148

💧 *The amazing Ian Botham had the mourners dancing in the aisles at Headingley last night with the greatest comeback since Lazarus.* 💧
PAT GIBSON

Ian Botham and Mike Brearley, the young vagabond and the grey sage, were at the heart of England's greatest hour. Botham had, on Brearley's recommendation, been appointed captain of England against the West Indies at home and abroad in 1980. A dreadful period for him followed, a period including heavy defeats and a court case. Worse, Ken Barrington, Botham's closest cricketing friend, died in the West Indies, leaving Botham alone in office. England's defeats led senior players to doubt Botham's capacity as captain.

In hindsight, Botham was too immature and too untrained to turn from footslogger to captain in a trice. He wanted to be loved and was full of bravado. Upon returning from the Caribbean Botham was tired and could not summon the energy to lead England with distinction in the first two Tests against Australia in the summer of 1981.

Scores of one and 33 were followed by a pair at Lord's, after which he left the field to an appalled and appalling silence, a reaction from the Long Room which offended his democratic swagger. Botham has never raised his bat at Lord's since that long walk back and vows he never will.

Botham knew he had lost the confidence of his selectors and accordingly resigned his position, minutes before he was to be dismissed. Mike Brearley, the *eminence grise*, was recalled to the colours. And so, with Australia one up, the teams met for a third time that summer of 1981, at Headingley.

Nothing changed for three days save that Botham's form returned. At the close of the first day Australia, after much playing and missing, had scored 203 for three with John Dyson constructing his first Test century. On a crusty pitch this was a powerful position. Botham had dropped two catches and seen one missed off his bowling,

which was not encouraging. Next morning, reacting to being nicknamed 'The Sidestep Queen', Botham took five wickets to end with six for 95 as Australia declared at 401 for nine.

In front of a large crowd eager to see them fight back, England lost wickets, Boycott and Gower falling to unplayable deliveries and others being undone by the movement of Lillee, Lawson and Alderman. Botham took guard on Saturday afternoon with the scoreboard reading 87 for five. Having informed his colleagues that he did not intend to sit upon the slice he duly made hay and hit 50 in 54 balls as England slid to 174, a score which Brearley considered to be satisfactory on such a pitch.

Hughes, reasoning that his bowlers

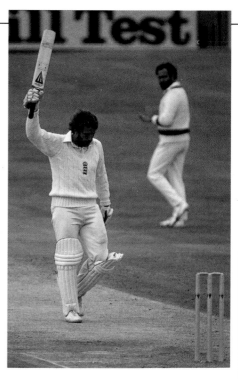

could rest on Sunday, enforced the follow-on and England lost Gooch that Saturday evening and were left to contemplate the hopelessness of their task.

Despite doughty batting from Boycott and Willey, England subsided to 135 for seven with only Botham and the tail left. At least, Botham reflected, he had been right to book out of his hotel that morning. England's plight allowed Botham the luxury of going pell-mell for his shots.

Dilley was his new partner and, with nothing to lose, the pair decided to have a thrash. Swinging hugely, but with God on his side, Botham now murdered Alderman, hitting him through mid-off and extra cover, past Bright at gully and, advancing down the pitch, into the sight screen for a straight six. Dilley was showing surprising form too, thumping drives through the covers as the experienced but weary Australian bowlers overpitched. Hughes had used his men in long spells and was reluctant to introduce Bright, considering his left-arm spinner too gentle for such a pitch. This was a mistake for Botham would certainly have tried to swipe Bright and might have been caught.

This pair added 117 in 80 minutes, including 76 in 44 minutes after tea on Monday. Exhilarated, as if woken from their graves, the crowd cheered and clapped, turning Headingley into an amphitheatre with gladiators doing battle. Everything happened at breakneck speed and Hughes lost control of events. Had his team been united his task would have been easier but the Packer dispute ran deep and emerged again as Australia came under pressure with arguments raging on the field. When Dilley was bowled by Alderman England were 25 ahead. Gambling happily, gambolling happily, England had turned the game and now it was Australian faces which were lined with concern. Another such partnership ... but it

was impossible. Wasn't it?

Chris Old joined Botham who told him: 'We've got 'em going; let's get a good lead' and promptly went berserk. Lawson, in his frustration, bowled two beamers and Botham simply guffawed. With mis-hits and thundering blows he charged towards his hundred which he reached, characteristically, by edging Lawson through the slips for four. Botham acknowledged the ovation which erupted from a crowd as hysterical as any Yorkshire crowd can be, or so people imagined, though the opinion was to be corrected a day later. Botham's hundred was saluted by the English players on their balcony with Brearley urging Botham to keep going.

In desperation Hughes introduced Bright at 309 but it was Lawson who bowled Old, leaving Willis to help Botham in the final 20 minutes. Another 31 runs were added with Willis allowed to face just five balls before the players trooped from the field with England 124 in front and Botham 145. Bob Taylor popped into the visitors' dressing room and was told to go forth and multiply.

Botham cover drives at Headingley – no need to run. It is impossible to imagine that there has ever been a more sudden or emphatic turn-round of fortunes in a Test match or a Test series, or that any innings has ever been played which so captured the public enthusiasm.

He reported back that the tourists were a beaten side. In three hours of carnage the mood of a team, a game, a series and even a country had changed.

Five more runs were added before Willis fell next morning leaving Australia to score 130 to win; and the rest, as they say, is history. Willis took eight wickets to give England an inspiring victory, a victory which was followed by joyful scenes and thousands stood in front of the pavilion cheering for their heroes and waving their Union Jacks.

Letters poured in to the heroes and headlines were written to confirm cricket's return as a sport of the people.

Botham had played an innings of a belligerent power seldom equalled. A fortnight later he did it again, hitting a majestic hundred at Old Trafford. This was a different innings, an innings of sustained mastery, of correct hitting, an innings which could be repeated. At Headingley Botham had been anarchic, violent and inspiring. Headingley was the noblest of them all.

IAN CHAPPELL

Australia v England, The Oval, 1972

SCORECARD ON PAGE 148

Ian Chappell plays a defensive shot to leg at Lord's in the 1975 Test match, a match in which Bob Massie made a brilliant Test debut with 16 wickets. It was Chappell's anxiety to prove that Australia really were a good side, and had not won merely by a freak bowling performance, which gave the succeeding Tests their significance.

It had been a rotten time for Australian cricket. Hammerings from the South Africans and Englishmen had provoked the selectors into dropping Bill Lawry, still an outstanding opening batsman, and giving 27-year-old Ian Chappell the task of rebuilding Australian cricket.

Ian Chappell was by instinct and temperament a hooker, but early on the 1972 tour to England he lost his wicket time and again to the shot. In Manchester, where the vital first Test was played, Chappell was out twice hooking, and Australia lost. Chappell stood accused of setting a bad example with his reckless batting. It was that time of challenge when a captain, by his actions, either grows or subsides in front of his men.

Before the second Test Chappell was castigated in the newspapers as a fool walking willingly into a trap. His grandmother, who had not hitherto been accredited with any profound understanding of cricket, wrote to tell him to throw the shot on a scrap heap. Just before he went in to bat in the second Test at Lord's Ken Barrington, a more likely source of useful information, also advised Chappell to stop hooking. This was the last straw. Chappell decided to hook and be damned, and scored 56 before losing his wicket.

Thanks to Massie's 16 for 137 and Greg Chappell's majestic 131, the series was levelled. Ian Chappell considered that 56 to be the turning point of his captaincy career because he had been brave enough to be true to himself.

A draw in Nottingham and a devastating defeat in Leeds meant England had held the Ashes and in their disappointment Australia could easily have packed their bags for home, in mind if not in body. Chappell was having none of this, for he was convinced that his team was strong, and urgently needed a victory so that others would believe him.

Doug Walters was dropped for the final Test whereupon he stood on a chair in the dressing-room and told his comrades to fight to the end. Chappell knew, though, it was a time for deeds and not words. As it turned out, the Oval Test was one of the greatest ever played and until the sixth afternoon it twisted and turned like a coiled snake.

England won the toss and, batting first, scored 284. Australia's reply stood at 34 for two when Greg Chappell joined his brother. Over the years in school, club and state cricket these brothers of contrasting technique and similar, ruthless temperament had only once added 100 runs.

Never had Australia needed more desperately a fraternal partnership. Snow was in aggressive mood and, using a white and bouncy pitch ideal for Test cricket, at once set about bouncing the brothers. Ian Chappell's respect for Snow did not demand subservience and he hooked at every opportunity, and found the shot easier to play on this firm, almost Antipodean pitch.

As the partnership built, Greg clipping to leg and Ian punching to off, Illingworth rested his fast men and introduced Underwood. This was a niggardly England attack in which Underwood was the meanest of all. Chappell could not use his feet, finding Underwood too fast, and so searched for another tactic to disrupt his enemy. Whenever Underwood pitched wide Ian Chappell swept, much to the bowler's irritation. Years later when it emerged that these fierce rivals had signed for Packer, they had a beer and Chappell joked: 'Bet you thought you'd seen the last of that broom!'

Despite Illingworth's bowling changes Australia advanced with authority. Just before tea, Ian Chappell reached 50, half-an-hour after his brother, who was dominating the strike. Slowly, carefully, and yet aggressively the score mounted until the brothers

were both approaching their hundreds. Ted Dexter had placed a hefty bet upon them scoring tons and stood to win £1,200 if they did so. Greg reached his target first, clipping another run through the leg side. No more than a word and a pat on the back passed between the brothers. Then Ian, moving down the pitch to drive Illingworth, misread the floater and edged to slip where, until recently, a man had been positioned all day. With the ball skidding off to the boundary Chappell raised his bat and lifted his cap to acknowledge warm applause from a crowd which knew Australia had been unlucky at Leeds, where a fungus called fuserium had turned the pitch into the stuff of Underwood's dreams. Chappell had led this fight back by example. It was a rousing innings, one calculated to take Australian cricket towards a fresh and promising day. Had Chappell failed Australia must have lost and years may have passed before his team dominated Test cricket. This day at the Oval was, for Chappell and his team, a turning point. Neither the hooking debate, nor the dreadful disappointment at Headingley had stopped Chappell and his men forming themselves into a tough, raw and defiant side.

Chappell finally fell to another rumbustious hook, Snow running in to take a fine catch at long leg. He had scored 118 and added 201 with his brother, who considers his 100 to be his outstanding Test innings.

Few innings have had as strong a sense of mission as this one by Chappell. It was an innings of will and of leadership; by continuing to hook and by constructing this hundred at a critical time Chappell had informed his men of his approach to the game and his expectations of them. It helped win the match both in itself and in the example it set. Only a feeble character could fail to find inspiration in so determined a leader.

TOP *Short leg ducks as Chappell sweeps to leg at Lord's in 1975.*
ABOVE *Knott behind the stumps,*

Roope at slip, as Chappell chips another delivery to leg in his Oval innings.

LEARIE CONSTANTINE

West Indies v Middlesex, Lord's, 1928
SCORECARD ON PAGE 149

Historian Gerald Howat relates that Learie Constantine was at the quayside in Port-of-Spain in 1919 when the survivors of the 1,500 men who had served in the West Indian regiment in the First World War returned. Twenty years later war broke out once more and this time Constantine was on an English dockside waving goodbye to the 1939 West Indian touring party as they went home. Between those years, and in his work thereafter Constantine proved himself to be a great man and a cricketer capable of occasional breathtaking efforts. Instinctive, imaginative, intelligent, Constantine lacked the application to be consistently magnificent, but he was outstanding at Lord's in 1928.

Lebrun, his father, was a foreman on a cotton plantation. The son of a slave, Lebrun toured England in 1900 and scored the first hundred in the mother country by a West Indian batsman. The game ran in the family. His mother could keep wicket, Learie thought, 'about as well as a Test 'keeper and my sister had as much aptitude for batting as I had'. His uncles were also fine cricketers. When the children were small they played constantly, using oranges for balls and coconut branches for bats. Curious pitches taught Learie to watch the ball and to react to it. And the family penchant for throwing crockery at each other improved his catching. Or so, at any rate, he said.

In any event the extrovert, bright Constantine was always a force in West Indian cricket. With George John as his fast bowling partner, Learie toured England in 1923. No Tests were played and Constantine recalled the tour mainly for its miserable weather, with chilly and damp fields and chilly and damp dressing rooms.

MCC toured the West Indies in 1926 and, the tour being a success despite Hammond's grave illness, a Test tour of England was arranged for 1928. It was on this tour that Constantine gave a display that established the standing of West Indian cricket and forced his own inclusion in the annals of folklore.

The 1928 tour was going badly. The crowds were poor and the weather dreadful. Constantine was unfit but the manager begged him to play against Middlesex at Lord's. Another heavy defeat might jeopardise the very future of Caribbean cricket. And with Headley incredibly left behind, the West Indians depended upon the effervescent, unpredictable all-rounder.

As if in sympathy the weather relented and the game began in baking sunshine. Without undue difficulty Middlesex reached 352 for six declared, with a hundred not out from Patsy Hendren. Their opponents duly collapsed and stood, at 79 for five, in danger of following on. Neville Cardus saw one West

Learie Constantine in the nets, showing his long reach as he comes forward to drive.

WEST INDIES 1928
*L.N.Constantine   F.R.Martin   E.A.Rae   J.A.Small   J.M.Neblett   H.C.Griffith   W.H.St.Hill   E.L.Bartlett
C.R.Browne   C.V.Wright   R.K.Nunes   G.Challenor   M.P.Fernandes*

The West Indian team in 1928, the first to play Tests. Back, left to right: L. N. Constantine, F. R. Martin (Constantine's partner throughout his first innings at Lord's), E. A. Rae, J. A. Small, J. M. Neblett, H. C. Griffith, W. H. St Hill, E. L. Bartlett. Front, seated: C. R. Browne, C. V. Wright, R. K. Nunes, G. Challenor, M. P. Fernandez (who partnered Constantine throughout his second innings). It is remarkable that in the first innings Constantine scored 37 per cent of his side's runs, and in the second innings nearly 40 per cent, yet each time he batted at number seven, and his innings were so fast that no wicket fell at the other end in either case!

Indian, dressed up to the nines for his day at Lord's, sitting disconsolately and alone near the pavilion. He wore a light grey frock-coat, striped trousers, a brilliantly spotted neckerchief, glossy shoes, white spats and a grey topper. But no smile.

Constantine took guard. In an hour he scored 86, an innings of ferocious driving, a primitive onslaught, said Cardus, savage in its destruction. He reached 50 in 18 minutes from 22 balls. Finding himself on 49, he tickled a single to fine-leg – the first single of his innings. His batting was a law unto itself. Shots cannoned onto boundary walls, or scythed through gaps in the field. It was the batting of a man on fire. At the other end F. R. Martin scored 11 while Constantine scored 86. C. G. Macartney, the Australian, was on holiday with his wife and saw the innings. He said Constantine was the hardest hitter he'd seen. For our glum West Indian it was too much. Far away at the Nursery End sat a group of West Indians rejoicing at the typhoon before them. Smiling hugely, the hitherto despondent spectator ran at full pelt around the boundary yelling, 'I'se comin' to join you boys, I'se comin'.'

A cricketer of inspiration, Constantine now had the bit between his teeth. On first innings, West Indies were 122 behind. Hurtling in from his short run, mixing bumpers with a clever googly, bowling with his sleeves rolled down and his cap still on top of his short-clipped hair, Constantine swept Middlesex aside, taking seven for 57, as the

county crashed for 136. By now his performance was of heroic proportions. And there was a game on.

Nor was Constantine done with yet. His team needed 259 to win. Again they slid, this time to 121 for five. Once more Constantine entered the fray: 138 to get, 90 minutes to get them in. He was cheered all the way to the wicket. Within an hour he hit 103 out of 133, leaving West Indies with five to get, which they did. His blows included one straight drive so uncompromising that J. W. Hearne, the bowler, could not avoid it. He did not play again that year.

Constantine simply exploded upon the match with cricket of fury; he was an irresistible force. His fielding was brilliant, he clean bowled five men with the ball, twice splitting stumps asunder, and he simply smashed respected county bowling all around Lord's.

Constantine had been awesome, brutal, possessed. The members in the pavilion and the entire Lord's crowd stood to him as he walked off. They cheered again in front of the pavilion at the end.

It was the performance of a lifetime. The West Indians lost the two Tests, but it was plain that West Indian cricket had arrived. Constantine brooked no argument.

Constantine grew in stature off the field as West Indian cricket rose upon it. Here, too, he would not compromise. In 1944 he was awarded damages from Imperial Hotels, London, who had refused to accommodate him because he was black. Constantine became an MP in Trinidad's first democratically elected Parliament after Independence in 1962 and was duly appointed Minister of Works. He was knighted in 1962, made a Life Peer in 1969 and served as a Governor of the BBC. To his people he showed what could be done, a message that, when the spirit caught, ran out loud and clear from his deeds upon the field. Lord's in 1928 was the beginning.

COLIN COWDREY

England v Australia, Melbourne, 1954–55

SCORECARD ON PAGE 149

ABOVE *Colin Cowdrey*

BELOW *The touring party leaving for Australia on 16 September 1954 on board the ss* Orsova *at Tilbury. Cowdrey is on the right of those crouching, with Evans half stooping to talk to him.*

Colin Cowdrey played in 114 Tests, scoring 7,624 runs and hitting 22 hundreds, an England record he shares with Geoffrey Boycott and Walter Hammond. His record is magnificent, his durability at Test level reaches far beyond Ted Dexter and Peter May, and yet, and yet. Every summation of Cowdrey's career is accompanied by that 'and yet'.

He was born in Bangalore where his father was a tea-planter, and was destined from the start for a life in cricket. Baptised with the initials MCC, he had 'barely eaten my first meal on earth before my father wrote off to friends in England asking them to put my name down for MCC membership'.

A private school education in time led to entry to Oxford University as Cowdrey's life moved serenely along an apparently pre-determined path. Impeccably correct in manner and in technique, if lacking a certain rumbustiousness in both, Cowdrey duly took his blue and was, as a 22-year-old undergraduate at Oxford University, called upon to take a long vacation in the form of an MCC tour to Australia.

Further, he was picked in front of Graveney and Wilson for the first Test of the series and, though England lost heavily, his debut was satisfactory (40 and 10). He retained his place for the second Test, which England won, but did not acquit himself well. In terms of runs he did not disgrace himself, hitting 23 and 54, but he threw away his wicket in the second innings with a slog off Benaud which Ron Archer caught at mid-on. It was a thoroughly immature shot and it provoked George Duckworth, a baggage man whose warm Lancastrian humour Cowdrey greatly enjoyed, to grunt upon seeing Cowdrey return from Church on the lay day: 'I should think you had a lot to tell 'im.'

So England arrived at the huge MCG for the traditional New Year Test with the series all square. Choosing to bat first before 70,000 spectators upon winning the toss, fearing the pitch might crack later, England were at once in trouble. Edrich was caught off Miller, and May dismissed for a duck by Lindwall which brought Cowdrey to the

Cowdrey off-drives Lindwall during his innings of 102 at Melbourne on 31 December 1954. Miller is at first slip and Langley behind the stumps.

crease to face the music. Surrounded by slips and short legs, he quickly hit three boundaries, two through leg gully, one past fourth slip, none of them convincing. But Hutton and Compton, last of the specialist batsmen, were soon out and Bailey joined Cowdrey at 41 for four (it had been 25 for four in the first Test at Brisbane).

Following his father's counsel Cowdrey had been concentrating upon watching the seam on the ball, reducing his backlift, and forgetting everything else. Those boundaries had taken him through his early nerves, greatly to his relief for at 22, as at 42, Cowdrey counted his runs from 1 to 3 to 5, 7, 10 and 11. To score five was enough to open a bottle of champagne for it meant abject failure had been avoided once more. A cricketer's insecurity should never be under-estimated. Encouragingly, the pitch was beginning to dry and the batsmen knew if they could last

till lunch a revival might be effected.

Survive they did. After lunch it was a different game. Miller was rested, Lindwall could find nothing more and it was left to Ron Archer's medium pace and Bill Johnston's springy bounce to break the partnership. Bailey fell for 30 at 115 but Cowdrey carried on, with his leisurely driving and secure back play. Godfrey Evans joined him, with Australia still pressing hard, and the MCG shouting for a wicket. Like Compton, Evans batted without a thigh pad but he was a game cricketer and he lent his youthful county colleague support as England fought back.

John Woodcock described Cowdrey: 'I can see him now driving England out of trouble in the classical manner, on a green wicket with Keith Miller's mane escaping in all directions.'

Then, as was to be his wont, Cowdrey entirely lost his way and for 40 minutes did not score. He'd reached 56, sailed to it as if he were an ocean liner moving massively through quiet seas, not a student facing a snarling tiger. Then, suddenly the runs dried up.

Australia had studied Cowdrey and had decided to apply a brake. They set a tight defensive field and put their best fielder, Neil Harvey, in a vital position blocking singles. Cowdrey hit several screaming shots and each was stopped. Cowdrey was flummoxed.

Utterly untutored in playing an innings though superb at playing every shot correctly, he knew nothing of placing singles. It was mid-afternoon and now Cowdrey was facing a crisis. In Sydney he'd lost his wicket trying to clear the field. Clearly the Australians were daring him to do it again.

Cowdrey could find no answer. Instead he waited upon Ian Johnson who was curling his gentle spinners away in the breeze, vowing to have a crack at anything tossed up. So he did. This time fortune smiled and he cleared mid-on by inches.

Having flirted with fate, Cowdrey now accelerated smoothly towards his first Test hundred. He reached 97 with a hook off Archer and then pushed a back foot shot wide of mid-on and ran like blazes. Around him he heard clapping as he ran one, a rising cheer as he scampered a second and a veritable roar as he turned for a third. Cowdrey was accorded a standing ovation. His hundred had been scored out of only 158 and had taken four hours. The youngster had sustained his team, given them hope, answered the call at a critical time.

To his immense disappointment he soon fell, a delivery from Johnson float-ing wide, pitching in some footholds and perversely spinning back between his pads to hit his leg stump. England were all out for 191, not much of a total. But far better than appeared probable when Compton was out.

England won the Test, and the series. Perhaps it was Cowdrey's finest hour. Life can be so simple for a rising player from whom runs are hoped for rather than expected. In his pomp Cowdrey was not to be the brilliant, composed, audacious player who took on the Australians that day in Melbourne but a heavier figure in whom, as Alan Ross has said, 'the jester and the monk share a gravity of vocation'.

⑥ I cannot think of a great player harder to coax into an awareness of his reserves. At his best he was a dolphin among minnows, gambolling between the green and the blue. Less good he seemed imprisoned by some internal gaoler. ⑨
ALAN ROSS

A typical weighty Cowdrey stroke as he leans into a square drive. Solidity and gravity were the hallmarks of the later Cowdrey. At his best, every movement was correct, every shot under control.

SUNIL GAVASKAR

India v England, Old Trafford, 1974
SCORECARD ON PAGE 150

Choosing one innings from the dazzling array played by Sunil Gavaskar is no easy task. Scyld Berry pointed unerringly towards Gavaskar's audacious, record-equalling 121 made in 94 balls against the full fury of the West Indian pace bowlers at New Delhi in 1983–84. Ravi Shastri spoke of

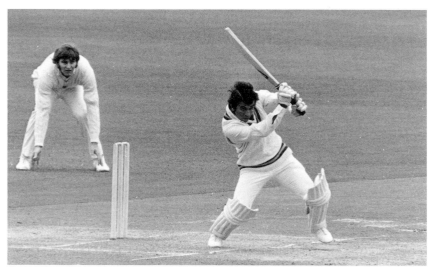

Gavaskar completes a back-foot cover drive during his innings at Old Trafford in 1974. Old is at forward short leg.

OPPOSITE *Gavaskar completes a square cut. Although a master of defence, Gavaskar played all the attacking shots with a wristy power.*

Sunil's unbeaten 236 later in the series as: 'Cool and ruthless, he ground them into the dust.'

Sir Leonard Hutton, apparently, regards Gavaskar's extraordinary 221 when India had been asked to chase 438 at the Oval in 1979 as one of the greatest innings he had seen. Michael Manly, no less, has praised Gavaskar's spellbinding debut in the Caribbean in 1971. For my part I saw Gavaskar play a majestic innings for Somerset and, like Asif Iqbal and Shastri, salute Gavaskar as the outstanding batsman of the post-war period.

Any of these innings, and a dozen others could have been picked for inclusion here. A chance encounter on an aeroplane gave me the opportunity of asking Gavaskar himself to nominate his finest innings. His choice, Old Trafford 1974, was surprising.

Gavaskar's rise had been meteoric.

Born in 1949 into a cricketing family (his uncle, Madhar Mantri, kept wicket for India), Sunil broke records at school, University and Ranji trophy level, yet was a surprise choice to go to the West Indies in 1970–71. He scored 774 runs in this series at an average of 159.8.

For three years thereafter Gavaskar struggled to carry the burden of his new found reputation. Every time he batted it was as if 900 million Indians were depending upon him. By the time he returned to England in 1974 the Indian selectors were growing impatient.

England had prepared a green wicket for the Old Trafford Test. Denness batted first upon winning the toss and was able to declare at 328 for nine. Throughout the innings the weather had been grumpy, with intermittent drizzle halting play and freshening the pitch. Cold gusts of wind bit through the thick sweaters of the forlorn Indians.

Now Gavaskar had to lead India's reply. He lost his opening partner Solkar that second evening, and early next morning nightwatchman Venkat and skipper Wadekar were dismissed. As Vishwanath joined his cousin India were 32 for three and urgently in need of a brave partnership.

Gavaskar was on song. In his pomp he would hoard runs, darting twos, punching singles, occasionally cracking mercilessly through the leg-side. No-one ever bowled at Gavaskar's pads, not deliberately anyhow. Here he settled in, played late, waited for the ball, leaving as many as possible.

England bowled well, Willis pounding balls in short, rearing them at Gavaskar's chin, Hendrick and Old spitting away at his off-stump, giving nothing away, probing for a flaw or a mistake. Slowly Gavaskar and Viswanath collected runs, punishing anything wayward, finding gaps in Denness' field. With so stubborn a partnership forming

Gavaskar in the white sun hat which he preferred in the field and sometimes when batting, driving through the covers in a World Cup match against Zimbabwe in 1983.

My greatest innings was my 101 at Old Trafford in 1974. Since doing well in the West Indies I had not hit a hundred in three years and my Test career was in jeopardy. I had to score runs. The pitch in Manchester was green and damp, and England had a strong attack in Willis, Hendrick, Old, Underwood and Greig. Once I took a century off them on such a wicket I knew I belonged.

SUNIL GAVASKAR

England turned to spin, and to his delight Underwood at once won some purchase from the soft pitch, though he did not enjoy bowling to Gavaskar and Viswanath. Both were superb through midwicket, and yet could cut anything drifting wide. There was little room for error against these hawk-eyed and wristy cricketers. Finally, at 105, Viswanath was beaten and bowled by Underwood. Denness at once recalled Willis for a vulnerable Patel and dangerous Engineer. Both fell quickly. Madan Lal followed and India stood in peril at 143 for seven with only the negligible Bedi and Chandra, neither destined to score a run in this game, still in the hutch.

Now Abid Ali joined Gavaskar who had, to his surprise, just reached his 50, a milestone acknowledged by a warm crowd. Abid Ali resisted gamely and Gavaskar made no effort to protect him. Staying in on this pitch against this bowling was hard enough. He could not bat for his partner too.

Batting without risk, giving no chances, Gavaskar continued to pit his inpenetrable defensive technique against England's top bowlers in conditions entirely in sympathy with them. Ever more he hardened his will, batting with a ferocious intensity which only Border and Crowe of modern batsmen could approach. It was as if he were on a different planet from everyone else.

Gavaskar's greatest worry, in fact, was that he had split his trousers. During the tea interval he tried to change them but Wadekar, his skipper, said 'nothing doing', so Gavaskar had to smile at Greig's innocent question as to whether air-conditioning was a regular feature in Indian trousers.

Unperturbed, immoveable, sand turned into stone, Gavaskar duly faced Underwood once more, and seeing one pitching short, he lay back and cut behind point for three. At once the crowd cheered and hundreds invaded the pitch. Gavaskar had no idea he was so close to his century, and tried in vain to avoid his supporters, and the gifts tradition demanded they press into a hero's hand. Play was interupted for five minutes, as these flag-waving supporters expressed their joy. Gavaskar took time to regain command of his mind and then settled back into his disciplined easy rhythm, allowing the fiercest waves to beat upon the rocks of his defiance.

He could be there still. It wasn't to be. Abid Ali, by reputation an optimistic runner, once more dropped a ball on his toes and darted off for a single. Springing from midwicket Denness picked up the ball and threw down the wicket. Gavaskar thought he was home but the umpire did not and that was that.

Despite more second-innings resistance from Gavaskar (58) and Viswanath (50) India lost the Test with 15 overs left. They lost the series too but could find succour in the confirmation that Sunil Gavaskar was not a one-series wonder. Far more importantly, Gavaskar himself knew it to be true. He wasn't a kitten, he was a tiger!

DAVID GOWER

England v Pakistan, Faisalabad, 1983–84

SCORECARD ON PAGE 150

Gower batting in India. A swivel on the left leg, and Gower swings the ball to the boundary with ten per cent strength and 90 per cent lazy timing.

Circumstance is often the hand-maiden of great deeds. David Gower has played many fluent innings for his country, innings to provoke a purr even from a cat not particularly fond of the game, yet his greatest effort, in some opinions at any rate, was a cautious hundred he made on a dead pitch in Faisalabad in 1983–84.

For years England had depended on Willis and Botham to win Test matches and now this pair was in decline. Botham's knees had collapsed and, bedevilled by scandal, he was going home for an exploratory operation. Willis was ill. England's recent tour of New Zealand had been blighted by dramatic tales of drug taking and other assorted dirty linen washed in public by an overwrought press. To top it off Pakistan had won the first Test match, beating England on their own soil for the first time. England had fought gamely in Karachi, Gower scoring 58 and 57, before losing a low-scoring match by three wickets. It was a Test played in a cauldron, as thousands of soldiers and policemen wedged themselves between players and protesting students, who were herded like cattle between iron fences upon which barbed wire had been laid. The dressing rooms had been moved to a safer part of the ground. Seldom can England cricketers have been in more urgent need of uplift.

It was not an opportune moment to succeed to the England captaincy yet because Willis fell ill this was the time that greatness was thrust upon David Gower.

Gower's life to date had led unerringly to this hour. Hailing from an ancient family of naval officers, lawyers and diplomats, whose most eminent member was Admiral Sir Erasmus Gower, Governor and Commander-in-Chief of Newfoundland in 1814, and whose motto was: 'You can break but not bend us', Gower had been raised in Tanganyika and educated in England's most proper schools before a skirmish with university education had failed to ignite a spark and, instead, propelled Gower towards a career in cricket.

Few thought Gower capable of strong captaincy. Too gentle, they scoffed, too dreamy. He had been appointed because he so closely fulfilled those

attributes commonly associated in England with leadership rather than through any proven qualities.

Faisalabad was not a city calculated to restore English morale; a polluted city full of textile factories, it was noisy and hot. Nor was Gower's diminishing squad in good fettle. They had brought water and food from Lahore and yet were still sick. Worst, he lost the toss and as his team took the field they drew comparisons with Napoleon's army in retreat from Moscow. Dilley's first over on a docile pitch included six no balls. Within minutes critics were confidently predicting that Pakistan would bat for a week. Actually they declared at 449 for eight at tea on the second day.

England's batting order was determined by health for now, ironically, it was the batsmen who were unwell. In the pavilion Gower padded and unpadded depending upon how he felt. There was an hour to play on the second day when, still unwell, he went out to join Randall. Zaheer declined to take the new ball and Gower, summoning his strength, kept the spinners at bay to reach nine not out as England went to the close at 233 for three.

❨ Seven weeks ago the bus carrying the England cricket team from Lahore to Faisalabad broke down. So, too, did their captain Bob Willis, thanks to some viral fever. And shortly afterwards he left Pakistan for home, leaving in charge a blond, curly-haired young man not yet 27 years of age, with intense pale eyes. ❩
SCYLD BERRY

Gower pulls between square leg and midwicket on a tour of India, where he has acquitted himself well.

Gower had seldom to date shown an inclination to play a long defensive innings and yet this was England's need now. Victory was impossible and morale at a low ebb. Gower had to construct a careful Test innings. Randall fell quickly on the third morning and Fowler joined Gower. Qadir was a handful,

A typical Gower scoring shot. He has just completed a half-cut, half-slash through gully, a shot which scores him many runs, but for which he is criticised whenever it costs him his wicket.

specially for Fowler.

Gower was less inhibited, though on 37 he appeared lucky to survive an appeal for a catch to silly point as he pushed forward to Qadir, who was to bowl 27 successive overs. Qadir's duel with Gower enchanted the crowd of 18,000, who were happy with the exchanges and yet strangely muted.

Lunch lasted 90 minutes to accommodate Muslim prayers. Fowler's were

unanswered and after lunch, harassed by the leg spin of Wasim Raja and Qadir he had a hit at the former and was caught by long off with the score on 361. Bob Taylor popped a catch to short mid-off without the score being increased, leaving Gower with Marks as his main support.

After tea Sarfraz returned, swinging the old ball as was his custom and so managing to inject life into the play. But Gower and Marks stood defiant and on 74 Gower became the 13th Englishman to score 4,000 Test runs, and before long he had reached his eighth Test hundred, so becoming the first England captain to score a century since Tony Greig at Calcutta in 1976–77.

Apart from one loud appeal Gower had made no mistakes and though he was exhausted as he left the field he had won the respect of his ailing teammates. Few had thought he could play so slow an innings in his team's interest.

England batted until lunch on the final day, by which time Gower was out, stumped off Mudassar at 528. He had spent 426 minutes at the crease for his 152, and faced 318 balls, hitting 16 of them to the boundary. Vic Marks fell for 83 and though England took three early wickets Pakistan held on for a draw.

Gower went on to score an unbeaten 173 in the Lahore Test which began two days later as England vainly tried to level the series. This, too was an innings of graft which, though it ended in a flourish, embraced seven hours at the crease. Gower had proven himself to his men and to his critics and appeared certain to rise to greatness.

It was not to be, or not yet anyhow. Perhaps, after all, it was easier to take over at such a tormented time. For once everyone was behind him and he took no worries to the crease with him. At home things were never so simple and while Gower did rule, his was a troubled reign.

GORDON GREENIDGE

West Indies v England, Lord's, 1984

SCORECARD ON PAGE 151

By July 1984 Test series against the West Indies had been a constant nightmare for England captains, selectors and supporters. So powerful were Lloyd's team, so merciless in their destruction that they commonly left a trail of devastation from which it took England years to recover.

Greenidge drives high over midwicket at Lord's in 1976. Knott is the wicket-keeper and Old is at slip. In this series Greenidge established himself as West Indies' opener.

Captains were sacked, rebel tours organised and confidence lost in authority as England desperately juggled their slim resources in search of a combination capable of sustaining a challenge against this formidable foe.

Any hopes England nourished for the 1984 series were quickly shattered in Birmingham where, thanks to fierce and highly skilled fast bowling and to rampant batting from Gomes (143), Richards (117) and a vigorously wagging tail, the West Indies won by an innings and 180 runs, and this despite their captain, Clive Lloyd, being hit on the head and forced to stay in hospital for several days suffering from blurred vision. Could England fight back in the second Test at Lord's, or were they doomed to a summer of discontent? Another humiliation, and morale would surely collapse.

Remarkably England played with immense fortitude and by the close of play on the fourth day a surprise victory was being predicted, and with it the enticing prospect of a tight series. England reached 286 in their first innings, whereupon Botham, recalling days of glory in a manner beyond all expectations, took eight for 103, bowling with a pace and a fire long since presumed extinguished.

West Indies subsided to 245, and England, recovering from a clatter of early wickets, strode towards 300, Lamb striking 110 and Botham, with 81, nearly reaching his first hundred against the West Indies. Gower was widely condemned as feeble-hearted when he declined to declare his innings closed that fourth night. In fact, he did not declare at once next morning either, for he had harsh experience of these West Indians and was not inclined to pin his faith upon a second collapse. Accordingly Gower did not declare until Pringle fell leg before to Garner, leaving Lloyd's team to chase 342 runs at over a run a minute. In the dressing room Botham doubted the wisdom of declaring at all.

Perhaps sensing that England were running scared, Greenidge and Haynes set about their task with a will, playing a couple of maidens and then punishing Botham, Pringle and Foster while playing Willis with respect. Greenidge had scored only 84 runs in his previous six innings against England and he felt he owed them a few. By now the pitch was good, its previous friendliness towards pace bowlers removed by a cool sun, which sucked away its green tinge.

With the score 57 after 15 overs, England had a stroke of luck, running out Desmond Haynes, who played

A typical Greenidge shot, the powerful square drive/cut. Almost England's last chance at Lord's in 1984 disappeared when Lamb failed to cling on to one such fierce hit.

Greenidge hooks mightily from what looks to have been a straight ball.

Pringle to Lamb at square leg and set off for a single. Sent back by an alarmed Greenidge, he was beaten by Lamb's underarm return which hit the stumps. For a time English spirits rose. They could scarcely suspect that this would be their solitary wicket this demoralising day.

At lunch the West Indians were 82 for one off 20 overs with Greenidge, deep in his crease on the back foot and yet reaching further forward to drive than any contemporary batsman, already in stentorian command. West Indies were moving at a run a minute and needed 260 to win in four hours.

Soon after lunch, off Foster's second ball in fact, Gomes was dropped at slip by Pringle, who injured his thumb trying for the catch and was prevented thereafter from bowling at his best. This was the decisive moment, for soon Gomes was tucking the ball neatly off his pads while his partner thundered like an offended deity. Between lunch and tea this pair added 132 in a miserable 25 overs, for England were desperately slowing their over rate. On 79 Greenidge, cutting fiercely, slashed a catch to Lamb at point. It was barely a chance, really, but England were in terrible trouble and Lamb's miss bit deep into their morale, for Greenidge had already hit two boundaries in that over. In their hearts England were in retreat, stiffening themselves for further blows. They had merely plucked the beard of this tyrannical enemy.

By tea Gower had tried all his bowlers and found Foster out of sorts, Pringle injured, Willis tiring and Botham, who had already done so much in the game, erratic. Gower persisted with two slips and a gully, believing that a wicket must, sooner or later, fall, aggression which was not, in the event, rewarded.

With scarcely a blink Greenidge strode past his 100 and, on 110, gave England one last chance of redemption, edging Willis, easily England's best bowler, to Botham at first slip, who dropped an awkward catch.

For the rest, it was murder. Botham's three overs after tea cost 29 runs and Greenidge's awesome assault continued as he struck boundaries through point, mid-off and square-leg, shots played with a dreadful power. Greenidge was to end with 29 fours and two sixes and after Botham's first over only Willis was able to bowl a maiden to him. From a position of apparent command England had, within hours, been routed; worse, they had felt powerless to do anything about it.

Needing only 129 after tea, the West Indians cantered home against a beaten side. By the time the final 20 overs began they needed only 43 to win, a task they managed with 11 overs to spare.

Gomes, running adroitly, the perfect foil, had scored 92 and Greenidge an unbeaten 214. His innings was the third highest ever recorded in a Lord's Test, being surpassed only by Wally Hammond and Donald Bradman. West Indies had chased 342 on the final afternoon and won easily without Viv Richards or Clive Lloyd being called upon to bat. As England left the field, footsore and thoroughly beaten, they must have been close to despair.

With his merciless batting Greenidge had, in four hours' work, destroyed England's last hope. Overnight they dreamt of victory, now they tasted the ashes of defeat. Seldom has any attack been so brutally torn to pieces; seldom has any team had its hopes so conclusively crushed. Broken, England slumped to heavy defeats in all three remaining Test matches, defeats which continued without interruption in 1985–86 and at home in 1988. At Lord's in 1984 Greenidge had slaughtered England's bowling, and the morale of English cricket too. Few innings can have had greater destructive force.

TONY GREIG

England v India, Calcutta, 1976–77

SCORECARD ON PAGE 151

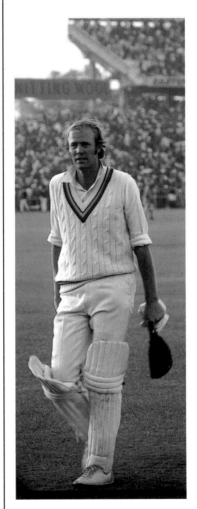

Tony Greig leaving the field at Calcutta after his century which captivated the Indian fans.

England had not won in India since 1933 when, under Jardine, they beat an inexperienced, even awed, Indian side 2–0. Howard (1951–52), leading a weak team, Dexter (1961–62) and Lewis (1972–73) had failed. Now England's new captain, Tony Greig, was charged with the responsibility of treading where many angels had feared to tread.

With typical pragmatism, Greig had picked players for their skill against spin. Barlow, a left-hander, might disturb the captivating spells woven by Bedi, Prasanna and Chandra, and with his nimble footwork and general cussedness Tolchard could score runs.

England's campaign began well with a win in New Delhi, only their fifth victory in 24 Tests on the sub-continent. Dennis Amiss contributed a skilful 179 in 508 minutes of determined batting, an innings played with a high temperature, an early sign of collective determination. Then John Lever, using a rogue ball, or greasing it with Vaseline according to your viewpoint, took seven for 46 and India were beaten.

Greig was not surprised, upon arriving for the second Test to be played at Eden Gardens in Calcutta, a ground built a hundred years earlier on swamp land by the Eden sisters, to find men hard at work scrubbing the pitch. India, evidently, intended to use their superiority in spin to level the series. Greig knew that this Test would be decisive, and knew that England had never won at Eden Gardens, though often the mists lurking over the nearby Hooghly River offered generous swing. Greig was determined to correct this gap in the records.

As usual, Calcutta teemed with life as play began. England's short bus trip had taken them through tens of thousands of people milling cheerfully outside the gates, hoping to find a ticket. As usual, supporters had bought tickets as a syndicate and used straws to determine their allocation. Entry for the final day, the dénouement, was regarded as the greatest prize.

Policemen packed on to the England bus, for security reasons they said, but really to take them inside the coliseum. Many, lathis in hand, hung on to the bus as it threaded through the masses.

Bedi won the toss but his batsmen frittered away this initial advantage and India were all out as lunch approached on the second day. With the ball already turning sharply, England batted stubbornly to reach 136 for four by the close.

Tony Greig was already 19 not out. He had announced his arrival at the crease with a straight driven four off Chandra, a shot which, to his horror, was lifted and nearly caught. Summoning his greatest powers, determined to crush the opposition, Greig immediately eliminated the drive from his repertoire. No risks were to be taken, and though he once hoisted a long hop for six, he concentrated upon using his pads to frustrate the spinners and protect his wicket. Nothing was to threaten a long tenure of the crease.

England needed a big innings from Greig because the ball was fizzing, dipping and spitting, and batting last would be difficult. Only with discipline could runs be scored and Greig, usually so aggressive, knew he must adapt or perish.

Unfortunately overnight he was sick, sweating with a fever which saturated his bed sheets; every hour he called for Bernard Thomas to provide medicine and he hardly slept a wink. Still feeling drowsy and ill, warming his shivering body with sweaters, Greig resumed his innings next morning. Throughout a day some considered tedious, others magnificent, a day on which 86 overs were bowled for 149 runs, Greig defied the spinners, adding 75 runs to his tally. As ever the ground was seething with noisy humanity and the extrovert, opportunistic Greig turned this to his advantage. Being a tall, blond South African, he was sensitive to charges of prejudice and wanted to be popular. For its part the crowd was astonished by the size and majesty of this freakish figure. Upon a firecracker exploding, Greig collapsed as if he had been shot and the crowd roared its approval. When Chandra, the local hero, bowled it was common practice for the crowd to chant as he ran in, building to a crescendo as he delivered. Greig was having none of this and stopped the game as the noise began. At first he was hooted but Greig cupped his hands together, begging forgiveness in the traditional Indian way, a gesture which brought roars of approval and a period of silence from the tens of thousands present. Chants only resumed when the realisation struck that they were playing into his hands.

Bedi opened with his spinners and early on Greig gave an awkward chance. Oddly, Bedi rarely crowded the bat and Greig was only surrounded when Gavaskar, taking charge when Bedi was absent, set the field. England were always eager for the turbaned spinner to return to the fray.

Only two boundaries were struck in the morning, Greig square cutting Bedi and Tolchard cutting Solkar. Tucking occasional singles backward of point, Greig reached 50 in 191 minutes of unbending self-denial, and this with an aching body.

Greig square cuts Bedi to the boundary while the close point protects his face. To Greig's satisfaction, Bedi rarely crowded the bat, and this sort of shot helped keep the close fielders at bay.

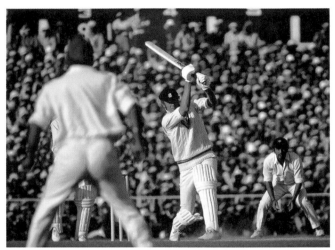

ABOVE LEFT *Greig hooks high for six down to very fine leg, the ball passing close to wicket-keeper Kirmani. Generally Greig was careful not to put the ball into the air during his innings.*
ABOVE RIGHT *Tony Greig off-driving in his innings at Calcutta. The Calcutta spectators were intrigued by this tall blond extrovert with the long reach for such shots, but Greig did not drive often, an early straight drive nearly being caught.*

After lunch Greig, still sick and unfed, continued his duel with Chandra, picking his bat up high and early, a tactic he had devised originally because it annoyed this formidable foe. Not once did the usually buccaneering Greig attempt a drive; he was bent upon a course of graft calculated to break his opponents, and he never strayed. Eventually Bedi trapped Tolchard and Alan Knott but Old held firm, even attacking Bedi as his partner's concentration never wavered. England were 285 for six at the close and Greig had batted all day, ignoring heat, men huddled around the bat, cheerfully partisan support and a turning pitch used by a great trinity of spinners. He had played a game entirely foreign to his temperament. And he had been wretchedly ill throughout.

England were now in total command and could smell victory. Greig spent the rest day in bed, happy in the knowledge that he had carried out his task and in doing so won the respect of his men and a Test series in India.

He resumed his innings a day later, driving Chandra to the fence to reach his 100. He had batted for 414 minutes and faced 320 balls, easily the longest innings of his career. Having changed tactics, he was soon out, leg before to

Prasanna. India duly collapsed and by the close of this fourth day were still 21 runs behind with three rabbits left.

With the game nearly over, only a small crowd was expected for the final morning. In fact, 50,000 turned up and the roar when Patel reached his 50 was surpassed only by an earth-shattering bellow when a Bedi snick forced England to bat again. England won by 10 wickets and were roundly cheered. In Bombay, later, they ran a lap of honour and Greig was presented with a garland of flowers. Orange peels and banana skins were reserved for the Indian selectors. Greig had conducted his campaign, his team, the crowd, like a conductor ruling orchestra and auditorium at a symphony concert.

Greig's innings, supported by Tolchard, had shattered India. In the circumstances, it was one of cricket's great defensive innings, not least because it was played by a cricketer reared on hard, bouncy pitches, who, in his youth, had been embarrassingly crude in his methods of combating spin. Greig had batted with an intense discipline few suspected to be within his capability, and his innings had decided a Test series. It was a triumph of mind over matter.

NEIL HARVEY

Australia v South Africa, Durban, 1949–50

SCORECARD ON PAGE 152

Neil Harvey leaves the field at the end of the match at Kingsmead, Durban, with hero-worshipping youngsters in attendance. Harvey turned almost certain defeat into brilliant victory with 151 not out.

By the time they reached Durban for the third Test of their series against South Africa Lindsay Hassett's Australians were already two up. Despite this a big crowd of 15,000 gathered at the Kingsmead ground to cheer on their men, and to see the mighty cricketers of Australia, who were paying only their third visit in 40 years. And the crowd had plenty to cheer on the first day as Rowan and Dudley Nourse took South Africa's score to 240 for two with batting of massive certainty.

For once the locals were in a reasonable position and need not fear a humiliating defeat. And as if their solid batting were not enough encouragement South Africa's stocks rose further when heavy rain fell overnight, soaking a pitch left open to the elements.

Suddenly 240 was a very good score indeed. Suddenly South Africa could contemplate winning, if they dared.

At 11.45 next day the captains inspected the pitch, Hassett in his street togs, Nourse in his whites. Inevitably they agreed to differ, whereupon the umpires, taking South Africa's part, decided play would begin at 12.15.

Hassett instructed his bowlers to concentrate upon containment and to avoid spinning the ball, for if Nourse saw the pitch misbehaving he'd declare. And so, cunningly, Australia bowled accurately but without venom as South Africa slowly collected runs. Only belatedly did Nourse grasp what a trick was being played and at once he ordered his men to hit. They were all out for 311, but precious minutes had been lost.

Determined to avoid losing too many good men in the 130 minutes left that day Hassett promoted tail-enders Johnston and Saggers and held Harvey and Loxton, his leading aggressors, in reserve, but the introduction of Tayfield caused an immediate collapse.

Australia limped to 63 for nine at the close and the partisan crowd went

Harvey, well down the wicket, cracks the ball just in front of square. Harvey's footwork, especially to the slow bowlers, was his strongest asset.

home happy. Nourse had the weekend to cogitate upon his tactics.

Upon dismissing Australia for 75 Nourse did not enforce the follow-on. It was his second mistake. The South Africans, batting judiciously, took lunch at 85 for three, an impregnable position. But after lunch wickets tumbled as Johnson and Johnston exploited the difficult pitch to take seven wickets for 14 runs in an hour's play. To Hassett this collapse was a mixed blessing because it meant his men had to survive for a day and a half to save the game, an awesome task. Victory was a childish dream.

Australia's batsmen defended stubbornly but slumped to 59 for three, their dim hopes barely alive.

Now entered Neil Harvey to play one of cricket's greatest innings, first helping Arthur Morris to guide Australia to 80 for three at the close of play.

With seven wickets to fall, and upon a crumbling worn pitch, Australia needed 251 runs to win when play resumed on the final morning. For a time Morris and Harvey survived, batting with extreme caution, countering the pitch's vagaries and Tayfield's ferocious spin. Morris lasted two and a half hours and made 44 runs before unluckily dislodging a bail. Australia were 95 for four with balls darting around like drunken elves as Harvey was joined by his chum Sam Loxton. With Loxton playing his natural game, Harvey began using his feet to pick holes and steal singles.

Spinners found him a difficult opponent because he wouldn't stand still. No man could move further forward at such speed and yet in his 125 Test innings Harvey was never stumped. Running hard and occasionally hitting out, lustily in Loxton's case, neatly in Harvey's, the pair rattled Nourse's bowlers. Harvey pulled a full toss from Tayfield to the boundary and Loxton drove Mann and cleared the fielders.

Shaken, Nourse took the second new ball immediately after lunch but was soon cursing again as Loxton was dropped at fine leg and edged between keeper and first slip. Minute by minute the South African morale dropped. They could scarcely believe they had not yet won. In three hours this pair added 135, and Loxton reached 54 before Mann beat and bowled him.

Colin McCool was Harvey's new partner, a gum-chewing leg-spinner who had scored a Test hundred and could cut spinners no matter where they pitched. With 106 runs needed, McCool chose this opportune moment to play his finest Test innings.

Harvey reached his hundred after four hours of careful restraint in which he had hit nine boundaries and given no chances. With McCool he took the score to 269 for five at tea, leaving 67 left to collect in two hours.

The South Africans had been disheartened by the audacity of Australia's challenge; Harvey's intrepid innings had hurt the confidence of the spinners, forcing them to bowl flat. Tayfield and Mann knew they ought to have dismissed Australia for 150 on this pitch, yet they could not even trap this nimble, intelligent batsman.

In truth Harvey had batted like a magician, defying balls whipping across his body with impeccable footwork and unfailing judgement.

Without undue difficulty McCool and Harvey took Australia to their incredible victory after tea with 25 minutes to spare. Harvey had made a chanceless 151 in 5½ hours on a pitch upon which any batsman would be proud to survive for an hour. His mastery had brought exceptional performances from Loxton and McCool and given his team an unimagined victory.

That night a tree was planted at the Kingsmead ground in his honour, in recognition of a disciplined and superbly crafted innings by a snip of a lad.

GRAEME HICK

Worcestershire v Somerset, Worcester, 1989

SCORECARD ON PAGE 152

B orn in Rhodesia in 1966, Graeme Hick appeared in England a few years ago as a batsman of evident calibre, capable of command yet civil and durable.

At the age of 20, Hick became the youngest man ever to score 2,000 runs in an English season, and throughout he batted without flamboyance, eschewing the macho and playing every ball on its merits, his game as pure as a punched hole. Moreover, he is a hungry batsman, as he conclusively demonstrated at Taunton in May 1988, scoring 405 not out, becoming the seventh man to reach 400 in a first-class innings.

Hick showed his mastery of every sort of bowling that year, collecting ten hundreds and hitting 2,713 runs, an aggregate which was the highest in English cricket since 1961. By now, Hick was scoring centuries every 5.29 innings. Bradman's average was 2.88, Ponsford and Woodfull's 5.00 and Vijay Merchant's 5.20. Hick is next.

As Somerset, somewhat warily, arrived in Worcester in September 1989, Hick felt he had not struck the ball well all season. His mother had told him to stop crouching, advice which had helped, and an injury to Ian Botham had allowed him to recapture a favourite bat which had been borrowed, and this, too, helped, but still he was unhappy. And now Worcestershire, with Essex breathing down their necks as the season approached its finale, had need of Hick at his greatest.

Somerset, under their new captain, Vic Marks, were in no mood for tame surrender and with rain snatching hours from the contest, the game resolved into a run-chase.

Hick had batted vigorously in the first innings and had appeared certain to take his customary hundred off Somerset's bowlers, when to their surprise, he had driven loosely and been caught at slip for 85, a dismissal which left Hick feeling annoyed with himself. In time, Somerset asked Worcestershire to chase 300 in 57 overs to win, a target Hick's colleagues regarded as too stiff, the pitch being unreliable. Only Hick, seeing a chance to redeem his first-innings mistake, considered it within reach and he made his view clear.

Worcestershire began slowly, taking the score to 50 in 15 overs before a wicket fell. Enter Hick, as usual striding to the crease and taking guard before his crestfallen predecessor had reached the pavilion.

Hick is not inhibited by batting or by pressure, and is disturbed only to be regarded prematurely as a great player. He likes batting with Curtis, 'an intelligent and practical cricketer who regu-

Graeme Hick plays square to the off against Hampshire near the end of the 1988 season, one of the most outstanding a batsman has enjoyed for many years – Hick became the seventh batsman to pass 400 in a first-class match and his season's aggregate was the highest since 1961.

OPPOSITE *Batting against
Middlesex in 1988 Hick gets the
ball high on the bat as he plays to
the off.*

ABOVE *In the 1989 season, the
second in succession in which his
batting had been a major factor
in winning the Championship,
Hick plays behind point and
starts to run in the match with
Glamorgan.*

larly gives him sound advice.

During the tea interval, with Worcestershire falling behind the clock, Hick was unusually agitated, pacing around and telling despondent colleagues that the target was still within reach. Plainly, Curtis' task upon resumption was to restrain Hick, to encourage him to bat normally, for he commonly scored at a furious rate and had no need to risk dismissal. To win the Championship, Worcestershire had to sustain a rate of seven an over for 30 overs. A growing and tense crowd considered the game to be slipping away.

To their consternation, Somerset were not extracting much life from the pitch and, worst of all, their spinner, Vic Marks, usually so difficult to hit, was out of sorts – 'bowling garbage', as he put it. Accordingly, with the Championship depending upon him, Hick could advance with dainty cuts and powerful drives to a deep-set field as he allowed his assault to gain momentum. Taking responsibility, Curtis hit boundaries while Hick settled and so kept the target in sight.

Building slowly, and yet with a terrifying certainty, Hick began to attack, moving into command with thunderous strides into areas previously uncharted in his first-class career. Changing tempo, he straight drove Jones, who had troubled him before and was still bowling with heart, for a glorious six, and, soon enough, picked up a delivery from Rose pitched barely short of a length and dispatched it to the distant mid-wicket boundary, a shot so clean and violent as to surprise even Hick.

Somerset recalled Mallender, dependable and accurate, and Marks sent his fieldsmen to protect the boundary. One avenue was left open, at mid-wicket, an area which Hick usually ignores, off the front foot at any rate.

Now, circumstance demanded innovation and, standing erect, detecting the gap and accepting the invitation, Hick moved across his crease to chip straight deliveries to the fence. Three times, he played this difficult shot unerringly, a devastating blow to his opponents who had thought it a chink in his armour.

Curtis fell and D'Oliveira soon followed but, thanks to Hick, Worcestershire scarcely missed a beat.

Hick reached his hundred in 110 minutes with a simple single, between times hitting boundaries apparently at will. Mallender was struck for a six and Marks' return to the bowling crease was unavailing. When Hick was facing, it was as if the pitch's anger had been silenced, as if the target were simple.

Only as his team approached victory, the home crowd cheering, nerves finally settling, did Hick play any wild shots, twice teasing outfielders with half-hit blows. For the rest, it was formidably inevitable, as if gentle deliveries were being served up for a master to dispatch at his leisure.

With five balls remaining, Rhodes cracked the winning runs and Hick left the field to an ovation tinged with awe. He had scored 136 runs in 168 balls in a masterly display timed to perfection. To his evident delight, he found his teammates, so unhappy two hours earlier, now full of joy. They slapped his back and poured him drinks as an unusually excited and drained Hick acknowledged their welcome.

Tim Curtis later reflected that it had been 'a magnificent innings, the best of its sort I've ever seen. Because of his absolute control, we hardly realised the magnitude of his achievement.'

It was the best chasing innings I have ever seen. In truth, Somerset's target was within the range of only one opponent, and, answering the call, he played an innings of destructive majesty, an innings entirely without flaw, an innings of breathtaking brilliance and, what is more, an innings which won a Championship.

ARCHIE JACKSON

Australia v England, Adelaide, 1928–29

SCORECARD ON PAGE 153

SCORECARD ON PAGE 153

❝ *When the great umpire gave Archie Jackson out at the age of 23 cricket lost one of the most graceful players it has ever known.* ❞

JOHNNY MOYES

A smiling Jackson after another great innings, of which there were to be too few.

The good die young, so they say. From the start Archie Jackson was fragile. Perhaps it was in hindsight that critics recalled the doomed, delicate air surrounding the boy. More likely they sensed a flame which though it burned fiercely might easily be snuffed. Archie was discovered by Arthur Mailey, witty, imaginative, pungent leg-spinner of Australia's greatest days. Mailey saw this tiny figure with pads half-way up his body batting with an ease and a poise utterly out of keeping with his situation. Crowds left Balmain's higher grade teams to watch the boy at work.

Quickly he was whisked away to higher things. At 18 he was picked to tour New Zealand with a Young Australia team. Victorian left-hander Karl Schneider, 22, was also in the party. Some of the lads went horse riding, and Schneider collapsed suddenly and began to haemorrhage. Jackson was one of those who helped to carry him to a mountain hut to recuperate. Archie may have contracted at this moment the disease of tuberculosis which was, five years later, to kill him. Schneider, himself a brilliant player, was dead within six months.

In any event Jackson moved serenely on towards Test cricket, being summoned to play in the fourth Test of 1928–29, when England were already three up. Around him, Jackson, aged 19 years and 151 days, found Bill Woodfull, gentle and modest, Stork Hendry and Jack Ryder, Oldfield, one Donald George Bradman, another stripling who had been blooded in the first Test, and Grimmett, giants of the past mixing with giants of the future. Also he joined forces with Alan Kippax, a lovely underrated batsman whose fluent, simple style Jackson had copied right down to the shirt-sleeves rolled low and kept in place by safety pins. Like Kippax, Archie was a deflector rather than a striker of the ball and he preferred fast pitches upon which he could persuade the ball to the boundary.

Chapman won the toss and elected to bat, as well he might that hot day in Adelaide. Once again Hobbs and Sutcliffe gave England a strong start, adding 143 before both fell. Hammond, fresh from double hundreds in both the previous Tests, scored 119 not out but, astonishingly, no one else did much and England collapsed to a satisfactory but scarcely intimidating 334.

Jackson opened with Woodfull and Australia made a dreadful start. Woodfull was superbly caught down the leg-side off Tate's fourth ball, Hendry fell to Larwood and then Kippax was fooled by White, who was already weaving his spells. And so Archie found himself 13 not out and surveying the wreckage of another Australian innings: 19 for three and only this kid Bradman to come. *Wisden* relates that this desperate position did not seem to bother Jackson in the least. Nor did it. It is not for youth to be inhibited by such things. A wily old pro would have put up the barricades. Jackson drove, hooked and cut with the utmost certainty. With Ryder he took Australia to 131 for three at the close, Jackson 70 and Ryder 54. Not that his batting was wanton. He was three hours at the crease before reaching 50. It was the apparent effortlessness which made time seem to skip by, at least to the members sitting in the pavilion square of the wicket, just the place to observe footwork so deft that Jackson seemed to glide rather than move into position. But it wasn't effortless. 'Stork' Hendry said later that Jackson was limp when he reached the dressing room. 'We had to mop him with cold towels', he said.

No, this was not a frivolous innings. You don't take easy runs off the likes of Larwood, Tate, White and Geary. At the close Chapman did not feel his team had been savaged, rather he felt that holes

Archie Jackson makes a swing to leg during practice. Archie, said Harold Larwood, who bowled at him during his Test debut century, 'was born to be great'.

had been picked with the courtesy of a fencer.

Next morning the game still hung in the balance. Ryder was trapped in front by White, whose length never erred, who scarcely spun the ball yet bowled his off-theory at such a pace and with such gusto that batsmen dare not get after him. Ryder and Jackson had added 126 in 2½ hours. Now Bradman arrived. Already people were comparing these two prodigies. Jackson, they felt, was the greater. Presumably this was Ryder's opinion. Why else bat Jackson at two and Bradman, who was nearly a year older, at six?

At lunch Jackson was 97 not out. To disturb him Chapman took the second new ball straight after the interval. Jackson promptly cut the first ball, from Larwood, to the boundary and the crowd cheered a hundred reached in four hours and 10 minutes. As if to say 'You ain't seen nothin' yet', Jackson now cut loose, adding 67 runs in the 70 minutes after lunch, using his feet to White, hooking Larwood, treating Hammond's medium pace with polite contempt. Finally at 287, after five hours, he fell to White, leg before wicket trapped off the pitch by the inswinger. His 164 had been chanceless, though he was nearly run out on 128.

It was an extraordinary first innings played against a powerful, experienced attack and in the tightest of corners. Certainly it heralded a brilliant career.

Sadly it was not to be. Jackson did not score another Test hundred, though he was to play until 1931. At times he simply didn't have the strength. He was not, of course, as good as Bradman. No one was. Nevertheless, it was acknowledged that in terms of beauty of execution this innings was the best played against England that season.

Jackson battled bravely against his disease. During the bodyline series he lay desperately ill in a Brisbane nursing home yet still found the strength to send a congratulatory telegram to his old rival, Larwood, after Harold had taken ten wickets in the first Test. England players visited Archie whenever they could, as did his Australian chums. Like Trumper he was universally beloved.

Jackson is still recalled with honour and reverence and this, as Irving Rosenwater has said, is a busy world.

KAPIL DEV

India v Zimbabwe, Tunbridge Wells, 1983

SCORECARD ON PAGE 153

I felt I could hit it anywhere. It all happened so quickly. Everything at my legs I scooped over mid-wicket. I just felt I could do anything, middle any shot.

KAPIL DEV

Kapil Dev leaves the Tunbridge Wells field surrounded by young admirers after his match-winning innings.

Kapil Dev Nikhanj was born in 1959 in warlike northern India. It was here, in the Punjab, that Mogul emperors were resisted and battalions raised for the Western Front. An indomitable and industrious spirit penetrates through the now-partitioned Punjab, a spirit which has brought wealth and health without ever losing its tradition of courage without calculation. Even now the Punjab erupts into anger as, with no outside foe to fight, brave men of different beliefs fight each other.

Kapil, tall, handsome and strong, his sparkling eyes hinting at panache, even foolhardiness, disdaining petty victory, proud and in search of glory, is in every respect a true son of the Punjab. His family was not especially prosperous but this is not, these days, nearly such a handicap in Indian cricket. Recently a groundsman's son and another from a lowly caste of milkmen have been picked to play for India. Beside these the 'Haryana Hurricane' as he came to be called, Haryana being an offshoot of the original Punjab, was well born.

His rise was spectacular. Furious at being told that no Indian could bowl fast, an opinion ignorant of great bowlers like Mohammad Nissar and Amar Singh, Kapil dedicated himself to leading India's attack and to smashing bowling around as if he were a cavalier on a charge.

It took him just 25 Test matches to reach his double of 1,000 runs and 100 wickets, a feat surpassed only by the no less vigorous, slashing and yet fundamentally sound Ian Botham. By 1983 Kapil was captain, because India too yearned for a knight in shining armour to lead it from darkness into light. Of course, it was a fantasy and, in time, Kapil fell, for players will follow reason not sentiment. Nevertheless, Kapil's reign was to include one glorious episode, probably the most glorious in the illustrious, colourful history of Indian cricket.

For in 1983 Kapil led India to an unpredicted, unsuspected World Cup victory. Yet when they arrived on 18 June at Tunbridge Wells to play Zimbabwe, their prospects were uncertain.

Before the game Kapil told his men that to be sure of qualifying for the semi-finals they must not only win but also score around 270. Despite finding a damp pitch he decided to bat first upon winning the toss, a brave decision founded upon an idea that defeat was an impossibility. With a large crowd, many of them Indian, filling this small ground so beautifully decorated with rhododendrons, Kapil felt at ease as he went out to practise. Just before play began he returned to the dressing room still in his track suit.

'I hardly', he says, 'had time to change.' Gavaskar went for a duck to the last ball of the first over. Srikkanth quickly followed. Hurrying into his whites, Kapil went in to bat with the scoreboard showing nine for four. 'I felt like I was in a trance. I'd had no time to think what I had to do. I simply decided to bat as if it were a five-day game.'

Another wicket fell and India were 17 for five. Already Kapil felt smooth, at ease. Careful in defence, denying the slips clustered around him eager for a catch, he found his aggressive shots skimming cleanly to the boundary. If only someone could stay in with him. Roger Binny, a veteran of other campaigns, held up his end, urged on by a crowd which slowly began to find fresh voice.

In the dressing room Ravi Shastri, due in next, and his glum team-mates watched, waiting for Kapil to lose his wicket. 'We thought he might be good for 50 or so but we were certain it couldn't last. We waited and waited but he kept hitting them in the middle.' In the field Zimbabwe also felt the end was

Kapil Dev during his great knock hitting powerfully through the off-side off the back foot.

nigh. They pressed on, dismissing Binny at 77 and Shastri at 78. Now Kapil, concentrating hard, restraining himself in every way and yet scuttling between the wickets, was joined by his comrade from the north, the old trooper Madan Lal, who said at once that he intended to stay in. Kapil could take care of the runs.

India took lunch at 106 for seven with the overs running out and the pitch drying by the hour. Upon play resuming Madan Lal hung on till 140 was reached and Syed Kirmani came in. With Kirmani battling gamely Kapil decided to hit out, striking three fours and three sixes in the following 18 deliveries. Zimbabwe turned to defence, hoping to contain Kapil and dismiss his partner. To cramp him, they aimed at his pads and Kapil, surveying the boundary, knowing their line, picked his gaps. He was still in a trance-like state, scarcely aware of time or moment.

A cunning bowler, Kapil bats by instinct or he fails. He sees the ball and he hits it cleanly, using timing rather than beef. Still wearing a long-sleeved sweater, he swung easily, almost lazily, entirely without the blurred fury of the possessed or the violent power of the brutal. Drives skimmed to the boundary with fielders hardly moving. Lofted hits soared into a nearby car park. From 17 for five India, unbelievably, marched in 266 for nine, Kapil scoring 175 not out and Kirmani 26.

It was, says Kapil, 'the innings of a life-time. Maybe I've played better but the situation here was so bad. It was my dream to do this. My aim hs always been to try to achieve the impossible.'

Fortified by Kapil, India won by 31 runs and went on to beat West Indies in the final, Kapil taking a courageous catch to dismiss Richards. He deserved nothing less, nor did India's supporters in England whose lives hitherto had been so difficult.

CLIVE LLOYD

West Indies v Australia, Lord's, 1975
SCORECARD ON PAGE 154

A typical Lloyd shot in the 1975 World Cup Final. Standing upright he lazily swings to leg. His strength and timing combine to send the ball to the boundary.

On Saturday evening, 21 June 1975, the longest day of the year and one of the hottest, Jeff Thomson was run out by Deryck Murray and the West Indians were champions of the world. Players bolted for the pavilion as the sea of excited humanity engulfed them. It was 8.42pm and after a sweltering, pulsating game, the climax to cricket's first World Cup was over.

Prince Philip presented the trophy to a shambling giant of a man who, blinking through horn-rimmed spectacles, held it aloft for all to see. Already the same fellow, who might have stepped straight from the crowd, had been named Man of the Match in recognition of economical bowling, outrageously athletic fielding and as ferocious an innings as has ever been played in any game, let alone one so important.

Clive Lloyd was born in Guyana in 1944; his father was a chauffeur and his mother had Lance Gibbs for a nephew. Lloyd had four sisters and a brother, all of whom he was called upon to support when his father died suddenly in 1958. Leaving school to be the family breadwinner the boy took a clerical job in a hospital. He was a long way from St John's Wood and Lord's.

Already Lloyd had suffered in an accident which threatened his slim hopes of a life in sport. Walking home from school he tried to stop a fight and a ruler was jabbed into his right eye. His sight deteriorated and he has worn glasses ever since.

Nevertheless, by 1967 he was playing cricket for the West Indies and by 1974 he was captain. Between 1965 and 1974 the West Indians did not win a single home Test and these humiliations left their mark upon Lloyd, who saw it as his task to rebuild West Indian pride and strength.

His first opportunity to do so was in the 1975 World Cup, a tournament which enchanted 200,000 spectators and countless millions following on radio and television. It was blessed by unremitting sunshine and steadily moved towards its climax. Lloyd's team stumbled on its way to Lord's, spluttering to 166 for eight as they chased Pakistan's 266. Fighting back, Deryck

Murray, Vanburn Holder and Andy Roberts took their side to an extraordinary and inspirational victory with two balls to spare. As the Cup progressed so critics could sense in Lloyd a mounting conviction. 'Nothing,' wrote Robin Marlar, 'nothing was to deter him. He was totally captivated by the ambition to win the Cup.'

Bright sunshine warmed a heaving and noisy Lord's as play began that July afternoon. All were hushed as Lillee thundered in to bowl the first over to tiny, puckish Roy Fredericks, resplendent in a floppy hat.

Off the last ball of the third over Fredericks, pivoting on his toes, hooked Lillee for a towering six, a shot greeted by a roar and a cacophony of trumpets, bugles and drums from the West Indian contingent. But they hadn't noticed that Fredericks had slipped and dislodged a bail and was walking back to the pavilion, a cruel blow.

Kallicharran was soon dancing like a demented elf but soon he and a tentative Greenidge had fallen and the West Indians were 50 for three in 18 overs. Now, down the pavilion steps and into the sunshine to join the greying Kanhai came a hulking figure, stooping slightly, wearing a maroon cap and carrying a bat like a forest timber. Everything now depended upon Lloyd. Great events, they say, bring forth great deeds, and here was a great captain ready to play his part.

Plainly bristling with aggression Lloyd hammered his bat onto the turf as the bowler ran in, an awesome, savage sight. Combining power with rhythm, Lloyd began with a hook smacked hard and high into the stands and again horns blew.

With Kanhai collecting careful singles, Lloyd let loose the dogs of war. Lillee beat him once and next ball Lloyd tried a pull which Ross Edwards dropped at mid wicket, a difficult chance. Lloyd was unruffled by these minor blemishes. Picking his bat up high he clubbed on and at lunch the West Indians were 91 for three after 28 overs with Lloyd on 34.

After lunch Kanhai did not score for several overs but it mattered not for Lloyd quickly pulled Walker over the boards and into the Tavern, and immediately smashed another drive through cover, the shot flashing precisely between two men stationed on the boundary whose exact positions and names Lloyd could remember a decade later.

Lloyd reached his 50 in 32 balls and acknowledged the thunderous applause. Hurrying back to his work, daring not to lose the moment, Lloyd continued his merciless assault upon Max Walker, who hardly bowled a wayward delivery and yet found himself deposited into the grandstand and cracked to the point boundary. Lloyd was oblivious to Walker's subtle changes and simply towered above the day.

In eight overs after lunch this pair added 73 runs, each one accompanied by a steady, rhythmical clanging of beer bottles and by immense cheers. And so the carnage continued.

Lloyd simply caught the mood of the day, batting not with abandon but with calculated ferocity and yet with joy and spontaneity not too far away. With Kanhai as a reliable partner, he took the West Indians from 50 for three to 199 for four in 24 overs, turning the game upon its head.

His century came from his 82nd ball, after which he was surprisingly adjudged caught behind off Gilmour. He retired to the sort of ovation commonly reserved for a Caesar entering Rome. Having hit two sixes and 12 fours he, too, had come, seen and conquered.

It was a great innings, as irresistible as a hurricane, and before 9 pm the West Indies were champions.

ABOVE *Lloyd on the field at Lord's with the first World Cup, presented to him by Prince Philip.*

✎ *To dwarf so many of the world's leading batsmen was a mark of greatness. To have such gifts of height and power is one thing; to use them at a time like this is another. Lloyd made the pitch and the stumps and the bowlers and the ground all seem much smaller than they were.* ✎

ROBIN MARLAR

Cricket lost its 18-stone (114kg), laughing Falstaff when, on 25 May 1969, just as the new season was gathering steam, Colin Milburn was involved in a car accident which left him with sight in only one eye. In his only Championship innings of that year he'd made 158 against Leicestershire. Milburn was never unconscious after the accident, but had nasty cuts on the face and seven stitches in his right knee, damage done by a shattered windscreen. On his right eye, which was never to be of use again, there was the merest scratch.

Milburn did try to return in 1973 but made only one 50 in 35 attempts. Not even his unquenchable thirst for life and for cricket could help him. Cricketers were left to remember Milburn, in Clive Taylor's words, as being 'as untidy as an unmade bed but as devastating as a hand grenade'.

Milburn learnt his cricket in Burnopfield, County Durham, where he played with his chums in a grim canyon between two streets of back-to-back houses. Burnopfield could already boast of Jim McConnon, another Test cricketer. Its other hero was Colin's father, Jack, a former league professional of massive size, geniality and legendary feats. Colin once said: 'I've always been a slogger and my father was a slogger before me.' It wasn't true, of course, because Colin was a fine batsman, but it catches the spirit of the fellow.

Northamptonshire heard of Milburn and soon he was launching their innings with rumbustious tirades. Test caps followed yet despite his dangerous hitting England picked him for only nine of 24 Tests played between début and accident. They said he could not field, needed to lose four stone (25kg) and was too prone to throw away his wicket. That he could win a match and hook any fast bowler game enough to bounce him was of less account.

So Milburn, like biblical prophets, was without honour in his own country. Australia, on the other hand, liked his cheerful spontaneity, and Milburn began to play Sheffield Shield cricket for the Sandgropers (Western Australia) in 1966–67. Les Favell wrote of his 129 against South Australia: 'Milburn became a combination of heavy bomber and an artillery piece as he bludgeoned my bowlers into a daze with his tremendous hitting from the crease.'

Western Australia were playing Queensland in Brisbane two years later and upon winning the toss they elected to bat. Opening with Derek Chadwick, Milburn started his greatest innings carefully, respecting the accuracy of Test bowler Peter Allan and wily seamer Ross Duncan. Off 33 balls he made four scoring shots, three singles and a boundary.

It was hot that day, 90°F (26°C), and Milburn by no means had a physique appropriate for the temperature. He couldn't push and poke much longer, for soon he'd blow a gasket. So Milburn began to play his shots, striking the ball to the fence, plundering four beefy boundaries off Duncan in one over, and three others besides. Rusi Surti, India's Test spinner, contained him for a time but another blow scattered his field.

By lunch Milburn had scored 61 off 92 balls and both teams left the field hot and bothered. So much sweat had seeped through Milburn's gloves he had difficulty holding the bat. He changed them for new ones. Twelve ineffective overs of pace after lunch forced Queensland to try leg-spinner Bob Paulsen. By now Milburn was in murderous mood. He clobbered two boundaries off Paulsen's first and perfectly respectable over, and four more off his second. A six and two fours were taken off the tall leg-spinner's fourth over and Milburn was now in total command. Surti, recalled to bowl into the wind, was Milburn's next

Colin Milburn, after his accident, drives for England Taverners against Australia Taverners at Arundel in August 1980.

Milburn pulls through midwicket during his fabulous innings for Western Australia in 1968–69.

⑤ *Ollie's unresting bat inflicted the heaviest punishment bowlers have ever suffered in one playing session here, despite the fact that this is the home of Peter Burge.* ⑤
RAY ROBINSON

victim, struck for 48 in 28 balls. Neither spinner could slow this fiery collecting of runs.

Once Milburn stepped back from his leg stump, intending a colourful offside force. Using the breeze, Surti drifted the ball away from the batsman, causing Ollie to scramble after it. From a prostrate position he chopped it behind point for four with, says Ray Robinson, 'all the grace of an animated armchair'.

His innings was not quite chanceless. On 131 Geoffrey Gray reached a hook with his fingertips and the force of the shot twisted him against the pickets, lacerating his chest and jerking the ball free. At 148 a cover drive nearly broke the hands of a fieldsman who dared to intercept it. At 228 Peter Allan just failed to grasp a ferocious return drive. None of these offerings was taken, for who could catch a meteorite?

Only 3,000 people watched this afternoon's cricket yet to a man they cheered as Milburn, representing Western Australia, and a Pom to boot, took 21 off Allan's tenth over: 6, 4, 4, 6, 1. In the two-hour session after lunch Mil-

burn scored 181 off 134 balls, breathtaking batting of a flow, a power and a calibre rare in any game.

Milburn's 242 off 226 balls in 230 minutes before tea has no parallel in Australia. Bradman (142), Ponsford (152) and Barry Richards (137) have all flayed attacks in a two-hour afternoon session, but none of them quite matches Milburn.

Not that he was out yet. During the tea interval Milburn, dripping with sweat, said he was absolutely exhausted (though this was not quite the word he chose). In the first over after tea he was caught by Morgan off another fierce drive. A chart revealed that he had hit the ball to every part of the Gabba, hooking, sweeping, cutting and driving to his heart's content.

Back in the hutch Milburn apologised to his team-mates and stood under a shower singing 'The Green Green Grass of Home' in what is described as a pleasant baritone. Peter Burge entered and congratulated him, most particularly for 'so obviously justifying the presence in the game of fat men'.

GRAEME POLLOCK

South Africa v Australia, Durban, 1969–70

SCORECARD ON PAGE 155

B orn in 1944 into a Scottish family – one grandfather was a Presbyterian minister – Graeme Pollock was one of cricket's supreme geniuses. Encouraged by his father, who was editor of the *Port Elizabeth Herald*, Pollock played Currie Cup cricket at 16 and at 19 became the youngest South African to hit a double hundred in a first-class match. At the same age he scored his first Test hundred, an astonishing 102 in Sydney which led Jack Fingleton to say that Pollock hit the ball harder even then Woolley.

In Adelaide a few months later Pollock struck an exhilarating 175, smiting sixes into the nearby Adelaide Cathedral, provoking Bill O'Reilly into describing his innings as 'Murder in the Cathedral'.

In Australia that winter of 1963–64 Pollock was scintillating, batting in his primitive style and constantly thumping boundaries. Touring England in 1965, he made a memorable 125 on a seaming Trent Bridge pitch, runs scored off 145 balls and out of 160 added while he was at the wicket. Returning home, Pollock now faced Australia and in the second Test played another great innings, scoring 209 out of his team's 353 as South

Africa vainly attempted to avoid the follow-on. But his masterpiece came in his next and, sadly, last series, against the Australians in 1969–70.

For Bill Lawry's team it had already been a hard trip, beginning with a controversial series in India which Australia won 3–1. On the road since October, the Australians were footsore and disgruntled when they arrived in the veldt.

Playing under Dr Ali Bacher, born Aaron Bacher, a Jewish doctor who worked in a hospital for non-Europeans outside Johannesburg, South Africa won the first Test by 170 runs and went to Kingsmead, Durban, determined to rub home their advantage. By now Bill Lawry – who had been called 'the corpse with pants on' by an English critic – was even more fed up. Nor did his mood improve when, agreeing to an early toss at Bacher's request, he found the pitch being cut and rolled after Bacher had elected to bat.

Barry Richards was playing in the second Test of his brief career and it was he who launched South Africa's first assault on this sunny day, delighting an enthusiastic crowd by tearing into the bowlers with batting of superb quality, adding 88 in even time before his partner, Goddard, skied a full toss from Gleeson to mid-off. Bacher joined a rampant Richards, who had taken 11 off Gleeson's first over and driven Freeman for consecutive boundaries. Bacher held on nearly to lunch before being bowled neck and crop by Connolly, leaving Richards stranded on 94 and the total on 126 for two.

After lunch Graeme Pollock joined the young master and for an hour the pair matched shot for shot to provide cricket with one of its most glorious episodes. One hundred runs were added in this hour with boundary upon boundary being struck and Pollock racing to his 50 in 57 minutes.

'Never' said Lawry, 'have I seen the

As soon as one looks at Graeme Pollock one thinks of how he could be improved. The stance is ugly. He holds his short-handled bat at the bottom. As he stands well over six foot he has to pop his posterior in the air to fit everything in, so forming an ugly, elongated, upside down figure of five as he stands awaiting the ball. In such a stance his head is far away from his feet. He cramps himself on the leg side. But suddenly his stance is immaterial as he blazes shots with ferocity across the turf.
JACK FINGLETON'S VIEW OF POLLOCK AT THE CREASE.

OPPOSITE *Pollock takes his left hand off the bat as he hooks in Australia in 1963–64, the season in which he first impressed Don Bradman.*

VIVIAN RICHARDS

West Indies v England, St Johns, 1985–86

SCORECARD ON PAGE 156

SCORECARD ON PAGE 156

RIGHT *Vivian Richards sweeping in a one-day international against Pakistan – a typical loose, free-flowing, powerful shot.*

OPPOSITE *Richards reaches 100 in 56 balls before his own Antiguan people – the fastest century in Test cricket. His joy is unconfined, as was that of the whole island.*

To Vivian Richards, a proud man, a combustible mixture of love and hate, humility and arrogance, a man capable of exploding into terrible anger and yet a man touched by faith, to play Test cricket in Antigua was the culmination of his extraordinary career. And to play there as West Indies captain, that was something besides. Who would have thought it, little Vivian Richards, child of a prison warder from an island ignored in the mighty West Indian firmament, a Test captain?

In 1981, as the West Indian and England teams arrived in Antigua, Richards was marrying Miriam, a childhood sweetheart, and it was local opinion that the celebrations would affect his batting. Ability to deliver goods to order was, however, one of Richards' most notable characteristics. Passionate, effervescent hundreds had been scored in cup finals and Test matches. Richards could explode upon the greatest stages as his entire body erupted in joy and menace, smashing

balls to the boundary or simply stroking one away and taking a languid single. On great occasions his batting was a splash of colour like some modern painting scorning the regimentation of past errors. It was not in Richards to pay respect to respectability, for it made him feel uncomfortable.

To the delight of his people Richards scored a sweet century that year of 1981, not one of his best perhaps but one of his most easily predicted.

England returned, no doubt warily, to the Recreation Ground in Antigua in 1986. They had lost all five Tests at home in 1984 and were now four down in this series, haunted by scandals and disappointments.

For Viv Richards this second homecoming against England was, if anything, even more packed with emotion than his first. His father had suffered a mild stroke and he was determined to play a torrential innings in honour of him. To his dismay he failed in the first innings, scoring 26 before falling to Ian Botham, but West Indies led by 164 runs.

With Greenidge indisposed it was another home town boy, Richie Richardson, who opened with Haynes in the second innings, adding 100 at a steady rate before Richardson fell trying to drive Emburey.

Now entered Richards, pausing till his protégé had left the field, and walking out to an ovation usually reserved for gods. Nothing had prepared the cricketing world for what was about to take place. Richards' form had not been particularly good and in the last couple of years he had been criticised for throwing his wicket away with extravagant shots, as if some unaccounted fury demanded expression. Whatever the cause it was plain that Richards owed the world a majestic innings.

There were 28 minutes left for tea. Richards defended against his first two balls and took three off his third, then

Richards, almost on one knee, cover drives. Richards has the ability to play shots all round the wicket, and the length and direction of the ball bowled to him does not necessarily inhibit his shot – he delights in the unorthodox and the outrageous.

⚬ *To play like that at any time, at any level, would have been within the scope of one batsman in a hundred, at the most. To come in and reel it off to order with a declaration pending in a Test was unimaginable, stupendous, awesome, magical.* ⚬

JOHN THICKNESSE

thumped Ellison and Emburey over mid-wicket for sixes with shots of awesome power.

Scenting Richards was in fierce mood Gower at once spread his field. Ellison concentrated upon bowling straight and Richards effortlessly clipped him off his toes and took singles, sometimes hurrying for a second. Emburey, too, quickly sent his men to the deep in the hope that Richards would be content with singles or frustrated into swinging a catch. Instead Richards collected 28 runs off his 15 balls before tea, a commanding start and yet, as it emerged, merely an aperitif.

To protect his young bowlers, and fearing the worst, Gower used Botham and Emburey when, accompanied by whistles, bugles, trumpets and chatter, play resumed after tea. Resplendent in his maroon West Indian cap Richards sauntered out and proceeded to bat with tigerish intensity. Botham sent three men back to the leg boundary and attempted to angle the ball outside his pads. In so doing he ·played into Richards' hands for now Richards' wicket was not under threat.

Richards began with a boundary, a thunderous shot, and then simply belted every ball to deep fieldsmen and strolled singles. Every run was greeted with a cacophony of noise as an excited crowd anticipated a mounting assault.

Richards reached 50 in 46 minutes off 35 balls, saluting this landmark with a devastating six over long-off off Emburey, a shot which landed far outside the ground. Later Jack Bannister measured the carry and thought it to be at least 125 yards.

Now Richards was on fire, feeding off his crowd, excited in his movements. Botham decided upon a bouncer barrage, a common tactic of his when wickets will not fall by orthodox means. As Botham bowled and Richards hooked so a song bellowed out from a

mobile disco in a stand: 'Captain, the ship is sinking'.

Nothing could stop the carnage. Richards had lost interest in singles and was intent upon destruction. Emburey tried a slower one and Richards, agitated, committed himself to a big hit and was beaten in the air. For the moment Emburey thought he had his man and his heart leapt. Realising he was in trouble Richards was forced to stretch for the ball one-handed. He connected and cleared long on with yards to spare. Richards had hit a one-handed six in a Test match.

Botham now tried his luck. If he stayed in, Richards was, by now, certain to score the fastest hundred in Test cricket, beating Jack Gregory who hit his in 67 balls. To take Richards by surprise Botham delivered a good length ball at off-stump. Richards' reply nearly parted Botham's hair and had the umpire taking urgent evasive action as the ball ripped over the sight screen.

Soon Richards was 93 and had faced 48 balls. His next four deliveries brought a single and a two as he approached his hundred with apparent seriousness. Another two and a single to deep fieldsmen took him to 99 off 54 balls. Was Gower to bring in his field? He did not, for only tanks could stop Richards now. Emburey bowled a wider ball, anticipating a move forwards by Richards, who instead, lay back and cut it to the boundary. A ground scarcely able to control itself for an hour now burst into an exaltation seldom encountered in any sporting arena. Richards had scored 103 in 56 balls and his last 50 had been scored of 21 balls against bowlers determined to contain him. No-one present is ever likely to forget it. Richards hit one mighty six against Emburey and promptly declared. No Test attack has been treated with such brutal yet joyous contempt and the West Indians won with time to spare.

FRANK WORRELL

West Indies v Australia, Brisbane, 1960–61
SCORECARD ON PAGE 158

SCORECARD ON PAGE 158

> ✆ *I have been blind for many years, Frank, but only once have I felt sorry for my disability and that was when I listened to Garfield Sobers play that unforgettable knock in Brisbane.* ✆
> LETTER FROM A BLIND MAN TO WORRELL AFTER THE TIED TEST

A famous picture of a famous match. Meckiff is run out, a Test is tied, cricket is revived and a man joins the list of cricket legends.

Sir Frank Worrell was the first cricketer for whom a memorial service was held in Westminster Abbey. Had not leukaemia taken him away at 43 his contribution, already huge, to cricket and to politics might have led to his inclusion amongst the greatest men of his time. As it was he was knighted, elected as a senator in Jamaica's first Parliament, appointed as the first black man to captain the West Indies on tour and, by the end of his career, universally beloved. It was Worrell more than anyone who united the West Indians and led cricket's revival in the 1960s, a revival which owed much to him and 'his happy band'.

Greatness in an innings is hard to define. A player may explode in an orgy of hitting, may defy extraordinary odds or an awkward pitch, may win a game off his own bat. In Brisbane 30 years ago Frank Worrell did none of these. He was 36 years of age, and his greatest days were behind him. Nor did he hit a hundred. Nor was he even the leading player in a partnership. Quite to the contrary, Sobers, his youthful partner and eventual successor, struck 132 in 123 minutes, an innings widely considered to bear comparison with McCabe's effort in 1932–33. Worrell scored 65 runs that time in Brisbane, and yet it must be judged great for he was a man who'd taken the tide of affairs at the quick.

By 1960 Worrell's career was nearing its end. Walcott and Weekes had retired, so breaking cricket's most famous trinity. Perhaps it was time to leave the game – after all the Caribbean was moving towards independence and Worrell might have a role to play. Then began a campaign in West Indian newspapers for Worrell to be appointed captain. The West Indies had been divided

A posed picture of Worrell. He made 261, 191 not out and 197 not out in Tests against England, but an innings of 65 is chosen here as the one which confirmed his greatness as a cricketer.

Worrell drives Davidson to the fence at Brisbane. Backing up is the young century-maker Garfield Sobers, whom Worrell coaxed into a great innings.

and disappointing under John Goddard, a white and an amateur, in England in 1957, and under Alexander, white and amateur, they had lost in Pakistan a year later. With self-government looming was it not time for a black cricket captain to be picked? Neither Headley nor Walcott, black professionals, men with superior credentials and characters, had been called to the post, and certainly the Cricket Board was conservative to the point of obstinacy if not prejudice (whether that bias be more against colour or status others must decide).

Nevertheless, as the campaign rumbled on, so the absurdity of the Board's intransigence became apparent. Finally, they had to bow to public pressure, and to the times what's more, and invite Frank Worrell to take the team to Australia.

It was immensely important that Worrell should succeed as a captain. Any stumble would be seized upon by the old guard with surreptitious sneers. In the event the tour was a triumph, so much so that Worrell and his team were sent home with an extraordinary motorcade through Melbourne at which hundreds of thousands of people paid homage and sang 'For he's a jolly good fellow'. Identifying 'he' was not necessary.

Worrell began by telling his team that they could bat, bowl and field as well as any Australian, but that to win 'we need to play as a team on the field and live like a family off it'. He split his party into groups of four, with each group having a leader. No one was ignored nor any problem hidden. Worrell told his men they must play as true sportsmen, win, lose or draw. Batsmen must cross on the field and never argue with a decision. If something was wrong Worrell told his men what was right and left it at that.

Unfortunately the tour began badly and a weakness against leg-spin bowling was immediately obvious. Worrell knew that the tour depended upon defeating Benaud. Talking was futile, the deed had to be done. And what better time than the first Test match in Brisbane?

West Indies were 65 for three when Worrell went in. His primary concern was for the tour, and despite the precarious nature of his position his main object was to prove to his partner, Sobers, and to his team watching in the pavilion that Benaud was not as great a bowler as they feared.

Notoriously Sobers could not read Benaud and strolled a single off him when there might, with haste, have been two, a sign of nervousness. Worrell played calmly, his very manner creating an aura on the field, an aura which filled his great partner with confidence. Sobers then tore into Benaud like a tiger let loose in a sheep pen, smashing four boundaries in one over. In 41 minutes the pair added 50, with Worrell scoring nine. At lunch the West Indies were 130 for three, having lambasted 94 runs in the second hour of this crucial first Test.

Sobers reached his hundred just after 2pm, bringing 10,628 spectators to their feet. He fell, lamely, for 132, lobbing a full toss to mid-on. Worrell soon followed, out for 65, snicking Davidson's outswinger to Grout. He had been in for 159 minutes. Seeing they had nothing to fear, the lower-order West Indian batsmen also batted superbly. Alexander hitting 60 and Wes Hall 50. They reached 453 made in 100.6 overs.

So began cricket's greatest ever Test series. So began, too, the building of one of cricket's most entertaining elevens. Had Worrell not risen to this occasion (and he hit 65 in the second innings as well as keeping his head as the match moved unerringly towards a tie) morale might have slumped irreversibly. Sobers' was the innings of a great player, Worrell's the innings of a great man.

MONUMENTAL MASTERY

DENNIS AMISS

England v West Indies, Kingston, 1973–74
SCORECARD ON PAGE 158

SCORECARD ON PAGE 158

PRECEDING PAGE *Barry Richards, who left South Africa and played his best innings in England and Australia.*

Dennis Amiss drives through the covers. A batsman capable of tremendous concentration and watchfulness, Amiss nevertheless could play attractive aggressive shots all round the wicket.

By January 1973 few doubted that Dennis Amiss, so secure and productive a batsman in county cricket, was a Test match flop. Beneath his pipe-smoking, phlegmatic appearance lurked a cricketer who could not control his nerves, a worrier, a pessimist, a man incapable of rising to the occasion – or so they said.

In India that winter he'd scored 46, 9, 11, 1, 15 and 8, a bewildering and humiliating series of failures which seemed finally to consign him to the dustbin. Roope, Birkenshaw and Lewis opened in his place that dismal January and if this was not the end it was something remarkably similar. A Test career which had begun against Sobers' tourists in 1966 and had spluttered ever since was closing not with a bang but a whimper.

In the year which followed Amiss was to score 1,356 Test runs at an average of 79.76 and to play one of cricket's greatest defensive innings. At last the thoughtful, self-contained man from Birmingham who was to be an undertaker in business life had defeated those nagging doubts.

Arriving for the second Test at Kingston, Jamaica, Amiss had already begun his rehabilitation with 174 in six hours 40 minutes in a vain attempt to save the first Test. England batted first at Kingston but with no-one playing a major innings slowly subsided to 353 all out, a total left far behind by the West Indians who, with Rowe striking his usual hundred in front of his home crowd, scored 583 for nine, declaring at lunch on the penultimate day, leaving England 10 hours to survive if they hoped to save the game and the series.

England's innings began dramatically, Boycott, the most reliable batsman, falling caught behind off a flier from Boyce, a surprising delivery on so benign a pitch, notwithstanding which setback England raced to 50 in eight overs. A wonderfully efficient player off his pads

Amiss had already tucked away four leg-side boundaries. Through his innings he was to score his runs in his usual way, with clips through mid-wicket and punches through cover, every shot so marvellously certain as to render earlier failures still more mysterious.

Jameson, batting at first drop, broke his duck with an edged hook which flew over slips for six. With this six and other more precise shots, England reached 100 in 25 overs. Regularly switching his bowlers, Kanhai introduced Barrett's leg-spin and at once Jameson played an indiscreet straight hit which ended in Rowe's hands at slip.

Amiss was batting staunchly, but when Denness was controversially given out it was a dreadful blow.

Hardly had spectators resumed their seats than another disaster befell England. Amiss called for a run and Frank Hayes had scarcely passed halfway as Lloyd picked up, turned and threw down the stumps.

England appeared doomed by a combination of self-destruction and plain bad luck. Tony Greig stayed with Amiss nearly to the end of this fourth day, only to be bowled between bat and pad by Gibbs. By now Amiss, punishing anything loose had reached a chanceless hundred and he was unbeaten on 123 as England took supper at 218 for five, still 12 runs behind and with only the tail left to support Amiss.

A huge crowd, noisy, irreverent, packed into Sabina Park for another scorching day as England set about its apparently forlorn task of trying to save the game. One mistake from Amiss and it was over.

As Amiss marched onwards, his permanence at the crease almost taken for granted by colleagues, opponents and spectators, so Underwood, too, began to resist gamely, lasting for 75 runs before Sobers, bowling his seamers now, beat him with an outswinger.

Amiss pulls to midwicket on the fourth day at Sabina Park. The wicket-keeper is Deryck Murray. Amiss ended the day at 123 not out, with England still behind and five wickets left to save the game on the final day.

England's hopes were rising, for Knott, next in, had a stout heart and a spirit which found a challenge in a crisis. And then, unbelievably, Amiss tried to pinch another single to Lloyd who, striking like a cobra, picked up the ball and threw down the stumps with Knott, who had uttered a yelp of despair while still in mid-pitch, a yard short of safety. Amiss hung his head in shame.

At lunch his team-mates urged him to forget the debacle and to concentrate upon saving the game. It could still be done. Amiss was utterly exhausted and sat in his corner barely able to sip tea or munch a cheese sandwich. Seeing his body, though not his spirit, sagging, a colleague compared England's last hope to a 'sack of potatoes', or some such, an image so apposite that the nickname 'sacker' stayed with Amiss for the rest of his career. To revive his spirits team-mates provided Amiss with nips of brandy, a ploy repeated at tea with no evident disadvantage. After lunch, Old was perilously close to dismissal first ball from Sobers who was distraught when his appeal was denied. Now he too rose to the occasion, batting for 118 minutes against an increasingly heart-broken West Indian team, lacking an explosive fast bowler to intimidate and demolish the tail. Finally at 343 Old was beaten by Barrett. England were only 113 in front and plenty of time remained for a result.

To Amiss' horror Pocock had a huge slog at Barrett first ball, a shot as inappropriate as singing a music-hall song of doubtful lyrics at a state funeral. Meanwhile Amiss, fighting fatigue, batting now as if in a trance, scarely aware of the passing of time, reached his first double hundred in first-class cricket with his 34th boundary, a cover drive off Sobers.

Slowly it became apparent that a wicket was not going to fall, that Amiss surely was not going to get out. Slowly the West Indians resigned themselves to their fate. It was, in truth, beyond comprehension that England, who had wasted two good men and whose morale was notoriously low, whose middle-order was fragile and whose tail was long, had not been beaten.

By the time Pocock was out, England were safe. Amiss faced 563 balls in 570 minutes at the wicket, hardly missing a delivery and giving only one chance, a difficult one to Sobers. It was an heroic effort which turned the tide. England drew the next two Tests and, against all the odds, squared the series with a brave, narrow win when the teams returned to Trinidad. For himself, Amiss simply continued pottering along collecting runs in his unswerving way, leaving as little as possible to chance, happy never to return to the bad old days.

DON BRADMAN

Australia v England, Lord's, 1930
SCORECARD ON PAGE 159

A happy Bradman on the ship arriving at Dover on 23 April 1930. Judging by his dress, he found the weather on his first tour cold. Before the end of May, however, he had scored 1,000 runs and warmed everybody up: fielders, fans and writers.

❝ *Every ball's the first ball whether I've just come to the wicket or have reached 200. And I never consider the possibility that anybody will get me out.* ❞

DON BRADMAN

Donald George Bradman, the boy from Bowral who was, in fact, born in Cootamundra, another hot, friendly bush town in rural New South Wales, the boy who practised alone by throwing a golf ball at a corrugated wall and hitting the rebound, was far and away the greatest phenomenon cricket, possibly even any game, has ever known. He scored a hundred every third innings or so, not by attrition but through aggression. On average his 117 hundreds took 128 minutes to reach. In the year the Second World War began he had 21 lines in *Who's Who*, only eight fewer than Hitler and 17 more than Stalin.

Yet he was no machine. To call him such is to be dismissive, to say that the game was easier for him, that he could simply walk out and start belting the ball around, an insult.

It was not a freak who arrived in England in the spring of 1930 but a nerveless, independent character who cared not a fig for style: 'Style? I know nothing about style. All I'm after is runs.' Moreover, he had crosses to bear. Had not Maurice Tate said, and Percy Fender written, that his cross-bat technique was bound to be his undoing on England's soft pitches?

By the end of May he had made 1,000 runs. His hundred on a soft pitch against Percy Fender's Surrey must have been particularly enjoyable. Can't bat on soft wickets eh? To rub it in he took his score to 252 not out. Douglas Jardine fielded throughout that innings and the experience left its mark.

By now Bradman was a hero and the demands upon him were ferocious. People followed him onto trains and stared at him wherever he went. The pressure was colossal. Then Australia lost the first Test. Bradman made 131 but England had by far the best of the conditions and won by 93 runs. So Chapman's men arrived in good heart for the second contest at Lord's.

Five days later England knew she faced the grim prospect of bowling to the greatest and hungriest of batsmen for another 20 years or so.

At first things went well for England. Duleepsinhji hit 173 and Chapman's men reached 425, a secure total in the ordinary run of things. In reply Woodfull and Ponsford began carefully, but by the time play was stopped so that King George V could meet the players, the Australians had taken the score to 162.

Immediately upon the resumption Ponsford was out, edging a catch to slip off Farmer White — 'the monarch's wicket'. And so at 3.10pm on Saturday, 28 June 1930, Don Bradman came out to bat for the first time at Lord's. It was a lovely sunlit evening. By the close he'd been batting for 155 minutes and had scored 155 not out. Tate, White, Allen and Robins had been flayed without mercy. Between England's top bowlers and this new Australian charger there was a vast gulf, and as they drifted home on their trains, everyone present that day knew it.

Bradman began by darting yards down the pitch first ball to White, which was supposed to be impossible as White bowled his left-arm spinners at a pace approaching Underwood's. Cardus recalled that first stroke as 'a flash of prancing white and yellow, with a crack that echoed around the ground and sent the pigeons flying'.

Bradman was on his way. At the crease he rarely talked to anyone and seemed to be in total communion with himself. His judgement was sharp and precise. Anything short was belted through mid-wicket with extraordinary power. If the bowlers pitched up to leg Bradman would tuck the ball away with a clipped stroke which sent the ball skating across the turf. To spinners White and Robins he drove down the pitch and ran with the shot, scoring off practically every ball. Later Bradman was to pick this innings as his greatest because 'every ball went exactly where I intended it to go'. Every ball.

Percy Chapman manœuvred his field, set traps, fought to stem the flow, but it was hopeless. When one gap was closed Bradman simply picked another. If Chapman moved a man from cover to mid-wicket the Don would hit the following delivery through the covers. It was a slaughter. Tate earned a huge roar

Bradman batting at Headingley in 1930. Two weeks after his brilliant innings at Lord's he made 300 in a day at Leeds and went on to the highest Ashes score of 334.

when he bowled a maiden to him. Bradman reached his 50 out of 66 in 46 minutes. By now the wise Woodfull, who had been going well, was content to take a back seat. At tea Australia were 244 for one with Woodfull on 105 and Bradman on a gleeful, murderous 59.

After tea Bradman continued carting feared bowlers to all quarters of an astonished Lord's. Cardus was to say that Bradman should be given out every time he missed the ball. By 5.25pm he'd reached his hundred. He'd been in 106 minutes and had so far added 152 runs with his captain. Bradman was dictating the course of the match. Just before the close Woodfull was stumped for 155 off a leg-break he could barely reach. Bradman left the field of destruction on 155 with Australia having surged on to 404 for two.

Bradman returned to business on Monday morning. He appeared certain to crunch his way past R. E. Foster's 27-year-old record Test score of 287. It was, in fact, to take Bradman a fortnight to beat 287 for, here, on 254, for the first time he lifted the ball. It went like a shot from a cannon but Chapman at silly mid-off took a marvellous, jumping catch. The Don left to a loud ovation. Bradman had been in for five hours and 39 minutes.

Australia won the Test easily, and won the decisive fifth Test too, thanks to Bradman's 232.

And so it went on, as England had feared, till finally Bradman retired with a Test average nigh on 100, far ahead of any rival. Everything predicted that Saturday evening at Lord's came to be. Bowlers were frightened of him. They crumpled in front of his eyes, even as he walked, sprightly and smiling, out to bat. They knew he was their master and could see only punishment, merciless punishment, in those determined unblinking eyes. The world of cricket changed that day in June.

ROY FREDERICKS

West Indies v Australia, Perth, 1975–76
SCORECARD ON PAGE 159

SCORECARD ON PAGE 159

Twenty thousand people crowded into the WACA ground in Perth when play began in the second Test match of the series between Australia and the West Indies in 1975–76. These were the two greatest teams of the era and their meeting had the atmosphere of a world title fight. Lloyd's men had won cricket's first World Cup a few months earlier and were expected to provide stiff opposition for Chappell's powerful eleven that, with fast bowlers Lillee and Thomson, had so destroyed England the previous winter.

Australia had drawn first blood in Brisbane, where the aggressive West Indians had hooked and carved their way to self-destruction.

Ian Chappell batted first in Perth and Australia were all out for 329 after 20 minutes play on the second morning. As Lillee marked out his run on his home ground the chanting built into a crescendo, as youth barracked for its Larrikin deity. Usually those chants of 'Lillee, Lillee' or 'kill, kill, kill' lasted all day as batsmen ducked and weaved, taking terrible blows on their bodies and losing all dignity as they sprawled on the ground in search of safety. This time the crowd was, within a few overs, transformed into a bubbling, excited audience roaring its approval of one of cricket's most dazzling exhibitions of batting.

Under a warm sun and upon a white, shining pitch Roy Fredericks took guard and cast a casual eye around the field. In his early years he had been a grafter, a typically nuggety left-hander in the John Edrich mould. Now he'd said goodbye to all that. If these fellows were going to rough him up they would at least know they had been in a fight.

Lillee's first ball brought Fredericks into watchful defence. Apparently concluding that his eye was now in Fredericks hooked at Lillee's second ball, a bumper, but he misjudged the bounce and edged the ball upwards and towards fine leg where Max Walker began to anticipate a catch. In a moment he was, instead, wondering how many rows back in the stand this shot would land. Fredericks had broken his duck with a six which returned from orbit to plop into a member's hands almost behind the sightscreen. It was to be his only edged shot in 212 minutes at the crease.

And so a whirlwind was let loose. Stirred by recollection of Fredericks treading on his wicket at Lord's, and of reckless hooking in Brisbane, Lillee continued to drop short and Fredericks continued to hook. Thomson was no less prodigal with short deliveries as the Australian captain, Greg Chappell, kept his ring of men around the bat, no matter how regularly the ball flashed through point or square leg.

After six overs bowled by one of cricket's greatest opening pairs the West Indians were 60 for no wicket. Time and again Fredericks lay back and cracked through point those 'not a man move' shots as they are called in the Caribbean. Seeing this small cricketer taking on the high and mighty fast bowlers aroused the crowd and they cheered loudly as scintillating shot piled upon scintillating shot.

At slip Greg Chappell stood beside his brother, apparently detached and certainly not prepared to change tactics. Why should he? England had been slaughtered by fast and short bowling.

Gilmour was brought on and almost at once Julien fell, caught at slip. With Fredericks he had added 91 runs in 10 overs, for already Fredericks had reached his 50 in 33 balls.

Rowe arrived and still the barrage continued, with Gilmour being mercilessly punished. At lunch, after 14 overs of extraordinary cricket, the West Indies were 130 for one. Soon afterwards Rowe fell to Thomson, caught by Marsh, which brought a second dimin-

OPPOSITE *Fredericks drives through the off-side in Australia during the West Indian tour of 1975–76, when he savaged Lillee and Thomson as they never had been before.*

utive left-hander, Kallicharran, to join Fredericks. Still Chappell and his bowlers attacked, and still the crowd bayed, intoxicated by the vibrant play.

Nothing changed, nothing stopped Fredericks' astonishing assault. At slip Ian Chappell was surprised to hear a louder round of applause than usual for a boundary. He looked at the board and was nonplussed to discover that after 22 overs of batting the West Indians had reached 200! And this in a Test match!

With another punching back foot shot Fredericks reached his hundred and the ground rose to him. He had faced just 71 balls. Only Viv Richards and J. M. Gregory have hit faster hundreds in Test cricket, and both were facing weaker bowling in very different situations.

Gilmour's five overs cost 61 runs, and he was removed and Ashley Mallett's off-spin tried. With Walker and Mallett in tandem and a defensive field set, Fredericks did slow down, for opportunities to hook and cut were fewer and further between. Moreover the sheer violence of his innings had tired him, as a boxer might tire after throwing punches for a few hectic minutes. It had been cricket at its rawest, as, for the only time in those few seasons when both men were at their peak, Lillee and Thomson were tamed.

Still cutting hard, and sweeping Mallett, Fredericks added another 69 runs off 74 balls, pedestrian by his standards this day, lightning fast in common company, until finally he tickled a vengeful Lillee to Greg Chappell at slip. Fredericks had been at the crease for 212 minutes and had faced 145 balls. His 169, which included one six and 27 fours, had been scored out of 258 and it had put his team in actual and psychological command of the game.

All present remember the innings and shake their heads still at the wonder of it, for it was barely within the bounds of possibility. Apart from his first shot no-one could recall Fredericks missing a ball and certainly the innings was chanceless. Seldom had ferocious fast bowling been defied so bravely and magnificently.

Fredericks hooks Lillee for six at Perth to begin one of the most thrilling innings in all Test cricket. Lillee's aggressive field includes a row of slips and two short legs, but Fredericks' shot landed in the stand high over deep fine leg.

W. G. GRACE

Gloucestershire v Somerset, Bristol, 1895

SCORECARD ON PAGE 160

W. G. Grace's stance. The Champion is wearing an MCC cap and has an MCC tie tied round his waist.

⑤ *Leaving the ball alone never won matches. I don't like defensive shots, you can only get three off 'em.* ⑨

W.G. GRACE

By 1895 W. G. Grace was already an old man. A year earlier he had averaged only 18 for Gloucestershire and the barrackers were quick to comment upon his vast bulk and his declining powers. Grace was aware of the calls for his retirement. Already contemplating a quieter life, the doctor decided to play only a few games that season. 'Cricket', he had said in 1884, 'interferes with my practice. I have a good practice which increases every winter when I am at home and decreases every summer when I'm away. It makes me wonder if I shall ever get to Harley Street.'

Eleven years later the old man, now 48, was still around, though his form was patchy, shadow where there had been substance.

He had been a great. At 18 years of age he'd scored 224 not out at The Oval for the Gentlemen against the Players and been forced to miss the final day to run in a 440-yard hurdle race, which he won. From 1868 to 1877 (when first the rumours began that he might be considering settling down to life in a surgery) Grace dominated the game as only Bradman has done since. It was said that only the arrival of touring teams from Australia kept him going. This is hard to believe. Men of Grace's temperament do not walk away from their stage. They have to be removed in boxes. Grace may have talked of retirement regularly but, like Nellie Melba, he never really meant it.

Grace virtually invented batsmanship. Till his arrival no one had used forward and back play so well. He was scientific in his approach, organised in his thought, scorning orthodoxy. Nor had anyone filled grounds as did Grace. An old advertisement outside one field tells the tale. 'Entry 3d. Sixpence if Dr Grace plays'.

For a decade the young, slim Grace demolished bowlers. Guided by his early coaching from Uncle Pocock he stood with the tip of his brown left boot raised and with his bat up early and ready to strike. One professional, upon dismissing him, habitually flung his cap in the air.

But this was all in the past by 1895. Only the shell of greatness remained. And then came the miracle of his life, 'the extraordinary rejuvenescence' as it was called. He opened with 13 and 103 for MCC against Sussex. 'Nice to see the old man scoring a few', said the pundits. It couldn't last of course.

He failed against Yorkshire – was it here he moved down to a bowler who'd dismissed him to squeak in his surprising voice: 'My boy, if you live to be 100 you'll never send down another one like that'? – and further decline was anticipated.

So, that May, Grace arrived at the County Ground, Taunton, wearing, as usual, white flannel trousers, a black coat and a black hat. On the field brown boots, by now out of vogue, hid those awesome feet, so big that an Australian once opined that he was worth £3 a week and his 'tucker' just to walk about crushing the cockroaches.

Somerset's standards had slipped since the pioneering days of 1890–93 when the club had forced its way into the County Championship. Not for the last time Somerset's bowling was a trifle friendly that year.

The teams met in Bristol. At first all went well for Somerset as Palairet and the hitter Fowler added 205 for the first wicket. But Somerset collapsed to 303, with W.G. taking five for 87 in 45 overs.

Nerves felt, but never shown, W.G. marched to the wicket and at once set to work. Two partners fell cheaply but Grace soldiered on, staying in his crease to play Tyler's flighty spin, moving forward to drive the ageing medium pace of Woods and Nichols (who wrote plays and died young). Behind the stumps

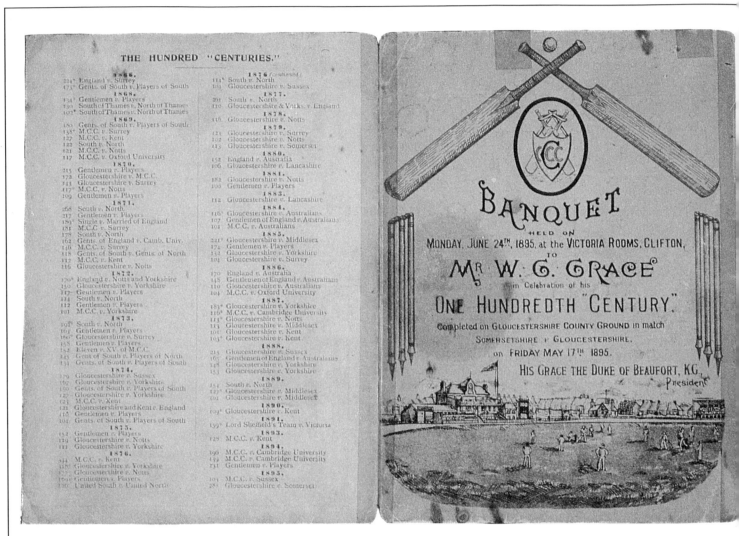

The menu/souvenir for the banquet held to celebrate W. G. Grace's century of centuries. The feat was performed on 17 May, and is the innings described here. The banquet was held at the Victoria Rooms, Clifton, on 24 June 1895.

was the Reverend A. P. Wickham, who wore brown pads, a famously celebrated butterfly collector who couldn't see much now behind W. G. Grace's vast posterior. Later Wickham was to say that he had no hesitation in describing this innings as the best he had ever seen (and he played and saw a lot).

W.G. drove Tyler's good length slows, pitching a foot outside off-stump, over mid-on's head and over the ropes. In those days this counted only four. You had to clear the ground to get six. To his death Wickham maintained that Grace allowed only four balls to pass the bat, one down the leg-side and 'three low ones to off'.

Grace made 288. When he reached 100 he became the first man to score 100 first-class hundreds, one reason this innings has been chosen. A magnum of champagne was brought out and the old man, whose appetites generally were massive, drank copiously, but those who hoped thereby to disturb his rhythm were sadly disappointed.

He was ninth out at 465, finally trapped by Woods, whereupon Somerset collapsed for 189 and lost by nine wickets.

Nor is this the end of the tale. Grace had promised, that third night, to attend a dinner in London for A. E. Stoddart, who had toured Australia so success-

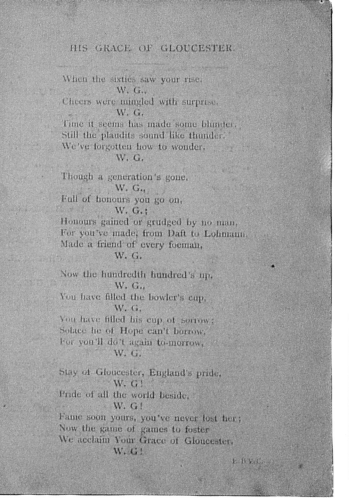

SOMERSET
v.
GLOUCESTERSHIRE,
TAUNTON,
JUNE 29TH, 30TH, 1896.

RIGHT *Less than a week after his banquet, Grace leaves the field with Sammy Woods, the captain of Somerset, just out for another 186 runs.*

fully the previous winter. Accordingly, he caught the first train at the end of the game without bothering to change. Nor was he put out to find a lady in his compartment. Her objections to his changing stopped as soon as he explained the circumstances and begged forgiveness. Grace arrived at the dinner at 8.45pm and everyone stood up and cheered him for two minutes. Apparently the old man beamed and was much touched.

W.G. went from strength to strength, fielding all day against Kent, hitting 257 himself and then knocking off the runs so that he never once left the field. When 30 May arrived Grace needed 153 to be the first player to reach 1,000 runs in May. Appropriately he was playing at Lord's when finally he pulled a long-hop to the fence. The crowd rose to him. National subscriptions were instituted by the *Daily Telegraph*, while *The Sportsman* set up a shilling fund. Grace ended £9,073 8s 3d to the good, not bad for an amateur. *Punch* and *The Times* agreed that he should be knighted, and so he should have been. Yet he never was.

Greatness lasts. By returning with such vigour W.G. silenced his critics, temporarily anyhow. He was too old really, it was just the lion reminding his people that if he could not hunt so well, he could still roar.

W. R. HAMMOND

England v Australia, Lord's, 1938
SCORECARD ON PAGE 160

In June 1938 German boys were marching along the Frankfurteralle armed with brushes and buckets of white paint daubing the Star of David on shops pointed out to them by adults. At school, speaking to Jewish class-mates was forbidden. In Austria the Nazis decreed that anyone who wanted to marry must prove his Aryan ancestry. In Vienna all Jews were given 14 days' notice by their employers.

As gradually, painfully, reluctantly Europe began to steel itself for war, yet, at the same time, tried to carry on, at least in its entertainments, Don Bradman's Australians arrived in England determined to hold on to the urn they had so narrowly retained against Gubby Allen's tourists in 1935–36.

Walter Hammond was leading the England eleven. Until the rise of Bradman, Hammond had been the great champion of cricket. Standing erect, he could thunder the ball down the ground off the back foot with an authority that brooked no argument. He'd burst into the England team in 1927 as a sleek, virile all-rounder and had appeared certain to dominate Test cricket for decades. So commanding was he and so brilliant that supremacy seemed to be his for the taking. And then Bradman had turned up, a merciless, efficient, chuckling batsman capable of scores beyond any other mortal. Hammond was an emperor denied an empire.

By 1938 Hammond was supposed to be in decline. But here he was, locking horns with Bradman, the greatest two of their time. The first Test was drawn after heavy scoring.

A fortnight later the struggle was resumed at Lord's. England, batting after winning the toss, lost Hutton and Edrich in a trice, Hutton being surprised by swing and lift into prodding a catch to short leg and Edrich edging a hook onto his stumps.

Hammond marched out from the

The scene at the end of play on the second day at Lord's in 1938, when Hammond played an innings about which C. L. R. James, the great West Indian cricket writer, said he had never seen a finer.

pavilion looking, thought Robertson-Glasgow, 'like a ship in full sail'. It was 11.50am and he was to play the greatest innings of his career. Barnett fell at 31 and disaster loomed. McCormick was bowling at a tremendous pace on a greenish pitch and had taken all three wickets. With green-capped, silent, gum-chewing Australians surrounding him, pressing even harder for another breakthrough, Hammond felt alone and responsible.

Paynter joined him at 12.04pm and his perky relish for the fight raised Hammond's spirit. Moreover, the bat felt good in his hands and his feet were moving easily into position. Of late Hammond's batting had suffered periods of nervousness during which the previously vibrant flames burned low. Cricket is not always so simple a game in adulthood. Politics, frustrations, disappointments, private worries, complicate the task which W.G. had defined as 'putting the bat upon the ball'.

Now Hammond was ablaze again. Moving back he punched McCormick to the straight boundary. Moving forward to McCabe's gentle medium pace, he drove in his measured, majestic way and the ball shuddered to the fence. Within 68 minutes he was acknowledging applause for his 50. To the crowd it was a remembrance of an earlier Hammond, a Hammond unbowed before the world. By lunch Hammond was on 70 and the total 134 for three. He had played every shot bar the hook, which Jardine claimed was bad for business.

Hammond's form continued after the break and at 3.06pm he reached his hundred with a single patted into a gap in a field by now retreating to protect the boundaries. He had been batting for two hours and 26 minutes.

Only the mean O'Reilly could now put any pressure upon the batsmen, as he roared in off seven long splay-footed strides, bowling too fast to allow Hammond to move down the pitch, and utterly unprepared to give second best.

Paynter fell for 99, leg before to O'Reilly. With his captain he'd steadied the ship and added 222. Ames took guard at 4.15pm with Hammond on 132. After tea Wally continued to scale the heights of batting mastery. Rarely had a bat looked so wide, rarely had cricket appeared so absurdly simple a game. Hammond was picking cherries from a tree. With a sense of inevitability Hammond's 200 was reached with a single after five hours and 14 minutes at the crease. At the close he stood invincible on 210.

Next day Hammond added a further 30 runs before McCormick tore out his leg stump. In just over six hours he had hit 32 boundaries. One off-drive thumped into the pavilion wall and returned nearly to the middle. The bowler picked up the ball lying near the top of his mark and carried on bowling as if nothing had happened. Hammond gave only one slight chance, a sizzling drive which split Chipperfield's finger. None that saw it ever forgot that innings. Those vivid bold shots played by a magnificent figure in a cream shirt spoke of greatness. C. L. R. James said he had never seen a finer innings. Vast crowds had watched the cricket – the gates were closed at noon on the first day and 33,800 were packed in before play began on the second, so many that hundreds had to sit on the grass beyond the boundary rope, which had to be moved forward a few yards. King George V watched some of Hammond's innings. Well may he have done so. It was a dish fit for the occasion.

HANIF MOHAMMAD

Pakistan v West Indies, Bridgetown, 1957–58
SCORECARD ON PAGE 161

Hanif Mohammad fled with his family at Partition to Karachi, where they found a bed in a refugee camp before setting up house in a disused Hindu temple, where they lived for a few years.

Standing at around 5ft 6in (1.68m) and weighing no more than $9\frac{1}{4}$ stone (59kg), Hanif was the middle of five brothers born into the Mohammad family which, until Partition, lived in Junagadh in the Kathcawar Peninsula, an ear of land which sticks out above Bombay. Beside the illustrious Mohammads this land produced Ranji, Duleep, Mankad, Mushtaq Ali and Amar Singh, greats of Indian cricket. Between them the quintet of brothers scored 10,938 Test runs and hit 190 hundreds in first-class cricket.

Partition drove the Mohammad family away from Junagadh and towards Pakistan, leaving their possessions behind, and their friends too. With his elder brothers working in Habib Bank it was Hanif who quickly rose to be the first star of Pakistan cricket. He was guided by an old Pathan wicket-keeper, Abdul Aziz, who would tell Karachi umpires in the 1950s to avoid giving Hanif out if at all possible, for nothing was to stop the rise of his prodigy.

Due to tour England in 1954 Hanif contemplated how to prepare and decided to take the last net practice each evening in the Pir of Pirago garden to accustom himself to batting in dim light. Incredibly Pakistan drew that series, but nothing had prepared their batsmen for Roy Gilchrist, when the team arrived in the Caribbean in 1958 to play West Indies. With no fast bowlers of their own, and brown, dead pitches upon which to bat, Pakistan, in facing Gilchrist, were meeting a ferocity and a pace far in advance of anything in their experience.

The teams met in Barbados for the first Test match. Batting first upon winning the toss, the West Indians pounded their way to 579 for nine with débutant Conrad Hunte hitting 142 and Everton Weekes 197.

In reply Pakistan were skittled for 106. Gilchrist's first ball climbed over Hanif, over wicket-keeper Alexander, and hit the Bridgetown sightscreen on the bounce.

Pakistan faced humiliation. A proud patriot with a realisation of his importance in these pioneering years, Hanif set about restoring his team's reputation in the second innings. It was an awesome task, for the tourists were following on 473 behind and had three days to bat.

As Gilchrist marked out his run again Hanif took guard, a Daniel facing a Goliath. He wore no helmet, of course, only a handkerchief around his neck; he did not even wear a thigh pad (the Pakistanis did not take to thigh pads until their 1962 tour of England), simply a piece of towel stuffed into his left trouser pocket.

Wisely Hanif, following Clyde Walcott's advice, cut out his hook shot when facing Gilchrist. No risks could be taken because only with a long innings could Hanif set an example to his teammates. This was a burden he was to carry throughout his Test career and it led to much barracking, for Hanif never played in a powerful Pakistan batting order. Had he done so his genius might have found a lighter expression.

Moving neatly and precisely into position Hanif reached 60 not out at the close of the third day. Alexander, the West Indian captain, tried bombarding him with Gilchrist but Hanif simply swayed out of the way; he tried his spinners, Denis St E. Atkinson, Valentine and Sobers, who between them were to bowl 158 overs for four wickets in this innings. Later he even tried Walcott, more commonly a stumper, but each was met with a straight and unrelenting bat. Gilchrist felt like a wave crashing against a tidal wall as Hanif resisted, every shot immaculate in conception.

By the close of the fourth day Hanif was '160-odd not out' and 'we started thinking we could save it'. In the evenings he repaired to his hotel room and sat quietly listening to sitar music before going out to see Muslim friends in Bridgetown for a bite to eat. This time, upon his return to his room he found a message from his captain Hafeez Kardar. 'You can save us. They can't get you out. You are our last hope.'

Battling on, troubled by Eric St E. Atkinson's medium-pace swingers, which he could not read, Hanif continued next morning playing every ball on its merits, for every ball is unique. In those days West Indian Tests lasted six days with five hours' play each day, so Hanif could not afford a mistake. He had to bat for another day and a half.

At the end of the fifth day Hanif was still unbeaten. By now his eyes were bloodshot. For his pains he was to have three layers of skin burned away from beneath those eyes by the harsh glare reflected from the pitch. More sitar music, another dinner with his friends and another message from Kardar: 'If you can play until tea-time we will be safe', and Hanif was off to a restless, weary and adrenalin-packed sleep. His brain kept replaying Gilchrist's bumpers. Could he save Pakistan?

He could and did. By tea he was '330-

odd and afterward the announcer said I'd beaten Bradman's 334, then Hammond's 336. There was only Hutton's 364 to go when a ball from Denis Atkinson popped a bit and went off the top of my bat as I tried to off-glance.'

A game had been saved. Hanif, by being caught behind, had missed Hutton's record but by batting for 970 minutes, the longest innings on record, he had entered the ranks of the immortals. Apparently insuperable odds had been defied, and he'd stood as a tiny man, refusing to give way no matter how awesome the bombardment.

This 337 was his masterpiece, an innings of courage, concentration and craft far beyond the scope of ordinary mortals. Like Sunil Gavaskar, whose technique and mannerisms his so clearly resembled, Hanif showed that subcontinental batsmen could, without any practice, against overwhelming odds, deal with the fastest, most hostile bowling and construct magnificent innings against it. For this reason this pair, forever batting in weak sides against powerful bowling, stand out as the two greatest batsmen of the post-war era.

A very young Hanif turns a ball through the leg trap during a private game at Osterley on his tour of England in 1954.

GEORGE HEADLEY

West Indies v England, Kingston, 1934–35
SCORECARD ON PAGE 161

George Headley: a snap from his private album.

From the time, in 1930, when George Headley played in his first Test match, scoring 21 and 176 as a youth of 20, almost to the time he retired, the cry in West Indian cricket was: 'Headley out, all out'. Headley had to carry a heavy burden. Disciplined, dedicated, brave, reserved, he carried the burden lightly, always playing Test cricket as if he were fooling around with his son in the back garden. Moderate and modest by temperament, he propped up the Caribbean batting so often that he won the nickname 'Atlas'.

By 18 he was planning to go to America to train as a dentist. Delays in the passport office allowed him to play against Lord Tennyson's tourists in 1927. In the first game he hit 71, in the second 211, and in the third another 71. Without undue difficulty, and with immense enthusiasm from a cricket-mad island, he was persuaded to stay.

Headley studied batting and worked to correct his faults with a fierce determination and with an intense concentration he kept largely to himself. Analytical and intelligent, he'd go to his hotel room at night and think about his innings next day. A true master did not leave anything to chance. And a master he became. His Test record is magnificent. Though he never played against weak countries, though he bore so much responsibility, he still scored 2,190 runs at an average of 60.83 and hit 10 hundreds. Twice he hit hundreds in both innings of a Test match against England. Asked to compare Walcott, Weekes, Worrell and Sobers with Headley one cricketer said: 'They could sit in the same cathedral as George, but not on the same pew.'

In 1934–35, when England sent their strongest team yet to the Caribbean, Headley was acknowledged as a giant. A comfortable victory was anticipated by the English authorities, but Headley put an end to all that in the deciding Test played at Sabina Park, Jamaica, in March.

For Headley the scene was set. He often reserved his best performances for his home crowd, which adored him and chanted his name. Love demands a response from the champion. It provides inspiration, driving the man on to still greater deeds. Not that Headley, taking guard on the first morning at 5 for one after Barrow had been bowled by Farnes, betrayed any notion or any sense, even, that this was an historic moment. Everything, of course, depended upon him. In 15 of his 25 innings for the West Indies he was top-scorer, in 11 making over half the runs.

Headley began imperiously. Wicket-keeper Christiani was bowled at 92 but

Headley cutting a ball through the slips. After deciding during a tour of Australia in 1930–31 that his favourite sizzling shots through the covers carried risks, he adopted a defter style, concentrating more on the leg side and on his cutting.

Headley was now set like concrete. Wyatt relied heavily upon his spinners Hollies and Paine. Headley moved his feet and chipped them through the leg-side. If they pitched short he rocked back and cut. To the quickies, Smith and Farnes, Headley shuffled into line, a technique he had mastered after tours to the Antipodes. He did not show them the stumps, did not flash, did not make a mistake. It was black excellence writ large. Anybody could see it. He wasn't the black Bradman, he was George

Headley, the great West Indian. This pair added 202 before Paine trapped Sealy. With Constantine swishing furiously the next pair added 58 in the blink of an eye before Constantine departed, quickly followed by Mudie and Fuller. Grant, the white captain from Trinidad, now joined Headley, whose bat was still resolutely straight. Headley had decided to bat for two days. The pitch was good, the bowling tired, and he had the strength. The pair added a further 147 and their opponents were broken.

Eventually Grant declared at 535 for seven. Headley was left unbeaten on 270, the highest score by a West Indian in Test cricket until 1973–74 when Lawrence Rowe cut past it. Headley had never really charged. Nor had he ever really looked like losing his wicket.

It only remained for Martindale and Constantine to finish the job. This they did, and handsomely. England lost by an innings and 161 runs, a staggeringly conclusive victory for the hosts, a nearly new entrant into Test cricket. England's team was powerful. The West Indian win owed nothing to chance. Their cricket had been excellent not freakish. And Headley towered above any other batsman in the game, even the awesome Walter Hammond, then at the height of his powers.

The West Indian cricketing board were as unwillng to appoint a black captain as England were to appoint a professional one. It was all the most appalling humbug. Headley certainly should have led his country. Few cricketers have been as quietly impressive. The West Indies did not choose a black touring captain (Worrell) until 1960.

Headley, head still, weight balanced, was allowed to carry his team but not to lead it. This 270 showed, at any rate, that West Indians could be not only brilliant, which everyone admitted, they could also be monumental.

CLEM HILL

Australia v England, Sheffield, 1902
SCORECARD ON PAGE 162

Clem Hill in a series of post-cards based on photographs taken by the famous cricket photographers of Hawkins of Brighton.

Clem Hill was a batsman capable of great deeds. Trumper used to say that he was the most difficult man of all to get out. His 188 against Archie MacLaren's tourists in 1897–98 remains the highest score by a man not yet 21 in Ashes Tests. Moreover, he hit 182 of them on that first day in Melbourne. No cricketer has scored more than this on the opening day of an Ashes Test in Australia.

Cricket ran in the family. In 1877 Hill's father scored the first ever hundred at the Adelaide Oval. The juvenile Hill scored 360 in a college game and, aged 16 and nine days, won selection for the South Australian XI. After this there was no stopping him.

Cool and self-possessed, Hill was an aggressor who used his brains. C. B. Fry thought that 'even his free and enterprising shots might be considered careful'. He did not bother to charm or to grace. Gripping the bat down the handle and round the back, crouching rather at the crease, he could hit all round the wicket, though the cut was his pride and joy. A small man of independent opinion he could hit fast bowlers to leg with a hook so pragmatic as to make the English aesthetes wince. These Australians, they thought, were really beyond the pale: that Blackham didn't bother with a long-stop, that Spofforth used short-legs and bowled at the pads, and this wretch Hill clouted straight balls to leg where no decent English captain would bother to station a man.

Hill was a scourge of the quickies, using nimble footwork to punch his back-foot shots, bottom hand firmly in charge, swing short and sharp. If the bowlers pitched up he'd slip his hands up the handle and hit hard and straight. Never did he lose his eye for the main chance. Yet, curiously, nerves did affect Clem in one situation. Five times in Test cricket he lost his wicket in the nineties.

In 1901–02 he scored 99, 98 and 97 in successive Test innings. Two matches later he scored 87. On other occasions he fell for 88 and 87 once more. Had he converted these eight opportunities into hundreds his record, already magnificent, would be almost incomparable, particularly in the light of the figures customary for the period.

In all this glory two innings against England stand out, one at Adelaide in 1907–08, and one at Sheffield in 1902. At Adelaide, Hill's eighth-wicket stand with Hartigan of 243 was then a Test record for any wicket, and Hill's 160 turned defeat into victory. But history points us to Sheffield as we pursue greatness. Never can players have been called upon to summon their mightiest efforts so often in so few games as they were in the final three Tests of that year's series. Trumper and Jackson at Manchester, Jessop and Hirst at The Oval, performed in a manner celebrated down the decades, as grandfathers told offspring: 'I was there.'

It fell to Clem Hill to begin these brilliant exchanges, for it was Hill, in the third Test at Bramall Lane, Sheffield, the only Test ever to be played on that distinguished arena, who put Australia one up in the series. Bowled out for 194, Australia nonetheless led on first innings by 49, thanks to good work by Saunders and Noble. Still they were in trouble. This man S. F. Barnes was eating away at their confidence. MacLaren had taken him from League cricket to Australia the previous winter and the Staffordshire wizard had been devastating, taking 18 wickets in three innings before injury struck. Now, silent, brooding, more skilful than Spofforth though not as menacing as a man, Barnes threatened to strike again. He'd taken six for 49 in 20 taunting, dismissive overs in the first innings. If the bogey were not laid to rest MacLaren might recapture the Ashes. Trumper, naturally, began

A photograph of cricket at Bramall Lane around 1902, the year of Hill's innings in the only Test played on the famous Yorkshire ground. The ground was used by Yorkshire from 1855 to 1973. Sheffield United Football Club still use it (although cricket and football never shared the same pitch) and there are prospects for a return of cricket there in the 1990s.

the riposte. Joined by Hill when Duff fell at 20, Victor hit 62 in 50 minutes, biting hard into the authority of the previously triumphant Hirst, Braund and Barnes. The pair added 60 in half an hour of which Hill made 16. Then Trumper was out caught behind off Jackson. Once again cricket asked a question of a player. 'Well', it said, 'he's out. What are you going to do about it?' Determined not to surrender the initiative, Hill hit 14 from Jackson's next over. Nor was the wicket at all easy. To the contrary, it was wet and gripping. Moreover, the light was funereal. Hill had reached 45 by the time lunch was taken. His captain Joe Darling had been dismissed by Barnes for a duck but Syd Gregory, a dynamic cricketer, was standing firm.

The pair added 107 runs in 67 minutes in a low-scoring game on a dodgy pitch in a delicate situation and in semidarkness. Gregory's share was 29. He applauded when, at 3.10pm, Hill cut Jackson to the boundary to reach his hundred after 115 minutes at the crease. For once he had not lost his head in those nervous nineties.

Jackson trapped his man in the end, MacLaren taking a brilliant catch at slip half an hour later. Hill had been in for two hours and 25 minutes. He'd hit 16 boundaries and survived two hard chances, one in the slips off Barnes on 74, the other at long-on off Rhodes when 77. He was out at 225, and from this point Australia collapsed to 289, but the damage had been done.

MacLaren asked Jessop to open, being himself indisposed. Jessop swept to 52 and England to 73 for one overnight but Trumble snared him leg before next morning and the game was over.

In all the great attacking innings which lit up this abysmal summer of 1902 Hill's was, perhaps, the coolest. It is certainly the most neglected, possibly because his team won so easily. But it was a vital innings played by a magnificent player. Barnes did not bowl another ball that summer. He'd cut through Trumper and Hill months earlier in Melbourne and Sydney. Scores had been settled between formidable opponents. Thanks to Hill, Australia were one up.

LEN HUTTON

England v Australia, The Oval, 1938
SCORECARD ON PAGE 162

Hutton being congratulated by Bradman after breaking Bradman's Ashes record of 334. Hardstaff is the non-striker.

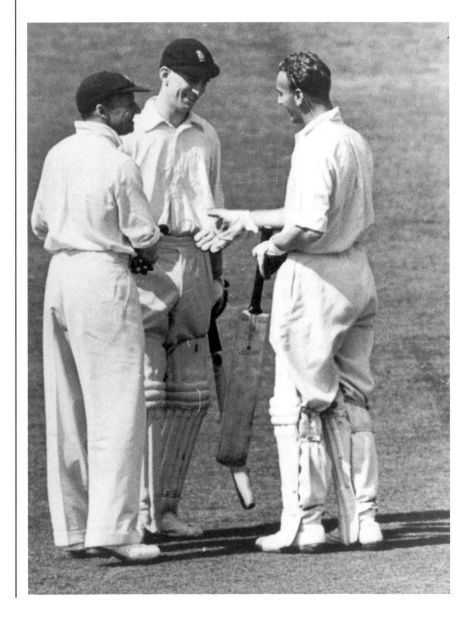

It is an old tale, of how a little 14-year-old boy from Pudsey was taken to Leeds for the 1930 Test against Australia, of how he sat, silent and grave, in his seat while a sprightly young man from far away, Donald Bradman, smote England's best bowlers as if they were chums of his serving up long-hops by way of friendship. Bradman scored 334 that day and continued to slaughter English bowlers for another two decades. It's a tale of how that little boy, one amongst tens of thousands present, helped England to revenge.

Len Hutton was born in Fulnock, a small Moravian Church community, a few miles from Pudsey, itself the birthplace of previous giants of Yorkshire cricket John Tunnicliffe and Herbert Sutcliffe. His father was a builder who raised his son in the stoical, silent traditions of these parts. Throughout his career Hutton was correct and restrained as if it would not do to let go, to betray emotion. Hutton spoke in enigmas, batted as if he had no artistic talent and yet expressed that talent with every sculptured, intense movement.

By 1938 Bradman was back in England and the locals glumly prepared themselves for the slaughter. Few were surprised when, thanks to Bradman's hundred and O'Reilly's ten wickets Australia held the Ashes by winning at Headingley. By the time the teams reached The Oval for the last Test, which was to be played to a finish, England could salvage only pride.

Both teams gambled heavily by picking seven batsmen. Hammond won this gamble, for he won the toss for the fourth time in a row. Bradman, who had not yet changed, chuckled as grim a chuckle as was ever chuckled, for 'Bosser' Martin's pitch was a belter. As Edrich and Hutton walked out to bat the words of their captain, Walter Hammond, echoed in their ears. 'Stay in forever', he had said, and what is more he'd meant it. However, with England on 29 Edrich fell leg before to the leg-spinner Bill O'Reilly, the greatest bowler of the era. This brought in Leyland, promoted to first wicket down by Hammond, the customary occupant of this position. The change worked superbly, for Australia did not take another wicket for 382 runs.

Hutton met every delivery with a bat so straight that the ball scarcely left the

Crowds stand in front of the pavilion and all round the ground to salute Len Hutton on his record-breaking innings.

🖐 *Well done, Len, but why ever didn't you score one run more – one for every day of the year?* 🖐
A WOMAN WHO MET HUTTON AS HE LEFT THE OVAL.

🖐 *Tell me, Denis, can you ever please a woman?* 🖐
HUTTON, TO DENIS COMPTON, WHO WAS WITH HIM.

cut part of the strip. At the crease his 'relaxed stance and time to play the ball' impressed Compton who had 'never seen anyone who looked less likely to get out'.

And then, incredibly, Hutton had a rush of blood. Down the pitch he danced, missed Fleetwood-Smith's googly and gave Ben Barnett a stumping chance. Pitched up, the ball skidded through and eluded Barnett who was never allowed to forget a mistake which cost his side 324 runs. Australia waited over 12 hours for a second opportunity.

At lunch England were 89 for one after a morning of solid batting. Hutton might as well have brought his sleeping bag with him, so calm was his occupation of the crease. During the interval, and the five which were to follow, Hutton nibbled quietly at a fruit salad and sipped tea; idle chatter might spoil his rhythm of mind and body.

Upon play resuming the Yorkshiremen continued to pile on the runs as the Aussies toiled in vain. O'Reilly was already muttering: 'Where's the groundsman's hut? If I had a rifle I'd shoot him now.' Hutton simply carried on crafting every shot, footwork precise and bat straight. He gave no more hope to the bowlers. Just before tea he reached his hundred and then for half an hour he forged ahead against the second new ball which Bradman had taken for change as much as anything. No mercy was expected by the Australians and none was given. This was contemporary batting, the batting of Ponsford, Woodfull, Kippax and Bradman, taken to its logical conclusion. Batting, the world now knew, was about scoring runs. Leyland, marooned in the nineties for half an hour, finally reached his no less meritorious century. And so the pair raced towards the close untroubled by Aus-

TOP RIGHT *Hutton sweeps to leg during his innings. It was a great achievement of technique, perseverance, patience and determination.*

tralia's weak bowling, applying themselves with the utmost dedication to their task. England were 347 for one at the close.

The Oval was bathed in colour as play resumed next morning. Hutton carried on, meticulous, precise, unwavering. Finally, at 411, Leyland was run out for 187, a surprising lapse as the pair had been running beautifully. Hammond marched majestically out, scarcely a sight to cheer the footsore Australians.

With scarcely a hiccup England moved onwards and at last, with his score around 250, Hutton began to contemplate Bradman's record. Contemplation was one thing, consummation quite another. Hutton, his body sagging with weariness, his mind numb, and yet every distraction ignored, continued, head down, picking off runs.

At the close of the second day England stood at 634 for five. By now Hammond and, in a clutter, Compton and Paynter, had lost their wickets, the latter pair for one run, a fate Compton had confidently predicted. Hutton had scored 300.

Sleep was impossible. Leyland told him to drink a port and a Guinness, and, though the teetotal Hutton obeyed, it was no use. 'Should have to drink six', he grumbled. Throughout the night he tossed and turned.

Next morning Hutton prepared as methodically as usual, left sock, left boot, left glove first: 'Mind, I'm not superstitious', he used to say.

On the field Bradman glared from short mid-off and O'Reilly moved in as 31,000 people and half the country tensed itself to await events.

Hutton had to work hard for his runs, and every one was loudly applauded as if the news of Mafeking's relief had arrived. Bradman took the fourth new ball at 670 and Hutton brought up 700 by late-cutting Waite to the pavilion.

He was within four of the record. Hearts missed a beat as he missed an O'Reilly no-ball and then, at last, it was over as he cut Fleetwood-Smith to the boundary. Around the ground a standing ovation began at once and somebody played 'For he's a jolly good fellow' on the cornet, the crowd taking up the refrain in lusty voice. At home, Hutton's mother broke down in tears while doing the family washing with the radio by her side.

It was done. Finally the tumult died and Hutton moved on till, on 364, he drove O'Reilly to Hassett at cover and was out. The Pudsey Parish Church rang a peal of 364 and during tea Hutton received 500 messages of congratulation.

With Bradman and Fingleton suffering injuries, Hammond declared, recklessly in 'Bosser' Martin's opinion, at 903 for seven, and England won by an innings and 579 runs.

Hutton had batted for 13 hours and 17 minutes, a record for England against Australia. He was 22 years of age and had endured formidable pressures, physical and mental.

CHARLES MACARTNEY

The Australians v Nottinghamshire, Trent Bridge, 1921
SCORECARD ON PAGE 163

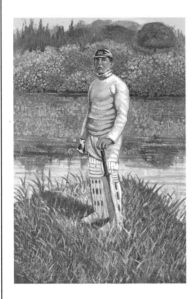

One of the paintings by Gerry Wright of cricketers from the earlier days of the game. 'The Guvnor-General', Charlie Macartney, on a river bank.

'In the long history of Nottinghamshire cricket there has, perhaps, never been such a deplorable match as this.' So began *Wisden*'s report of the game played in 1921 between Armstrong's powerful Australian tourists and the supposed might of Nottinghamshire cricket. Nor were *Wisden*'s words inappropriate. After bowling Warren Bardsley for a duck in the first over of the first day the locals were slaughtered. They lost by an innings and 517 runs. Charlie Macartney, 'The Governor-General', jaunty, cocksure, square-shouldered and square-jawed, played the innings of a lifetime, an innings which destroyed a powerful county eleven led by one of cricket's most ruthless captains.

Cricket ran in the Macartney blood. His grandfather played on the Melbourne Cricket Ground when the wickets were pitched east to west and bowled his slow roundarms with the sun at his back. Later he bowled green apples to Charlie in his orchard, friendly deliveries which the child tried to smite with a little bat made from cedar wood. Charlie was mad on the game. Regularly he'd wag school to practise with his chums. Like W.G. he had a dog which loved to chase after the ball. In time Macartney fought his way through the hard schools of grade and shield cricket until, in Sydney in 1907, he played the first of his 35 Test matches.

He had a brilliant career. Killer instinct added to flair, he was, in these early years, impudent, even arrogant as he went about his work. In 1912 he took 99 off Barnes bowling at his best on a helpful pitch, an insolent innings in which, as usual, he opened fire from the start.

By 1920–21 Macartney was in his pomp, hitting 170 in four hours against J. W. H. T. Douglas' England tourists in an innings seen by a boy called Bradman, upon whom it had a great effect.

Much was expected of Macartney in the old country the following summer and much was delivered.

Australia were already two up in the Tests when the tourists arrived at Trent Bridge for the county match. Armstrong and Collins, captain and vice-captain, decided to rest, leaving Warren Bardsley in charge. He won the toss and, in scorching weather, decided to bat. The rest, as they say, is history.

Upon Bardsley being bowled Macartney marched out, evidently meaning business which was, in fact, his customary state of mind. Jack Fingleton opened with him once and was told to watch out for the first ball which was duly smashed back down the ground nearly bringing the lives of those at the bowler's end to a premature conclusion. Mid-pitch, Macartney told his youthful partner that it was a good idea to aim the first ball at the bowler's head as 'they don't like it, it rattles 'em'. Macartney looked straight in the eye of those to whom he talked. And he hit straight, often and very hard.

Short and stocky with a blacksmith's forearms, Macartney began this innings without bothering to assess the pitch, which was so obviously a belter.

His very arrival had been impressive. The way he raised his bat high after taking guard, the way he stretched himself. This early aggression only confirmed the worst suspicions of the bowlers; Macartney was in the mood.

In truth, he murdered the bowling in a way seldom, if ever, seen. True he was, on nine, missed in the slips. 'Nottinghamshire', said *Wisden*, 'had to pay a terribly high price for one blunder.' In under four hours Macartney hit 345 runs, an innings including four sixes, 47 fours and only three threes. It was, thought Macartney, too hot to run. The weather was tropical and the outfield was fast. On 213 he gave a hard chance to mid-on but this was the only other blemish in a dazzling display.

Under the fierce stewardship of Arthur Carr, a man tough enough to use bodyline in county cricket before it was ever taken overseas, Nottinghamshire fought hard. Their groundfielding was excellent, but Macartney pulverised them, moving perkily into position as

The Australian team in 1921. Charlie Macartney is second left in the second row. W. W. Armstrong, the captain, is on Macartney's left, and H. L. Collins, the vice-captain, on the other side of Armstrong.

⚫ *Any batsman worth his salt should let the bowlers understand at once that he is the boss.* ⚪
CHARLIE MACARTNEY

small men can do, and cutting and hitting to leg with awesome power. He was a pocket battleship. Perhaps his ferocity was provoked by his size. In his cotton socks Macartney stood 5ft 5in (1.65m). He carried himself like a giant.

Throughout the morning and into the afternoon Macartney trifled with the attack. At one time Carr seemed to lose control in the field, with fielders running hither and thither like headless chickens. Leadership was urgently needed. Carr decided to bowl an over himself so his real bowlers could change ends. 'I thought it would look well in the score sheet. A. W. Carr, 1 over, 1 maiden, no runs, no wickets. I was going to bowl so wide that Charlie couldn't reach them.'

What actually happened is recorded in *Wisden*. Arthur Carr, one over for 24 runs. Every ball he bowled was hit to the

boundary. And here is something still more remarkable. Carr's recollection is wrong. Macartney did not face that over. It was his team-mate Pellow who treated Carr so disdainfully. Moreover, Macartney was, at the time, wondering if he was scoring quickly enough. Seeing Pellow cut loose raised Macartney's hackles. Certainly, he thought, I've been an old tortoise today. Accordingly he went for his shots. Only later did he realise that his command had been total from first to last. His greatest shot was the half-volley chopped late and square of third man, a shot Desmond Haynes played in Perth in 1988 but a shot in the repertoire of few others. First to last, Macartney exuded a terrifying certainty that he would obliterate the bowling.

As the slaughter continued so Macartney began to contemplate chasing Archie MacLaren's 424 made, rather rudely, against Somerset in 1895. And then, suddenly, he was gone, leg before to Joe Hardstaff, an occasional bowler, the seventh tried. If not totally disgruntled – he had, after all, made 345 – Macartney cannot, to borrow from P. G. Wodehouse, be considered entirely gruntled by this turn of events. By all accounts, the decision was a shocker. With two hours left to play and the bowling at his mercy Macartney might easily have scored 500.

Macartney was to torment Arthur Carr again in 1928. In the third Test Carr, by now England captain, put Australia in. Bardsley fell for a duck this time too, first ball in fact, whereupon Macartney hit a wonderful hundred before lunch. It cost Carr his job.

Macartney was dropped once on that occasion, by Carr in the slips, whose comments are not recorded. It was George Gunn who dropped him on nine that searing day in Nottingham. His observation has been handed down: 'They ought to have a collection for me', he said.

PETER MAY

England v West Indies, Edgbaston, 1957

SCORECARD ON PAGE 163

Peter May meets the West Indian party at the beginning of the 1957 tour. The West Indies had won their first series in England in 1950, and had drawn the series in 1953–54. The 1950s success had been based on the calypso heroes 'those little pals of mine, Ramadhin and Valentine'. Valentine had since lost his form, but Ramadhin still struck terror into batsmen.

Six feet (1.83m) tall, raw-boned and immensely strong, Peter May was a gifted and fiercely competitive games player. From Charterhouse he joined the navy and at 21 made his first Test appearance, scoring 138 against South Africa. At Cambridge he won blues at soccer (being a great footballer was his heart's desire) and fives as well as cricket. Appointed captain in 1955, he led England, ruthless streak to the fore, in 41 Tests, winning 20 and losing 10. With 4,537 Test runs to his name, at an average of 46.77, his status as one of England's pre-eminent batsmen brooks no argument.

None of which mattered a jot as England gathered to meet John Goddard's West Indians in Birmingham in 1957. Slow bowler Sonny Ramadhin had been devastating in England in 1950, when the West Indies won 3–1. His name was on everyone's lips as the new series began. To the astonishment of Walcott and other West Indians, the English had no idea which way Ramadhin was turning the ball.

Then a tactic emerged. Someone had heard that Lindwall had taken the long handle to Ramadhin a year earlier and been told the spinner had left the field in tears and not bowled again in the series. Evidently England had to attack him before he opened his box of tricks.

On the first day May entered at 61 for two, as determined as usual to impose himself on the game, playing to win with every fibre in his body, his batting an expression of will and nervous energy. England moved to 104 for two with apparent serenity and with nothing to fear save fear itself.

Within half an hour Ramadhin had taken five wickets for nine runs. England's tail wagged cheerfully but they were bowled out for 186 in 79 overs on a track as flat as any in the kingdom. Ramadhin had taken seven for 49 as England's tactic backfired horribly.

In reply, the West Indians batted for two days and scored 474 before allowing England to bat again. There were two days and one evening left to play and May's men were 288 runs in arrears. Someone had to do something.

Miserably, England lost Richardson and Insole both to Sonny Ramadhin that night, and adjourned at 102 for two. Overnight May and Cowdrey talked to Bill Bowes, fast bowler turned reporter. Bowes advised them not to try to read Ramadhin, but to play every ball as an off-spinner while keeping a canny eye open for the quicker one. This method, he argued, would protect the stumps and allow leg-spinners to pass harmlessly across the bat.

Next day Close went early, and at 11.55 Cowdrey joined May. They were not to be parted until, going for a six, Cowdrey was caught at deep mid-on at 3.25 next day.

As usual Ramadhin pitched to a perfect length and, varying his trajectory and speeds cleverly, he bowled five maidens in a row as May and Cowdrey eyed him suspiciously. They played and

May cuts through gully during the first innings at Edgbaston in 1957. Richardson is May's partner. This was the innings when the policy of attacking Ramadhin failed. May and Cowdrey's partnership in the second innings was the last available rock on which Ramadhin's ship finally foundered.

missed time and again, but were not alarmed. By lunch England had reached 176 for three, May 62, Cowdrey 25.

Cowdrey defended with his pads. Time and again Ramadhin appealed. To this day he believes he was sorely betrayed by the umpires in Birmingham. For his part Cowdrey argues that he had mastered the art of positioning his foot on middle and leg so that anything striking his pads was likely to miss leg stump.

Not yet reading the spin reliably, May reached his hundred by driving Ramadhin to the mid-on boundary. Utterly intense, batting with a fierce passion, May carried on relentless and yet vigorous, gradually breaking the spirit of this teasing, glorious spinner.

In $3\frac{1}{2}$ hours the pair added 150 runs, of which Cowdrey hit 49. Only one wild shot was played, May suddenly launching himself at Atkinson, and driving the ball onto the second floor of the Edgbaston pavilion. Two balls later he just fell short with another searing straight hit. At the end of the over Cowdrey went down to ask May if he had 'any idea what the ruddy hell he was doing?' Both men laughed and have recounted the tale ever since.

At the close, after $5\frac{3}{4}$ hours of defence the pair had taken England to 378 for three. England had a good chance of saving a game which, a day earlier, had appeared beyond redemption. The pair had built an apparently impregnable

partnership defying a supposedly magical bowler, and had repaired English morale with a titanic partnership founded upon clear thinking and general cussedness.

Goddard, perhaps insensitively, used Ramadhin until lunch next morning. Ramadhin had, by now, not taken a wicket in eight hours. Was this not a certain way of destroying a most potent weapon? Had not Goddard played into England's hands?

Next day, May and Cowdrey simply carried on, Cowdrey moving to his hundred after $7\frac{1}{4}$ hours of disciplined resistance. By lunch England were 467 for three, and obviously safe. Pretty soon Ramadhin bowled his 98th and final over, having taken two for 179.

Free to attack at last, May raced to 250 and Cowdrey to his 150, before the bulky youngster finally hit a catch. May and Evans added another 50 against kinder bowling before May declared with his own score on 285 not out. With Cowdrey he'd added 411, England's record partnership for any wicket.

A champion bowler had been broken and a strong team demoralised. England won the series 3–0 with Ramadhin taking only five more wickets, and these at a considerable cost.

May's 285 not out was one of the greatest innings ever played by a captain. It was an innings calculated to inspire a team. Where there is a will there is a way.

BARRY RICHARDS

South Australia v Western Australia, Perth, 1970–71

SCORECARD ON PAGE 164

OPPOSITE *Richards was a fine upright hard-hitting striker off both front foot and back, here crashing the ball through the covers.*
BELOW *Barry Richards played much of his cricket in England for Hampshire. Here he off-drives.*

Around 3,000 people gathered at the WACA ground in Perth to see their State team play Ian Chappell's South Australians in 1971. Chappell had brought a strong team which included Barry Richards, the South African Test opener who was being paid a dollar a run by Coca-Cola, a move calculated to whet his appetite for runs.

The locals were powerful too and were beginning to dominate domestic cricket. Tony Lock was their fiercely competitive captain and his attack included an ageing Graham McKenzie and a young Dennis Lillee. Ian Brayshaw, a skilful into-the-breeze bowler, Tony Mann and Lock himself rounded off a formidable and highly motivated attack. These 'sandgropers' were a proud side, for distant Western Australia had a powerful sense of neglect for which they were eager to make their rivals pay.

Ian Chappell won the toss and elected to bat on a hard, white and shining pitch, upon which the ball would certainly fly for an hour.

This was Barry Richards' first Sheffield Shield season. Already he had played in his only Test series, scoring 508 runs against Bill Lawry's tired tourists in the winter of 1969–70. Since then his hopes had been frustrated and for him Shield cricket offered the compensation of pitting him against the great bowlers he had wanted to meet in great arenas.

McKenzie's first ball this day was a gentle outswinger which Richards missed. Behind the stumps Rod Marsh took the ball and said, none too quietly, to John Inverarity at slip: 'Geez, I thought this bloke was supposed to be able to play a bit.'

Richards survived the over, a maiden, and watched Lillee open with a maiden too. Only four of the following 91 overs in this 5½-hour day were to be scoreless.

After 12 minutes at the crease, Richards took a single off McKenzie and an over later he pushed a back-foot drive square of the wicket and was surprised to see it skim to the fence.

Twenty-five runs were taken off two overs, prompting Lock to summon Brayshaw to bowl into the wind, which he did economically, delivering five

overs for 11 runs before being rested. His next seven overs were to cost 58.

Already Richards felt superb and later he reflected: 'Recalling that innings now is like a dream. Somehow I managed to sustain for a complete day the sort of form that usually materialises only in short, glorious, moments.'

South Australia reached 50 in 47 minutes and soon enough Richards was acknowledging his own 50. Only Lillee had disturbed him, Richards misjudging two hooks which luckily fell safely. This apart, he took the score to 100 in 83 minutes, forcing Tony Lock to change his bowling.

Tony Mann was a leg-spinner with a googly few could detect, but Richards had played with him in club cricket and was his master. Now he glided down the pitch and stroked the ball into gaps, sending it humming between fieldsmen whose determined chases were invariably unavailing.

Graceful and effortless, Richards avoided violence, batting as if in a dream. His game was charming and accomplished rather than explosive and the fieldsmen, glancing at the board, were regularly surprised by his score.

Lock quickly grew hot and bothered, his temper restored only when Causby fell for 38 at 109, but by lunch Richards had moved to 79 and South Australia were already approaching 150.

If the locals had not enjoyed the

morning, the afternoon was to be far worse with Richards and his captain adding over 200 runs in a torrent which Lock could not arrest. He bowled with five men in the covers and time and again Richards strolled forward and threaded the ball through. Nor did Chappell's sweeps improve the mood of a sweating, cursing, thoroughly betrayed skipper.

Lock recalled Mann and stood at mid-off, hoping for tranquillity and an informed view of proceedings. Richards stepped out and three times placed the ball inches beyond Lock's despairing dive. From a prone position, Lock looked up like a whipped dog.

Richards reached his 100 in 125 minutes and his 150 in 176 minutes, of which 84 had been scored with graceful boundaries. On 169 he gave his only chance, lifting McKenzie to mid-on where Ian Brayshaw dropped a straight-forward catch. For a time Richards contemplated having a thrash but decided he was enjoying himself too much and returned to his former pattern.

Tea was taken. Lock's men had bowled well and yet the scoreboard, and it is a big scoreboard in Perth, told its cruel message. They had been slaughtered.

Word was out in Perth that something extraordinary was happening and the crowd grew. Nor were they disappointed as Ian Chappell and Richards took their partnership to 308 in 170 minutes before, with 5 o'clock approaching, Chappell was superbly stumped. Richards had just hit his only six and the field was now spread far and wide.

With an hour left, South Australia were 417 for two and Richards was nearing his 250. Greg Chappell joined him and Richards, who had been content to take easy singles, began to dictate once more. With Greg Chappell failing, South Australia 'collapsed' to 447 for three. Richards reached his 300 with a shot over cover which was nearly caught by Bob Meuleman, a fine squash player who narrowly failed to take a sprinting catch. Richards had been in for 317 minutes and had become only the third man to score 300 runs in a day in Sheffield Shield cricket, his predecessors being Charlie Gregory and Bill Ponsford. No-one had thought it could still be done.

Had he defended in the closing minutes Richards would have been excused for he was exhausted. He did nothing of the sort, striking four more boundaries and striding out to the final delivery bowled by Lillee and cracking it into the sight screen. Richards followed it, leaving the carnage behind and strolled toward the pavilion. Inverarity turned to Marsh and said: 'I suppose he can play a bit.'

Richards batted 42 minutes next morning before falling to a poor leg-before decision, being hit on the toe by Mann's googly. Richards was out for 356. Lillee had bowled 18 overs and taken none for 117.

It was, perhaps, as scintillating an exhibition of batting as has been seen since the Second World War. Sadly politics prevented Richards showing his curious combination of charm and contempt in the hotter atmosphere of Test match cricket. He had batted for 372 minutes and his score included 48 fours and one six. For South Australia he scored 1,528 runs, a tally exceeded only in an Australian season by Don Bradman.

LAWRENCE ROWE

West Indies v England, Bridgetown, 1973–74
SCORECARD ON PAGE 164

OPPOSITE *Lawrence Rowe clips to leg and begins to run all in one movement. Rowe was a fluid, compact batsman.*

BELOW *The end of 612 minutes of mastery. Rowe drives high after reaching 302 and wicket-keeper Knott watches the flight of the ball. It was caught by Geoff Arnold and Rowe had to leave at last.*

Few Test cricketers have whistled while they worked, and fewer have been allergic to grass. That these two characteristics met in Lawrence Rowe may explain why the little Jamaican toyed so long with greatness without ever quite grasping it. Rowe was a humble man born with a sublime gift who lacked the resilience and the health to turn talent into deed. If the force was with him he was devastating, if not he could fail ignominiously. He needed to feel wanted and, significantly, until 9 March 1974, all ten of his first-class hundreds had been scored in Sabina Park, Jamaica, on his home ground, where Lawrence was lord of all he surveyed.

Rowe's Test career began against New Zealand in 1971 and at 23, he scored a dazzling hundred and double hundred in the same Test. His batting was described as artistic and yet ravenous with nothing mechanical, just simple footwork and crisp shots which burnt tracks across the turf.

Injury and loss of form led to a decline and Rowe owed his selection against England in 1974 to the absence of other candidates to open with Roy Fredericks. As usual, Rowe scored 120 at Sabina Park in front of a crowd packed to the rafters and beyond. Men hung on to light pylons, sat on brick walls and roared their approval of this nonchalant hero with a troubled mind.

Arriving in Barbados with England one down, Rowe knew that he must, sooner or later, convince the sceptics from rival islands that he could succeed in a bigger world. Otherwise obscurity beckoned.

Losing the toss and being asked to bat on a humid morning, England were rescued, not for the first or last time, by Tony Greig and Alan Knott and by the second day they had reached their final total of 395. The West Indian reply lasted from tea on Thursday afternoon until 3pm on Sunday with the rest day intervening. For all but the final hour of this onslaught, Rowe held sway with batting as majestic and flawless as any seen in Test cricket. Here, surely, private doubts were erased.

England were none too pleased with Rowe before his innings began, for he had survived a confident appeal for caught behind against Geoff Arnold in a previous match, an injustice upon which England brooded. Accordingly no sooner had Rowe taken guard and begun whistling than he was bom-

Rowe returns to the pavilion after being dismissed in a one-day international in South Africa in 1983. After an on-off Test career bedevilled by injury, Rowe by now was seeking some financial security for the future.

OPPOSITE *Many of Allan Border's best innings have been played when Australia was in trouble.*

barded with bumpers. With his short backlift and alert eye Rowe was a brilliant backfoot player and as England belaboured him so he hooked and cut and hooked again.

Undeterred, England continued the barrage, confident that Rowe would soon lift a catch. With each boundary came a roar from an enchanted crowd and with each defensive shot a cry of 'no'. Judged by his confidence, Rowe might have been in Sabina Park, and his scornful batting brought him 48 runs by the close, upon which he was carried from the field like a king amongst exhilarated subjects.

Huge crowds swarmed to the ground next morning for Rowe had a rare magnetism. Kensington Oval was vibrant and eager to salute a new idol. Thousands were locked out, thousands too many let in, and play resumed to a cacophony of noise.

Wisely, England had abandoned its aggressive tactic and Greig contained the batsmen with his off-cutters. Nevertheless, Rowe was in charge and with Kallicharran he added 249 on a pitch upon which no-one else played with any freedom. It was a command performance.

His innings was chanceless and as England tried to shake him the bowlers constantly overstepped their crease. Rowe once thumped Old through point where Greig gave chase and, forgetting himself, leapt over the boundary and into a group of spectators and found himself facing a drawn knife and an angry man growling 'don't do that here, man'.

Once Old made a ball rear and hit Rowe on the chest, causing the astonished batsman to roll his eyes but otherwise the day was notable chiefly for the smooth certainty of Rowe's work. Once Kallicharran was out wickets fell steadily but to the chagrin of England and the trumpeted delight of everyone else,

Rowe had reached his double hundred by the time the bails were removed to end another day.

All Barbados was ablaze with talk of Rowe. Writing for the *Nation* newspaper, Tony Cozier recalled how, with Rowe unbeaten overnight, the crowds poured in to see history being made. Nor were they disappointed for Rowe batted on, punishing anything loose, hitting on the ground and using his feet to Pocock. England had little difficulty in dismissing Lloyd, Kanhai and Sobers who, between them, made 26. Only Deryck Murray stayed with Rowe as he moved onwards. Denness had spread his field far and wide and Rowe still punched boundaries, scarcely sweating and apparently unmoved by the hysterial scenes around him. Rowe reached his 300 with a blazing off-drive and at once held his bat aloft to acknowledge the chanting, bedlamatic crowd who promptly invaded the pitch. Soon afterwards, Rowe lifted Greig into Arnold's hands at deep mid-wicket. He had batted for 612 minutes, faced 430 balls and hit one six and 36 fours. Of the 116 runs added in the morning, Rowe made 72 and only Willis troubled him.

This was only the second triple century by a West Indian, the first being hit by Sobers. George Headley, in whose footsteps Rowe now seemed destined to tread, Kanhai, Hunte, Lloyd, Nurse, Worrell and Walcott had all hit substantial double hundreds.

Another hundred soon followed on a spinners' pitch and every so often in the next decade Rowe would do something extraordinary, yet this remorseless innings was by far his greatest hour. Enigmatic losses of form as well as confidence-sapping illnesses took their toll as Rowe failed to embrace his talent. He left us with wonders such as this to behold and with a sense of emptiness too that these wonders were so few and far between.

COURAGE AND GALLANTRY

ALLAN BORDER

Australia v West Indies, Port-of-Spain, 1983–84
SCORECARD ON PAGE 166

A picture which shows Border's determination. A forward defensive stroke from The Oval, 1989, when Border, by now captain of his country, recovered the Ashes from England. Russell is the wicket-keeper, Gooch first slip.

OPPOSITE *A bearded Border hits high in the air, for once batting without feeling some sort of responsibility on his shoulders, as his opponents were the eleven of Lavinia, Duchess of Norfolk, at Arundel Castle in 1989.*

Arriving at Port-of-Spain for the second Test of 1983–84, having narrowly escaped defeat in the first, Australia found to their consternation that the pitch was damp and green. Moreover idiosyncratic diplomacy by Kim Hughes in the game with Trinidad, when he blocked up in protest at a cautious home town declaration, had alienated an entire island. If Hughes lost the toss his men could expect a hostile reception on and off the field.

Australia had a torrid morning as Garner roared in. Ignored for a recent tour of India, hearing rumours that he was considered over the hill, Joel Garner made even Marshall look ordinary, charging in with his head down before gathering his arms and legs in a final surge. Australia sank to 16 for three.

It was not a happy time to begin an innings, especially for Allan Border, who had developed 'a mental block' about Garner after previous encounters. But Border had been in tight corners before. At 11.56 he took guard and at once began a duel with Garner which was to illuminate the match and which Border was to win, a victory probably beyond the capability of any other contemporary batsman.

Hughes fell caught behind just before lunch, by which time Australia had struggled to 55 for four off 16 overs, with Garner having taken four for 19. Thankfully, from the Australia perspective, no further play was possible until Saturday morning, when hostile battle resumed. Plainly the West Indians had picked Border as their principal obstacle and so set about removing him. David Hookes, his new partner, took 16 off one Marshall over but he fell at 85, bringing in debutant Dean Jones.

After lunch Border could not score and it was Jones who picked up the pace. Border was in physical trouble too, defying waves of nausea which made him dry retch by the side of the

wicket. Eventually Richards was forced to rest his pace men which allowed Border and his young partner to collect runs. But Jones, to his intense annoyance, contrived to hit a long hop back to Richards after scoring 48 in 109 balls and adding 100 runs in 159 minutes with Border.

Lawson arrived to face a barrage from Marshall which he survived and it was left to Daniel to take his wicket and that of Hogan. Dogged by interruptions Australia's innings had reached 248 for eight by the close of the second day by which time Border had scored 92 not out. Early next morning he lost Hogg and was 98 when joined by Terry Alderman. Could he score his 100? Garner was determined to deny him and with Border on strike he delivered one of cricket's greatest overs. Four times he beat Border, who was forced to duck and dive as he endeavoured to keep body and wicket intact. Soon Alderman was caught at slip off a bumper to leave Border stranded on 98 and Australia all out for 255.

Gerry Gomez, former West Indian captain, said this was one of the best innings he had seen on this ground. Jeffrey Dujon, Jones and others present hold it in awe. Border had batted for 310 minutes and hit ten boundaries. And yet it is not necessarily even his greatest innings in this match. For, on the final day, Border constructed another epic which merits inclusion in this list.

Six hours play had been lost on the first two days and it was with a day and evening left that Richards declared at 468 for eight with a lead of 213 runs.

Once again Australia started badly and they did not improve next morning. Australia were 114 for four with five hours left for play as Border took guard, and were soon 115 for five when night watchman Hogan left. But Garner was suffering from food poisoning and now

A helmeted Allan Border plays to mid-on during the 1989 tour of England, when for once he was on the stronger side and attacking, instead of being called upon to show his grit, which was his lot in many Tests early in his career.

❦ *It's a war of attrition, and you really don't have any option but to tough it out with them. The trap a lot of players fall into is trying to fight fire with fire. My approach to batting is to wait for them and score off the bad balls.* ❦
BORDER ON BATTING AGAINST THE CARIBBEAN FAST BATTERY

OPPOSITE *Allan Border drives through the covers.*

Wayne Daniel left the field complaining of a stomach virus.

Richards brought on Gomes and himself. They bowled 52 overs between them this day. Hookes fell to Gomes at 153, spooning a catch to cover and at 162 Jones followed, yorked by Richards' quicker ball. There were 3½ hours left to play. With the West Indians still 51 in front Australia had precious little hope.

Yet the West Indies continued to rely on spin. Perhaps those easy wickets mislead them. Lawson and Border played their shots, adding 34 at a run a minute before Marshall's return signalled Lawson's departure.

With 55 minutes remaining until tea and only Alderman, a true rabbit, in the hutch, everything depended upon Hogg and Border. To widespread surprise they survived in some comfort till tea, Border doing most of the scoring, punching shots through gaps in the covers. But when Hogg was removed by Richards straight after tea, everyone began to pack their bags. Yet Alderman offered a straight bat as Border continued to collect runs, forcing Richards to take the second new ball.

Minutes ticked by, and incredibly, no wicket fell. Richards returned to spin and Alderman prodded forward, taking care to miss anything wide. Both men struck boundaries as Richards crowded the bat. Border was simply Border, predictable, secure, unemotional, a battler from birth.

With only four overs remaining it was plain that Australia, led by Border, had executed one of cricket's greatest escapes. Sportingly Richards did not call off his effort as Border approached his hundred. Finally, he tossed the ball to Logie, inviting him to turn over his arm, Border straight drove a four to reach three figures and Richards strode across, shook his hand and called an end to proceedings.

Naturally the Australian camp was jubilant, though the reprieve was to be temporary. Border had batted for 630 minutes and had not lost his wicket. He had batted on a damp pitch and against furious bowling and had stood his ground. He had faced spinners throughout a hot afternoon without losing concentration. Truly this was one of cricket's greatest draws and these were two of cricket's greatest innings.

DENIS COMPTON

England v Australia, Old Trafford, 1948

SCORECARD ON PAGE 166

Denis Compton as represented on a 1938 series of cigarette cards. At the time he was 20, but had already scored a century against Australia – in his first Test encounter with them. In 1947 he returned from the war and had a magnificent season, but knee trouble (he had also played for Arsenal) restricted his career in the 1950s.

Versatile, handsome, smiling Denis Charles Scott Compton was the golden boy of English cricket, and the man who, starting his career just before the war, restored morale after 1946 with batting of an impish, laughing genius. He was courageous, disarming and as capable of artistic flair as technical mastery. Few sportsmen have been as popular, few so warmly greeted as they left the pavilion, for few have fought so valiantly when battle was at its hottest. And it was hot in 1948, for the Australians were back and Bradman, for the first time in his career, had great fast bowlers at his command.

For Compton, as for his friend Bill Edrich, 1947 had been a glorious year. Between them they recorded 7,355 runs, Compton's share being 3,816, a tally including 18 hundreds, six of them against the South Africans. Never coached, Compton made his runs by moving back (he seldom ventured forward) behind the ball and either using powerful forearms and a short backlift to hook, cut and drive boundaries, or a delicate touch to glide and glance runs free of the wicket.

For two Tests the English batsmen were battered by the Australian fast bowlers. Compton scored 184 in the first, but Australia had won both comfortably. The teams moved to Manchester where, to widespread astonishment, England dropped their premier batsman Len Hutton.

In disarray, in danger of demoralisation, England batted first upon winning the toss as the third Test began at Old Trafford. For a few overs the pitch was distinctly lively and on 22 Washbrook was beaten and bowled. Emmett had already survived one nasty crack and now Edrich too was hit. Soon Emmett departed, caught off a flier at short leg.

Enter Compton. Rarely had England been so in need of a rousing innings from its favourite son. At once Lindwall began to bump him, firing balls around his head, testing his mettle, and striking Compton on the arm. Unperturbed Compton hooked at another and top-edged the ball onto his forehead. Perhaps he heard the call 'no-ball' and lost concentration. He staggered around with blood spurting out of a wound by his eyebrow, which made the injury appear even worse than it was. Escorted from the field, his shirt sticky with blood, Compton was ordered to rest and two stitches were inserted.

Compton sat, faintly nauseous, in the dressing room as England desperately tried to prevent further damage. But when the second new ball was taken, three wickets fell quickly and at 119 for five Compton, who had batted briefly in the nets to test his eye, walked jauntily, head swathed in bandages, to a reception even warmer than usual.

It was Compton at his best who now revived England's innings. Deflecting to fine leg, chopping to third man, his score was at once ticking merrily along as if he had not a care in the world. Yardley fell and it was Evans, a gambler evidently determined to enjoy every moment of a life which had not been scuppered by war's gross regime, who provided Compton with support.

In 70 minutes this pair added 75 runs and took England to 216 for seven, a disappointing score but not a hopeless one. On 50 Compton was missed behind the wicket by Don Tallon moving low to his right to collect an edged outswinger. Otherwise his batting was flawless. Just before the close he lost Evans, but retired for the evening to a stirring ovation, acknowledgment of his courage in returning from a blow which might have intimidated a lesser man.

Incredibly a third new ball was due as Compton and Bedser resumed England's innings at 231 for seven next morning. Little was expected of this pair as Lindwall and Johnston bent their backs into their work. But Compton was soon moving easily, glancing boundaries to fine leg. At 73 he was again dropped by Tallon, this time off Johnston, whereupon Compton reacted by twice hitting Toshack through the covers, as if stung by his own carelessness.

Meanwhile Bedser, propping forward, occasionally using the long handle, delighted another capacity crowd of 30,000 by holding firm.

Bradman tried to contain Compton, sending his only slips to deep cover for Toshack and Johnston, hoping to cut off Compton's darting, nimble cuts. Unruffled Compton duly reached his second outstanding hundred of the series with an on-drive off Toshack which also brought up the 300. Compton's hundred was greeted by a loud cheer and by a dog straying onto the field. Bedser then brought up the 100 partnership with a tickle to third man.

After lunch Compton found Johnston in his most fierce mood so he counter-attacked. The greater the odds the greater the challenge. Lindwall was recalled, and Compton played him circumspectly, defending those aimed at his ribs and ignoring everything higher.

Nothing appeared likely to break the partnership. But Compton had one serious weakness in his game. 'He was the only player,' wrote John Warr, 'to call his partner for a run and wish him good luck at the same time'. Bedser was duly run out leaving England in relative clover at 337 for eight. Pollard was soon bowled and Young caught at extra cover, leaving Compton unbeaten on 145 after 5½ gruelling hours.

Certainly he had been dropped twice at least, but *Wisden* said this was 'a great display of skill and courage'. It was a great innings, not merely because of the injury, or the collapse, but also because this was the third Test in a series which had already demanded unflinching courage in the face of dangerous, explosive bowling directed by a captain prepared to use his fast bowlers fully.

A lesser man might not have had the stomach for another fight.

The shot that was Compton's peculiar trade-mark, the sweep to leg. Nobody has played it better before or since. The wicket-keeper in this 1948 match is Hampshire's Neil McCorkell.

BEV CONGDON

New Zealand v England, Trent Bridge, 1973

SCORECARD ON PAGE 167

New Zealand had played Test cricket against England for 42 years but not a single Test match had been won. They could find good cricketers but never field a strong enough eleven to challenge England. Such, at any rate, was the accepted doctrine when the seventh New Zealand team to meet England on their own territory landed in 1973.

Not even the craggy features of captain Bevan Congdon, whose deadpan and disapproving expression recalled a Scottish presbyterian minister in a gloomy mood on a wet Sunday afternoon, could turn this Kiwi team into a threatening unit. A man of stubborn intent, he was respected by colleagues

Congdon (left) and Glenn Turner come out to bat on the second day of the Trent Bridge Test. Although things went badly from here until the third afternoon, New Zealand finished with reputations firmly made.

as a cricketer rather than beloved as a leader. As the teams came to Trent Bridge for the first Test, there had already been murmurings of discontent at his aloof attitudes and cautious tactics. He had much to do to convince his team of his standing.

At first things went well. Batting first on a hot, sunny day England slipped from 92 without loss to 191 for nine as the New Zealand bowlers plugged away, bowling line and length to an unrelentingly defensive field. Only a late flurry from Alan Knott and Norman Gifford took England to 250.

On the second morning the air was heavy as New Zealand were hustled out for 97. Humiliation, ever a threat to Kiwi cricketers of this era, was once more in prospect.

Fighting back, New Zealand quickly restored the balance to the game by reducing England to 24 for four, but once more the door was to be closed, as Amiss and Greig, the careworn and the cavalier, added 210, allowing Illingworth to declare 478 runs in front. Only the wildest New Zealand optimist at Trent Bridge was forecasting anything more than 200 second time around.

When Turner and John Parker were brushed aside with only 16 upon the board everyone's worst fears appeared merely to await their confirmation. With over an hour left for play that Saturday night and with his hopes in tatters, Congdon took guard and prepared to face Snow and Arnold. With runs to spare Illingworth had set an aggressive field and Congdon was quickly able to open his account and take ten off an over from Snow. And then, as if his load were not already enough, he mishooked Snow and edged the ball into his face, which was bruised, swollen and cut.

Congdon's face was still in disorder as play resumed on the Monday morning. Within 18 minutes his team was in greater disorder still, for, at 68, Hastings

Knott behind the wicket, Fletcher at first slip and Roope at second slip saw plenty of Congdon at Trent Bridge in the second innings. Here he turns Willis to leg during his knock of 176 which set New Zealand cricket on an upward path.

fell to Arnold. Mark Burgess entered and at once began to play his cultured shots. Moving impassively Congdon reached his 50 in 106 minutes but lost Burgess for 26 at 130. At lunch New Zealand were 146 for four with Vic Pollard hanging on grimly, and it was not until after the break that this pair began to take charge. As, with watchful defence and occasional aggressive shots, they built their partnership, so a change came over the game, a change detectable in the hushed pressbox and fascinated crowd, for both men appeared impregnable and, quite suddenly, England were in a contest.

Between lunch and tea 87 runs were added taking New Zealand to 233 for four, a marvellous fightback but still a hopeless position. Already Congdon had kept England at bay for five hours, hours during which the merest slip on his part would have meant inevitable defeat. Upon his shoulders had rested not merely this game but the very reputation of New Zealand cricket. At last, with the bowlers losing control, Congdon and Pollard were able to advance with fierce cuts, pulls and drives as the game slowly turned. Congdon had reached his hundred after 220 minutes of hard-headed and practical batting, and now he was surging on, with Pollard still resolute in support.

As the close approached, and Pollard passed his 50 after 203 minutes at the crease, Congdon continued as if nothing on earth could shift him, for he hab-

itually hid his emotions and here he was disguising that dangerous combination, exhilaration and exhaustion. Finally, and even surprisingly, Arnold threaded a ball through his defences and with only 15 minutes left to play, he was out.

New Zealand were 307 for five. Congdon had scored 176 runs in 412 minutes and hit 19 boundaries. He left to a warm, even moving ovation. It had been an innings born in despair which died in hope, an innings played against overwhelming odds on behalf of a weak team in a dreadful state against a formidable enemy. It had been an innings of great skill and, most importantly, immense psychological courage.

Nor did its significance end with that shattering of stumps by Arnold, for Congdon had filled Kiwis' hearts with fight. From 317 for five overnight Pollard and Wadsworth took the score to 402, just 72 short of victory. At lunch, New Zealand needed 70 with four wickets left.

To his bitter disappointment Pollard departed leg before after lunch and, breathing defiance to the end, the Kiwis' heroic struggle fell 39 runs short of the target. Thoroughly inspired, New Zealand outplayed England in the following drawn Test at Lord's.

Congdon's innings showed New Zealanders what could be done, and helped to build a resistance and a spirit within New Zealand cricket which was to take them from the bottom rung of the Test cricket ladder nearly to its top.

BASIL D'OLIVEIRA

England v Australia, The Oval, 1968
SCORECARD ON PAGE 167

D'Oliveira pulls Gleeson to the boundary during his century at the Oval in 1958 which, despite twistings and turnings by authority, finally was to bring about the isolation of South Africa on the cricket field.

❖ *I wanted to be a cricketer who had been chosen as a cricketer and not as a symbol.* ❖
BASIL D'OLIVEIRA

As he walked out to bat at the Oval on 22 August 1968 Basil D'Oliveira knew that his extraordinary career had reached a moment of truth. MCC were to tour South Africa that winter, to tour the land of his birth. If he could do well this day he was bound to be picked. A Cape Coloured playing against the mighty whites of South Africa! What would Mr Vorster and his companions make of that? And what a way to repay those nameless friends who had scraped and saved to raise his air fair for England those few years earlier!

For D'Oliveira was no ordinary cricketer and this was no ordinary situation. Behind the scenes all manner of political shenanigins had been occurring, for MCC had forseen the pitfalls of picking a coloured cricketer to tour South Africa. Lord Cobham had met Dr Vorster, South Africa's senior politician, and reported back that it was highly unlikely that D'Oliveira would be allowed to play there. Rumours spread that people of influence intended at all costs to avoid picking D'Oliveira, and so endangering cricket relations with South Africa. Why else had D'Oliveira been dropped after scoring 87 not out in the first Test of this Ashes series?

Dolly was not named in the party for the fifth Test. Then Cowdrey, the captain, noticed that the Oval pitch was green and likely to suit medium-pacers. Accordingly he asked for Tom Cartwright and Barry Knight to be added to his squad. Neither was fit so, eventually, D'Oliveira was summonned. Then, unbelievably, fate intervened once more, striking down Roger Prideaux, forcing him to withdraw. D'Oliveira was in the team.

D'Oliveira's early cricketing successes had been on primitive Cape Coloured pitches. At 19, he had dared to write to John Arlott seeking opportunity in distant England. A Lancashire League club, Middleton, had in their turn dared to employ a virtually unknown and middle-aged cricketer as their overseas player. Local subscriptions had paid D'Oliveira's passage to England. At first he had failed, but in time he grasped the niceties of the English game and conditions and returned home to a ticker-tape reception. In time, too, he moved to Worcestershire and in 1960 was picked to play for England.

To save the Ashes England had to win this final Test at the Oval. D'Oliveira joined Edrich at 238 for four, with an hour to play on the first day. That evening he batted confidently as if he had not a care in the world. Resuming next morning, with a Test match still to win and a tour place still to book, D'Oliveira was, at once, dropped on 31. This was his only blemish. That morning Dolly had rung his wife Naomi and told her to sit in front of the television as he was

The end of the Oval Test in 1968. All the players are in the picture as Underwood gets Inverarity out lbw. The other England players are, from the left: Illingworth, Graveney, Edrich, Dexter, Cowdrey, Knott, Snow, Brown, Milburn and D'Oliveira, who had earlier broken a stubborn partnership to help set up this finale.

going to be in all day. He had steeled himself to score a hundred and was convinced he would make his target.

D'Oliveira made no more mistakes. He and Edrich advanced smoothly until finally Edrich was bowled by Ian Chappell's leg-break for 164.

With Illingworth as his partner D'Oliveira now took command, using his small backlift and formidably powerful shoulders to thump anything short through the covers. Wickets fell as England's innings faded, but D'Oliveira soldiered on, intent upon his target which, to a tumultuous roar, he at last reached. It was as if the entire crowd had been willing him on.

Cutting loose now, with only the tail to support him, and yet never appearing flustered, never putting a hair out of place, D'Oliveira threw his bat at everything, and gave three more chances before he was ninth out, caught by Inverarity off Ashley Mallett. There now

followed an emotional scene rarely equalled on an English cricket ground, for D'Oliveira was clapped and cheered all the way to the pavilion. As usual he appeared nerveless, raising his bat in acknowledgment but betraying no other sign of emotion. He had won the hearts and the minds of English cricket supporters, who wondered if he would be given a fair go, for the air stank with appeasement.

In a dramatic finale England won the Test, D'Oliveira, given five overs, getting a wicket at a vital time. He was the hero of the hour.

That night the selectors picked their team for South Africa. D'Oliveira, who had just scored 158 and taken the most crucial wicket to save the Ashes, was not included. It is worth naming these selectors. They were Insole, Bedser, Kenyon, May, Cowdrey, Amiss, Gilligan and Gubby Allen. Ordinary people were outraged. Distinguished members of

Basil D'Oliveira driving. As a young player all he knew was hitting sixes. In England he developed his all-round game, but not at the expense of his natural power.

the MCC resigned. David Sheppard and others demanded a special meeting of MCC members and though they lost the vote they certainly won the argument.

In the furore, Penny Cowdrey sent a bouquet of flowers to the D'Oliveiras with the inscription: 'Thinking of you very much today, love to you both'. Ted Dexter put it down to good honest bungling by good honest men. Probably this is unduly generous, for the decision speaks of feeble-mindedness.

Nor had the wheel finished turning yet. To Cowdrey's astonishment Tom Cartwright withdrew from the tour with a sore shoulder, and in the prevailing climate, the selectors could scarcely do otherwise than name D'Oliveira in their party. Dr Vorster's reaction was

predictably brutal. 'It's not the MCC team, it's the team of the anti-apartheid movement,' he said. 'We are not prepared to have a team thrust upon us.'

So the tour was cancelled. D'Oliveira was not welcome to play cricket in South Africa. A wicked government had been smoked out.

This was a great innings. Apart from helping to win a Test against Australia and to hold the Ashes, it also embraced humanity and morality. For his supporters D'Oliveira had to succeed. He rose magnificently and with dignity to the occasion, let deeds speak louder than words and left the pusillanimous politicking to others.

In 1969 D'Oliveira was awarded the OBE.

GRAHAM GOOCH

England v West Indies, Bridgetown, 1980–81

SCORECARD ON PAGE 168

To the England cricketers Ken Barrington was a coach, confessor, counsellor, cockney comedian and chum. It was at the players insistence that he was added to the party for the Caribbean tour of 1980–81, for every player understood his importance and enjoyed his company. Throughout the early weeks of this West Indies trip, weeks of bombard-

Gooch plays a ball past Haynes at midwicket and starts to run during his courageous century at Barbados made in the shadow of Ken Barrington's sudden death.

ment from Holding, Croft and Garner, weeks of political bickering, weeks of crushing injuries to Willis and Rose, days of eternal waiting and heavy defeat, Barrington had remained cheerful, his vast smile shedding cheer upon every circumstance, no matter how grim.

And then, quite suddenly, he was gone. Frank Keating caught this time of tragedy: 'He had been so hale and full of beans. So dynamite-chuffed at the end of the West Indian innings in the morning. His smile illuminated the jammed pavilion long room. If, batting first, a side could not make at least 300 in this place they could consider themselves well and truly stuffed. Choked he was about England's afternoon collapse but always first with a great big consoling arm and

some perky get stuck-in encouragement for the outgoing batsman.'

Barrington had suffered a heart attack overnight, brought on perhaps by the strain upon him and his beloved team, for England were already one Test down and in trouble.

To lose Barrington was as devastating a blow as any cricket team or any individual cricketer, has suffered. At 7.30 am manager A. C. Smith and skipper Ian Botham appeared at Gooch's door and at once he could tell something dreadful had happened, for their faces were lined with pain.

Gooch and his wife wept unashamedly before joining their friends and colleagues in the manager's room at the end of the pier in their Barbados hotel. Shocked, saddened, empty, the players were at first silent, hiding their anguish, but slowly a resolve built to carry on with the game, and so to honour Ken Barrington. To leave now, or to surrender, would have disappointed that patriot and cricket lover.

That morning players of both teams and the entire crowd stood in respectful silence, saluting a departed friend. Now England faced the grim prospect of carrying on with the cricket. By now the West Indians were in command. Bowled out for 265 on a typically fresh Bridgetown pitch (the groundsman was a bosom pal of Joel Garner's), they had taken an intimidating lead by skittling England for 122, to which lead they built handsomely on the third day, scoring 245 runs in 79 overs, thanks largely to a steady 100 from Vivian Richards. Next morning Lloyd and his men plundered a further 134 runs, as Richards and his captain treated Dilley and Botham with something approaching contempt. Lloyd declared at lunch leaving England an afternoon, an evening and a day to bat to save the game.

At once Holding disposed of Boycott, whose two innings in this Test

DOUGLAS JARDINE

England v West Indies, Old Trafford, 1933

SCORECARD ON PAGE 168

Jardine's autocratic bravery allowed him to withstand hoi polloi *criticism. No amount of democratic heckling could persuade him to forsake his brightly coloured Harlequin cap.*

OPPOSITE *Jardine swings the ball round to leg. His long angular body was a provocative target for Constantine and Martindale in the 1933 Old Trafford Test.*

Douglas Jardine was the most controversial man in the history of cricket. Opinion about him was strongly divided. Jack Fingleton saw Jardine as 'a dour remorseless Scot 130 years after his time. He should have gone to Australia in charge of a convict hulk.' Colleagues took a different view. Bill Bowes, a fast bowler on the bodyline tour, felt that 'he revealed all the qualities one hopes to find in a leader of men'. Hedley Verity called his first son Douglas after him. Following that famous Australian tour, when Jardine's policy inflicted injury on a number of Australians, he returned to England to tumultuous welcomes in Scotland and Yorkshire but to an increasingly embarrassed silence from those who had appointed him.

Friend and foe alike were, however, united in acknowledging one quality in him. Jardine was courageous. Bowes recalled Jardine being hit on the hip in Queensland during the 1932–33 tour. Momentarily his team thought their leader was going to fall. So did the fieldsmen who rushed to his aid. In fact he straightened himself, thanked his opponents for their interest and carried on batting as if nothing had happened. At the close of play he strode haughtily through the usual barrackers, but upon reaching the privacy of the dressing room he staggered to the physiotherapist and, speaking through clenched teeth, revealed upon his hip a bruise the size of a saucer, the centre of which was nearly raw.

A powerful friend and a relentless enemy, a man with a loathing for Australians, Jardine asked no quarter and gave none. In 1932–33 cricket saw at work a ruthless man who played to win, a man who used any weapon and any tactic, a man who disdained popularity and ignored advice, a man in short who thought the ends justified the means.

After Australia one question re-mained. Evidently Jardine could dish it out but could he take it? The West Indians arriving in the summer of 1933 for a three-match Test series meant to find out.

Jardine led England to an easy victory in the first Test for which Nelson refused to release their professional, Learie Constantine. At Old Trafford Constantine *could* play, joining forces with Martindale, a fast bowler of the Lindwall school, of medium height with a smooth, long run and a simple delivery, who was to break Wyatt's jaw in 1935. He and Constantine were a formidable pair.

Winning the toss and batting, the West Indians made 375 thanks to Barrow (105) and George Headley (169 not out). And then the fun started. Constantine believed that Hammond and Jardine in particular had shown no enthusiasm for his bumpers in 1928. Jardine, in fact, had walked away from his stumps and patted down the pitch in a marked manner. Constantine scented a weakness. Once Jardine had let loose the dogs of war in Australia it was a weakness he could exploit.

Accordingly Martindale and Constantine at once set a field with six men on the leg-side. Jack Hobbs, now a reporter, smiled as he sat in the Press box. Finally, he thought, English crowds will see what bodyline was about.

The English batsmen had a torrid time and Hammond was hit three times before his chin was split open and he was forced to retire hurt. Naturally it was at Jardine that the most venomous attack was directed. What was good for the goose was plenty good enough for the gander. Jardine did not flinch. To the contrary, *Wisden* states that he 'played it probably better than any other man was capable of doing'.

Standing on his toes, using his full height, time after time he dropped balls directed at his chin down to his feet.

A general view of the Old Trafford Test in 1933, with Jardine at the wicket during the innings in which he answered his bodyline critics.

Sometimes the point of contact was so close to his face that he was forced to take his right hand from the handle to lift the perpendicular bat above the ball. All the while fieldsmen huddled around the bat eager for a catch. It was like huge waves crashing against an inplacable rock.

After tea, with the arrival of a second new ball and Langridge at number 7, the attack was intensified still further, a fifth short leg being called up. Jardine managed to take most of the strike and still he ducked and weaved and defended without flinching. After two hours and 50 minutes of resistance he suddenly hit Martindale for ten in an over to reach his 50.

Next morning he and Robins added 140 in two hours, taking advantage of a storm which had slowed the wicket. Jardine finally reached the first and only Test hundred of his short career. He'd shown that runs could be scored against bodyline though, of course, neither the pitch nor the bowling were quite so hostile as in Australia. Eventually, his point made, he was taken by Constantine at deep gully off a catch so low that Jardine hesitated and stared hard at the fieldsmen before somewhat reluctantly

❛ He had so much guts he'd have tackled a lion single-handed. The players used to say 'If it ever comes to a fight for my life I hope skipper is on my side'. ❜
BILL BOWES

he went on his way.

Jardine had shown to the West Indians that he had no intention of running away from their attack and that, what is more, their tactics would neither break his morale nor take his wicket. It was not a happy episode yet it was an impressive one.

Jardine missed the final Test but with considerable reluctance was asked to lead England in India that winter. He did, then withdrew as captain, for the Australians were due in the summer of 1934. He'd bowled bodyline, then he'd defied it. Now they could bowl half-volleys all day to Bradman as far as he was concerned.

According to the star he followed, Jardine had proved himself as a leader and as a man. He had won battles against overwhelming odds. If they didn't like it they could all go to blazes. Actually, he probably put it stronger than that. Jardine cannot be properly understood without the realisation that, when roused, he could swear like a trooper kicked by a mule. But letting himself go was not his habit.

As with this courageous, pointed hundred, it was all a matter of will.

JAVED MIANDAD

Glamorgan v Essex, Colchester, 1981
SCORECARD ON PAGE 169

Javed about to sweep on the way to his 200 for Glamorgan against Essex at Castle Park, Colchester, in 1981. His magnificent innings on a difficult wicket was in vain.

OPPOSITE *Javed stands straight and drives through the covers off the back foot in Sharjah in 1987.*

Only those who have driven through the streets of Karachi can hope properly to understand Javed Miandad. Imagine a baking sun, smoke and noise, picture a scene like bedlam and place in it a boy in tatty clothes with flashing eyes threading his battered and croaking rickshaw through non-existent gaps, darting on to pavements, cheerfully shouting abuse at pedestrians so that they might grant him a thoroughfare for he is not king of much but he is king of the road.

Picture a man in his element, a master of his rickshaw, happy in his work. He senses the quickest way and takes it time and again for all drivers are rivals and a man must win. It's a dog eat dog world and only a fool would deny it. See a boy who will, one day, be rich, for this boy is going to make it.

At 16 this rude youth scored 311 for Karachi Whites against National Bank and at 19 he scored 100 in his first Test innings for Pakistan. By the time he was 22 he had scored six Test hundreds and was captaining his country, a position for which, having not yet turned from lawbreaker to policeman, he was not ready. At the crease Javed still lives on his wits, moving behind the ball and pinching singles or nipping down the pitch to strike boundaries.

He is cricket's most creative batsman, detecting a run in every delivery, finding a gap and styling his shot accordingly. From unpromising material, a mean delivery supported by a tight field, Javed will take a run, like an urchin on a scrap heap finding a crust of bread.

Swaggering and unapologetic, he pretends to be an intrepid aggressor and yet is, in fact, a master of survival who uses his reflexes to adjust to every delivery no matter how late its movement.

Throughout his career he has been Pakistan's greatest batsman. His range is extraordinarily wide. Permitting no bowler to contain him, Javed can attack with gusto off front and back foot and to all parts of the field; spinners in particular find him a difficult opponent. Moreover, he has an appetite for big scores, for his background instructed him in the wisdom of making hay while sun shines.

Javed had, by 1981, joined Glamorgan, an ailing county side used to propping up the table. That year he hit 2,083 runs at an average of 71, and in scoring eight hundreds passed Gilbert Parkhouse's county record of seven made in 1950. Throughout he played with infectious enthusiasm and conspicuous skill.

Colchester was his finest hour. Essex were, as usual, pressing for the championship and they had prepared a strip calculated to deteriorate rapidly under the hot sun of this late summer, a strip, moreover, which the umpires contemplated reporting on the first morning.

Surprisingly, Essex were tumbled out in their first innings for 187, collapsing ignominiously to Glamorgan's mild attack. In reply, the Welsh county made 274 thanks, largely, to Javed who defied spinners already finding sharp turn to score 81 before being stumped off David Acfield. Batting again 87 in arrears, Gooch and Hardie humbled Glamorgan's spinners who failed to use friendly conditions, perhaps because they had been so long at the bottom and froze with victory in sight. Finally, Essex declared, inviting Glamorgan to chase 325 at a run a minute. Essex's spinners were an experienced and gifted pair, Acfield and Ray East, who anticipated an early finish because the ball was now turning 'at right angles'. Later East recalled: 'They had no chance. The pitch was tinder dry and could have been reported. Batting on it was impossible.'

Glamorgan duly lost two early wickets and were 7 for two as Javed took guard. In the following 315 minutes he gave an extraordinary exhi-

❂ *I've seen lots of good hundreds on flat tracks, saw Javed's 200 in a Test match when he made it look so easy. But his innings in Colchester was incredible. He kept running past the close fieldsmen and hitting against the spin into open spaces. It was the best knock I've ever seen.* ❂

KEN PALMER, UMPIRE DURING JAVED'S INNINGS

bition of batting, an exhibition described by East as 'easily the best I've ever seen. He never looked like getting out – it was as if he was batting on a different wicket. We simply could not believe our eyes.'

Curiously, Javed was troubled early on by Lever and Phillip who coaxed steep bounce from a pockmarked surface, quickly reducing Glamorgan to 44 for four so that an early finish now appeared certain. Fletcher crowded the bat as balls began to behave like fat in a frying pan.

Javed did not miss a ball. At once he set about disrupting the bowlers, flicking East through deep mid-wicket against the spin and against all manner of odds and then reverse-sweeping Acfield to third man. Between times he darted forwards, yards in front of short leg and silly point to pierce gaps with booming drives or gleefully to pinch a single. Javed's mastery disturbed the bowlers who imagined they were bowling dreadfully, and it inspired his partners to hang on.

East was forced to put a man at deep mid-wicket, a humiliation on such a pitch, while Acfield stroked his chin agitatedly at the outrage of good balls landing on off stump, rising and turning sharply, being reverse-swept to the fence backward of point. Only someone daring and blessed with extraordinary talent could play with such audacity.

Glamorgan had reached 155 before another wicket fell and 224 before Eision Jones was out. They needed another 100 runs and, astoundingly,

Javed was still going strong. By now he was tormenting the bowlers, feinting to dash forward and then sitting back on his stumps to pull or cut, and all the while nagging at the bowlers, playing on their nerves, provoking them into something stupid.

Another wicket fell at 227, apparently scuppering Glamorgan's hopes. Robin Hobbs, next man in, was out first ball, not at 227 but at 270. For eight overs Javed faced every ball, though Essex tried to give him singles early in each over. Instead Javed struck shots wide of fieldsmen and scampered two. Off the final delivery he played tip and run, tapping the ball at his toes and scampering home.

Hobbs was held at short leg which brought captain Malcolm Nash in with 53 needed and two wickets to fall. By now the Essex spinners had been destroyed, causing Fletcher to recall his fast men, who dismissed Nash at 291.

A further 32 runs were needed as young Daniels joined Javed, who was growing desperate. Javed whispered to umpire Palmer: 'Palmer, can you give us some wides or some no-balls because we are running out of time.' Twenty runs were added and then an appeal rent the air, whereupon Daniels was adjudged leg before, a decision universally regarded as shocking by eye witnesses. Essex had won and Javed's brilliance had been in a lost cause.

He was left unbeaten on 200, an innings including 22 boundaries and lasting 315 minutes. East said: 'He made us look ridiculous.'

DEAN JONES

Australia v India, Madras, 1986–87

SCORECARD ON PAGE 169

SCORECARD ON PAGE 169

OPPOSITE *Jones in India on another famous occasion – the winning of the World Cup in 1987. This is a typically aggressive square drive.*

Until his innings in Madras in 1986 Dean Jones was a batsman who flattered to deceive. Time and again he threw away his wicket when he had the bowling at his mercy, as if a devil had whispered in his ear that he could, if he wanted, do the impossible. Jones would then play an outrageous shot and surrender his wicket as sages shook their heads. This streak of self-destruction caused him to be left out of the Australian party to tour England in 1985. It was a bombshell, but he forced his way back into the team for a short tour to India in October 1986, a tour upon which he simply had to restore his reputation.

Play in the first Test began in scorching heat and under an unrelenting blue sky. The Chepauk ground in Madras was packed to the rafters. So intense was the heat that one holidaying Australian couple could stay for only one hour without feeling ill.

Marsh and Boon opened, adding 48, playing the bowling easily enough and yet battling hard against the elements. Then Marsh, utterly drained, had a swish at Yadav and was caught in the deep. For Marsh it was an ungodly shot and yet unsurprising too, for no man could think straight when his body and brain were so overheated. Kiran Moré, India's wicket-keeper, had already departed to hospital with a fever.

Enter Dean Jones to play one of cricket's greatest innings. Within an hour his boots were full of water which squelched through the lace-holes. Drinks were taken every 20 minutes. Defying fatigue, he and Boon stayed in nearly to the close. They batted defensively, conserving their energy, trying to break the bowlers.

Boon fell to the second new ball just before stumps, bringing in night-watchman Ray Bright to join Jones, who returned to a cold shower after $4\frac{1}{2}$ hours in the inferno having scored 56 runs. He resumed fresh and eager next morning, determined once more to build his score carefully.

It was again hatefully hot. Ray Bright fell for 30 and promptly collapsed in the dressing room and was treated by a doctor for heat exhaustion. Border joined

Dean Jones, helmeted, booking in the first Test against England in 1989. Jones was showing courage here, too, for the helmet and grille were protecting a recently smashed cheekbone, which was still tender.

Jones. Lunch was approaching and for the first time, Jones was feeling wobbly. In truth, he was sick with fever. From now on his innings took on a force and a courage which sets it apart.

Running between wickets was out of the question so Border and Jones decided to walk singles and hit boundaries. Finally Jones, to his undisguised elation, reached his hundred. Border warmly congratulated him and instructed him to carry on for his job was not yet completed.

But Jones was ill now. Drinks were useless because he could keep nothing down. Regularly he vomited beside the wicket. Twice he urinated into his pants. Heaving and drained, white as a spectre, Jones was now in a trance. Around him his opponents kept asking after his health and recommending remedies. They could see he was poorly and, this day, possessed of greatness.

With no strength left Jones decided to hit out. His range of strokes was limited. Cramp prevented a bending of the knee to sweep and he was also inhibited by pins and needles in his arm. Accordingly he decided upon a tactic of blocking two balls and belting the third. In this manner Jones hit his second hundred in 84 balls. He cannot remember much about it. Everyone else present recollects the graft and the bombardment as something extraordinary.

Having catapulted to 160, and hardly able to stand, Jones tottered down to Border to say that since the team's position was now secure and since he was feeling as if he were at death's door, he was going to retire or perhaps throw his wicket away. 'All right,' Border said, 'if that's the way you feel let's get a real Australian out here; a Queenslander.' Greg Ritchie was due in next.

Border's insult stung. So Jones carried on and reached an incredible 200 just before tea, a score saluted by colleagues, opponents and by a crowd which roared and clapped long enough to shake the crammed stands.

During the tea break Jones' teammates stripped him off, cooled him down with iced towels and tried to goad him on. He lacked the energy to stand under a shower. Upon the bell ringing, these same chums dressed him and put on his pads, unfortunately omitting to include in their otherwise helpful contribution Jones' box and thigh pad. Jones still does not know if this was an oversight or a joke. It'd probably be best not to tell him.

Twenty minutes later Jones was out, bowled by Yadav for 210 having a hit. Now emerged the true horror of this innings, for this man had pushed himself to his limit.

Back in the pavilion Jones sank into a tub of iced water prepared by physiotherapist Errol Sheetly, who also felt his pulse. Feeling fine, he stood up in the bath, to wake in hospital on a saline drip.

Jones had lost seven kilos and was suffering from dangerous dehydration. It took him seven months to return to his fighting weight and to recover his full strength. Nevertheless, he discharged himself from hospital that night because he wanted to be with the boys. He asked Border if he'd reached his hundred. Border looked at him as if the question was unnecessary and replied, 'Yes, mate.'

As chance had it this was, too, a great game of cricket, the second Test to be tied, the last wicket falling on the fifth ball of the last over. But that's a different story.

Back home a month later Dean Jones showed his pictures to his wife. She flicked through them and happening upon an unfamiliar face, a wild face with eyes popping out, like a man from whom a devil had been exorcised, she sought identification from her husband. Who was this odd creature? Dean Jones looked at the photograph and replied: 'It's me.'

STAN MCCABE

Australia v England, Sydney, 1932–33

SCORECARD ON PAGE 170

McCabe was nicknamed 'Napper' because his balding head and visage bore a marked resemblance to those of Napoleon Bonaparte.

⑤ *If I happen to get hit out there, keep Mum from jumping the fence and laying into those Pommy bowlers.* ⑤

MCCABE TO HIS FATHER ON GOING OUT TO BAT IN THE FIERCE ATMOSPHERE AT SYDNEY.

From the start England's intentions were clear that dramatic winter of 1932–33. 'If we don't beat you', Bill Voce said to Vic Richardson, 'we'll knock your bloody heads off.' In the event Jardine and his professional fast bowlers from Nottingham did both.

It was a time of high scoring. Batsmen with broad bats, fastidious techniques, and a holy patience collected double, triple, even quadruple, hundreds on flawless pitches. Fit, strong bowlers threw themselves into the fray and yet found only sweat and despair. Batsmen took no chances in their remorseless pursuit of vast, cruel totals.

For years great bowlers like Larwood and Voce worked against overwhelming odds. Then finally they found a skipper and a tactic which gave them the chance no longer to be the slaves of the game. Quite simply they were going to scorch the Australians by bowling at a terrifying pace at their bodies and heads.

Only a batsman of outstanding courage and talent could hope to counter the bodyline bowling. Ordinary mortals were not up to facing ball after ball rearing at their noses with men stationed in the deep to catch the hook and others squatting on the edge of the bat to pick up catches off glove or bat handle.

Stan McCabe was a country boy from Grenfell, New South Wales. Sent to a Catholic boarding school in Sydney, he'd left early to begin work and to play cricket. A gifted games player, he became golf and billiards champion of New South Wales. He was a simple, humble and self-contained man with a rare talent for back-foot batting.

To widespread disappointment Don Bradman could not play in the first Test, where Woodfull won the toss and elected to bat. At once Larwood and Voce made their intentions clear. Traditionally Australian wickets had been too genial. But things had changed. The grass now used did not produce the polished surface upon which the ball skidded through and hardly left a mark. No longer were the wickets graveyards for fast bowlers. On these new pitches the ball would grip and so lift.

The SCG was heaving. To improve their view the hordes sitting on the asphalt in front of the Sheridan and Brewongle stands pulled most of the palings off the boundary fence. Across the ground the Hill was packed. People were hanging on to the steel fences around the Ladies Stand. It had the atmosphere of a bull-fight.

Woodfull went first, caught behind off Voce. Then Larwood struck, bowling Ponsford and trapping Kippax in front. Brushing away the sweat, he began to see the bumpers fly past the ears of desperately ducking batsmen who stood and stared, stunned by his pace and bounce. Soon enough Fingleton followed and Australia were 87 for four when Richardson and McCabe joined forces. McCabe set about attacking the bowling. Unlike his contemporaries McCabe did not bother with figures. He was a cricketer of inspiration and instinctive brilliance. In his career he played three of cricket's greatest innings. This was to be the first.

At once he hooked Larwood, an audacious and dangerous stroke. Yet really he had no choice. A fellow out there was either a punch-bag or a boxer and Stan didn't care for the passive role. Mind you, he preferred to cut. One quarter of all his runs in Test cricket were made with this shot. He was not, though, prepared to back away from anyone and so, with Jardine ordering a leg-side bombardment, he had to risk everything by hooking. When McCabe hooked he did so not with Bradman's tight, clipped shot but with panache, no holds barred. The shot brought about his downfall in nine of his 43 Test innings. It also, on occasions, took his batting to the rarefied

Stan McCabe (right) going out to bat after tea on the first day during his great innings. His partner is Vic Richardson.

heights beyond greatness and into genius.

Nobody thought he could last long yet the hooks kept falling out of reach, much to the evident irritation of Jardine. Bodyline was under threat. Had all those months of planning been a waste of time? And Bradman, for whom the tactic was devised, wasn't even playing.

Then Richardson lost his wicket to Voce. Later he was to lament: 'If I hadn't got out we'd have killed bodyline stone dead.' Oldfield didn't last long, which brought Grimmett in to join McCabe. As McCabe's assault continued the crowd cheered madly. Finally, at 5.35pm, McCabe drove Gubby Allen to the cover boundary to reach 100 in 161 minutes against bowling of a kind so terrifying as to intimidate anyone without guts from toe to temple.

McCabe took his score to 127 and Australia's to 290 for six by the close. He left the field to a rousing ovation. Jardine and his men walked off tired and uncertain, yet knowing full well they would not, that summer, see a more compelling innings. It was the stuff of which dreams are made. And Jardine did not intend to be beaten by dreams.

Next day Grimmett was caught behind off Voce and Lisle Nagel bowled first ball by Larwood, who sent the off stump cartwheeling away as the Victorian giant picked up his bat.

Without ever quite seeing the ball O'Reilly contrived to score four but it was last man Wall who, joining McCabe at 12.22pm with the total on 305, managed to lend him the support he urgently needed. McCabe's batting was thrilling. When Jardine, varying his tactics, tried off theory McCabe produced off-drives and cuts of scintillating power. He seemed to have a better bat than his colleagues, which was always the case when he was on song.

The last pair added 55 in 33 minutes, of which runs McCabe hit 51. When, finally, Hammond had Wall caught, McCabe had scored 187 out of the 278 runs scored during his four hours at the wicket.

He had nearly, but not quite, brought bodyline to its knees. No one else had attempted to bat in this buccaneering way because no one else thought it could be done. McCabe had stood up to terror tactics without flinching and had batted in a manner calculated to raise the dead from their slumbers.

In the end it did not work. England won this Test, lost the second, then, having worn down the reserves of their opponents, they sealed the Ashes with easy victories in the third and fourth. Neither Bradman's genius nor McCabe's reservoirs of bravery could stop a captain armed with ferocious bowling and a bold strategy.

NAWAB OF PATAUDI

India v England, Headingley, 1967

SCORECARD ON PAGE 170

One Bank Holiday evening in 1961, Robin Waters and his chum the Nawab of Pataudi drove out of the Hove ground where they'd been playing for Oxford University. Out of the blue, a car appeared on the wrong side of the dual carriageway and smashed straight into them. Waters was hardly hurt at all. Pataudi had time to turn his shoulder and felt only a sharp pain on his head which he feared might prevent him leading Oxford in the varsity match. But a splinter of glass had entered his right eye and Pataudi learnt that it would be practically useless.

Discharging himself from hospital, Pataudi went straight to the nets and found that he could see two balls seven inches apart and could not always remember to hit the right one. But was not 'The help of God and a quick victory' the motto of the Pataudis? He was blowed if he'd be beaten.

Within months he was playing for India. Within a year he was captaining India in the West Indies, a post he inherited when Nari Contractor was nearly killed by a bumper.

So it was Pataudi who brought India to England in 1967. 'Never', said *Wisden*, 'has a touring team endured such misfortune as befell the Nawab of Pataudi's combination' on this trip. His two main fast bowlers Guha and Mohol were fit for one Test between them and his preparations were upset by endless rain, preventing India's batsmen adjusting to damp, soft, and seaming pitches.

After two days of the first Test at Leeds, England stood at 550 for four declared and India at 86 for six. In the papers next morning Ian Wooldridge wrote that were this a heavyweight fight the referee would have stopped it. Godfrey Evans opined that ticket prices should be reduced.

Before Saturday's play Pataudi stood in front of his team and told them that if they could not bat on a pitch such as this they might as well give up. Because his team had no common tongue Pataudi had to speak in various languages. He told his men: 'Indian cricket is down and out. People are saying we are no hopers, unfit to play Test cricket and, worst of all, that we lack guts.' His message was easily understood. Asked what language he'd concentrated upon he replied: 'Abusive'. Thanks largely to Pataudi's 64 India reached 164 and followed on 386 runs adrift.

In the second innings Surti quickly fell so that Wadekar joined his Parsi chum, Engineer, at 5 for one. Now began one of cricket's noblest retorts. This pair added 168, taking charge of the match with aggressive cricket. Engineer, fearless, intrepid, hit 14 boundaries in his 87. Wadekar, his usual composed and elegant self, flirting only occasionally with the slips, stroked his way to 89 not out as India reached 198 for two overnight, Engineer hitting a return catch to Close just before stumps. Despite the fightback, press-

The Nawab of Pataudi, in white mackintosh and suede shoes, with a chilly-looking Indian party arriving for the 1967 tour of England.

Pataudi cuts through the gully during his magnificent captain's innings at Leeds in 1967. Close is at leg slip, where he missed Pataudi early in his innings. Graveney is at short leg in front of the bat, D'Oliveira is at slip and Murray is the wicket-keeper.

men checked out of their hotels Saturday night, thinking the match not worth hanging around for till Monday.

Indeed, on Monday morning India lost Wadekar for 91, caught by Close at leg slip off Ray Illingworth, and Borde for 33, bowled trying to pull the crafty Yorkshireman. Pataudi, wearing a cap and a long-sleeved sweater, came in at 12.30 to join Hanumant Singh with the score 228 for four. Close took the new ball, thinking the one-eyed Pataudi was vulnerable to pace. He wasn't that day.

Pataudi was feeling fine. Snow was England's best bowler and having played with him at Sussex, Pataudi felt he could predict Snow's moves even as he ran in to bowl. Higgs he regarded as a steady county bowler and no threat on that pitch. Moreover, India had far superior leg-spinners to Hobbs, and Illingworth was not spinning it much. Why should he not make runs? Ever since his accident he had batted aggressively, reasoning that his eyes made him susceptible in so many ways and at any time he might be out.

To the delight of a sympathetic crowd this pair fought back heroically, although not without luck when Pataudi was dropped by Close at leg slip soon after lunch. When Hanumant pulled Barrington for six the cheers were as if Leeds had won the Cup.

Close shuffled his bowlers to no avail until, finally, Hanumant tickled Illingworth to slip. They'd added 134 in the grand manner and India were only 24

runs adrift. Soon Saxena snicked Snow and England had to bat again.

Saxena did not last long but Pataudi was in charge now. He did not hook nor on-drive, could not trust his eyesight enough for these shots, but, sometimes moving down the track to the spinners, he played everything off the pitch, collecting runs with firm drives and occasional cuts. On 62 he passed 1,500 runs against England in Tests, and he took India to her highest score against England. In time he reached his hundred, his sixth against England, and he was still unbeaten at the close when his team stood at 475 for eight, a lead of 89. It was an extraordinary fightback, hugely applauded by a crowd which recognised an underdog giving its all when it saw one. Indian supporters, too, were relieved and delighted. Seldom had any captain so magnificently answered his own call or any team so conclusively restored its own reputation.

On Tuesday morning, Pataudi was at last fooled and bowled by Illingworth to end a glorious innings of 148, an innings saluted by a warm crowd. Eventually, England were left to score 125 to win. Morale restored, India took four good wickets before conceding defeat. In the papers, Brian Chapman was now saying: 'Book your tickets for Lord's now'.

This was, perhaps, the greatest innings ever played by a captain. With two eyes and proper preparation it would have been outstanding. With one eye, it was simply extraordinary.

EDDIE PAYNTER

England v Australia, Brisbane 1932–33

SCORECARD ON PAGE 172

Eddie Paynter as represented in the Players cigarette card series 'Cricketers 1938'.

Eddie Paynter was surprised to be picked by Jardine to go to Australia in 1932. He wasn't a fellow who expected much from life. At 5ft 5in (1.65m) and 10st 5lb (66kg) he'd had to fight his way up from club cricket in Lancashire and had for seven years toiled away in the second XI. He was in his 30th year before he scored his first hundred in first-class cricket. Incredibly, a year later he was on a boat heading for Australia – no matter he owed his place to Duleepsinhji's withdrawal.

Perhaps Jardine regarded Paynter as a reserve and thought he might as well bring someone jolly along. And Eddie *was* jolly. He was also, of course, a superb player of competitive temperament, a man capable of averaging 60 in his 31 Test innings, an average surpassed only by Sutcliffe of English contemporaries.

England won the first Test, in which Paynter did not play. They lost the second, and Paynter was still not playing. Had Jardine not fallen out with the Nawab of Pataudi Eddie would probably never have played at all. In Melbourne Pataudi refused to move to short-leg when Jardine decided to apply his bodyline tactic. Scornfully Jardine observed that 'His Excellency is a conscientious objector' and sent him elsewhere.

The third Test in Adelaide was one of the most tumultuous ever played. Even *Wisden* was driven to remarking that 'the whole atmosphere was a disgrace to cricket'. So hostile was the feeling against Jardine by now that in the days before the game England had to practise in private. In time Woodfull was hit on the heart – drawing a 'well bowled, Harold' from his captain – and Oldfield upon the head. Spectators hurled abuse.

Amidst this passion Paynter had a marvellous game. Batting at number seven he added 96 crucial runs with Verity for the eighth wicket. England won. Suddenly Paynter mattered.

Paynter was sick before the game at Brisbane but, fearing for his place, dared not tell his captain. Nor was his condition helped by the fierce sunshine which glared its harsh rays upon the wilting England fieldsmen throughout the first day. For once pitch and weather

Strube's cartoon of Paynter's bed.

On board the ss Orantes *on the way to Australia. Paynter (with cigarette) and Tommy Mitchell (with spectacles) are seated on the deck. On the chairs are Harold Larwood, Leslie Ames (snoozing), Maurice Leyland and George Duckworth. The shy Paynter took Leyland and Duckworth with him when he went to collect the cheque which the Australian public presented to him after his heroic innings.*

⑨ *Paynter seemed like a stowaway, found hidden among the team's baggage and put to work his passage in the hope of a pardon.* ⑨

RAY ROBINSON

removed Larwood's sting. In the field Paynter suffered terribly. His throat was sore and his temperature was soaring. He was taken off to hospital.

Australia ended the first day on 251 for three, but Larwood bowled Bradman and Ponsford early next morning and Australia slid to 340 all out.

England, in turn, edged to 216 for six. The game, and the series, hung in the balance. Already Jardine had decided to send for Paynter, whose illness had now been diagnosed as tonsillitis. Doctors had ordered him to rest for several days. Warner told Jardine that it was wrong to take so sick a person from his bed.

Jardine had his way and when England's sixth wicket fell the name PAYNTER was hoisted on the scoreboard to the astonishment of the crowd. As the Lancastrian walked out, apologetically, as if still not certain he deserved to be in such company, the crowd cheered. Here, at last, was something English they could salute.

Stooping at the crease, settling with both feet pointing toward mid-off and, as usual, apparently ready to burst into tears, Paynter began his famous innings. Sportingly the Australians had offered him a runner but Paynter declined. They might bowl him out but he was blowed if they were going to run him out. Pale, tired and feverish, he hung on to the close. The beating sun drained him terribly during his 90 minutes at the crease but the bowlers scarcely took a trick against him.

After another hot night in hospital (survived on cold chicken and iced champagne) Paynter resumed his innings next morning. With only Hedley Verity and Tommy Mitchell to help him, he decided that the time had come to attack. With Verity offering stout resistance and picking up singles here and there, Paynter went for his shots. In a further $2\frac{1}{2}$ hours he added 67 to his score. By the time he was caught by Vic Richardson off Ironmonger, a

The stricken Paynter, with his floppy hat protecting him from the fierce sun, on-driving high during his great knock at Brisbane.

weary shot, a chip when the full potato had been intended, England were 16 runs to the good.

Paynter's courage inspired his teammates. Larwood steamed in to take three wickets, including Bradman's. Allen and Verity were roused too and Australia, out for 175, were beaten.

Rain was falling as Paynter himself made the winning hit, a clouted six. So popular was his triumph over adversity that the Australian public subscribed generously to a testimonial launched to recognise his deed. Back home when a speaker in the House of Commons men-tioned his name there was cheering throughout the chamber. Most significant of all, England had won the Ashes. An unconsidered cricketer, a minnow amidst salmon, had saved the day.

In retirement Eddie was invited to fly to Australia for the Centenary Test in 1977. Tickled pink, he accepted and boarded an aircraft for the first time in his life. Once in Melbourne he chatted merrily to everyone and made only one complaint. This beer the locals drank. It was too cold. He wanted his warm. Iced drinks were only appropriate when you had the fever upon you.

BERT SUTCLIFFE

New Zealand v South Africa, Johannesburg, 1953–54

SCORECARD ON PAGE 172

Cultured, charming and charismatic Bert Sutcliffe was the most beloved of New Zealand's cricketers in those early, formative years when, in the view of their Antipodean neighbours, to play them was to break a butterfly upon a wheel.

In fact, Sutcliffe was destined never to play in a victorious New Zealand Test team. Quite simply the islands could not field 11 strong cricketers and were too dependent upon the valiant deeds of a select few. In particular, their bowling was not powerful enough, not until the arrival of Richard Hadlee, and no matter how determined their batting New Zealand could rarely dismiss their opponents for a manageable total. Sutcliffe belonged to this pioneering era in which individual deed could inspire as the team lost again. And it was Sutcliffe who, in Ellis Park, Johannesburg, on Boxing Day 1953, played as brave an innings as was ever played for New Zealand, or for anyone else for that matter.

Sutcliffe was a wonderful batsman. Enterprising by temperament, he used a high grip on the bat and a correct left-handed style to belabour bowlers at every opportunity.

Sutcliffe scored 2,627 runs in England in 1949 and three hundreds in his only three games in Australia in 1954. Yet it was this innings in Johannesburg which lingers in the mind after all those brilliant efforts have passed into the books. Fortunately Ray Robinson was present to catch the occasion and upon his recollections this account leans heavily.

South Africa had won the first Test by an innings, Sutcliffe scoring 20 and 16 as an opener. He was moved to second drop for the second Test which began in Johannesburg on Christmas Eve. South Africa made 259 for eight on the first day. Overnight terrible news arrived from home of a train disaster at Tangiwai between Wellington and Auckland in which 151 people had died, includ-

ing the fiancée of Kiwi fast bowler, Bob Blair (22). Flags were flown at half-mast at Ellis Park and, of course, the New Zealand players were devastated, sharing the grief of their team-mate. Cricket hardly seemed to matter any more, but a Test match had to be played.

In Neil Adcock South Africa had discovered a dangerous fast bowler, and the Ellis Park pitch was hard and green, ideal for a man prepared to bend his back, so the cricket was tough enough on its own. With their opponents all out for 271, New Zealand at once found the ball crunching into their ribs and whistling past their noses as they ducked and wove or took body blows. Chapple was bowled off his ribs and, soon enough, Miller taken to hospital, coughing up blood after a blow on the chest. Two others were to collapse beside the wicket during an innings played in conditions entirely unfamiliar to New Zealand players.

It was 9 for two as Sutcliffe began his innings. At once a ball from Adcock smashed into his head as he tried to flick it away. To the horror of the 22,000 crowd, Sutcliffe sank to the turf, one hand pressed to his left ear. A stretcher was rushed out and the silence around Ellis Park was forbidding. After five minutes of urgent attention, Sutcliffe staggered to his feet, waved away the stretcher and was helped from the field by his captain. An ambulance rushed him to hospital where Sutcliffe fainted while the injury was being treated. Nevertheless he insisted upon returning to Ellis Park and, upon doing so, found New Zealand had subsided to 81 for six, though wicket-keeper Mooney was staunchly protecting his wicket.

Sutcliffe decided to go in because New Zealand still needed 41 to avoid the follow-on. His arrival was greeted by a roar from the crowd, in recognition of his determination and their relief. Usually dapper and full of laughter, Sut-

OPPOSITE *Bert Sutcliffe pulling the ball through midwicket. Sutcliffe's innings in Johannesburg, in the context of a hopelessly lost match and a real national disaster, taken with the additional sauce of the bravery of Bob Blair, represents just about the most courageous innings ever played in a Test match – gallantry for its own sake.*

cliffe was now swathed in bandages and absolutely ashen.

David Ironside was bowling his swingers and Sutcliffe, to another huge roar, swung his third ball over square leg for six. So began one of cricket's most thrilling onslaughts.

Adcock was recalled and Sutcliffe, with regal disdain, cut him for four. Tayfield, who had been lethal a fortnight earlier, was twice smacked over the fence. Such violent batting loosened the bandages and attendants had to run out to tighten them. With Sutcliffe swinging lustily, 50 runs were added in half-an-hour of graceful violence. They were batting not merely for their team but for

Bert Sutcliffe posing in studied forward defensive mode. There were not too many defensive strokes played in Johannesburg.

OPPOSITE *Gary Sobers played many a captain's innings for the West Indies.*

a country so touched by tragedy and for their chum who was hiding his pain in his hotel room. Ironside bowled Mooney and MacGibbon fell for a duck, leaving New Zealand on 146 for eight, the follow-on saved, but still a wretched position. Guy Overton joined Sutcliffe who had what he presumed to be a last fling, smiting Tayfield over long on for six to reach 55 before Overton was beaten by Ironside. At once the players moved towards the pavilion. No better description can be written of what now took place than that already provided by Robinson.

'Then there was a sudden, almost chilling silence, as Blair came out to bat, giving a dramatic day its most poignant moment. He had heard at his team's hotel that his team was in trouble, and somehow had summoned the courage to come to the ground. It was distressing to see how much trouble he had trying to get his gloves on, how he tried to brush them over his eyes as Sutcliffe came to meet him in the sunshine, and to put an arm around him.

'Then it was all action. With the sweetest of timing, the most deft of footwork, Sutcliffe hit three more sixes in an over from Tayfield, then took a single from the seventh ball. Blair clearly did not feel in need of such protection. He hit the last ball far into a half-demented crowd.

'They were together only ten minutes but added 33 before Blair was stumped. So they went off together, arms about each others' shoulders into the tunnel.'

Sutcliffe made 80 runs out of the 106 added in his time at the crease, and he hit seven sixes. New Zealand lost, of course, for they were out-gunned, and Sutcliffe was never quite the same against fast bowling again, but he had done enough already. As Robinson wrote, until Sutcliffe played it such an innings did not exist outside schoolboys' dreams.

TRICKY WICKET TRIUMPHS

JACK HOBBS

England v Australia, The Oval, 1926

SCORECARD ON PAGE 173

SCORECARD ON PAGE 173

RIGHT *A happy Hobbs with his England blazer and cap and, what was much commoner with sportsmen in 1926 than it is today, a cigarette.*

❁ *Sometimes I'd just plug them down at him and hope he had a fit or something.* ❁
SYDNEY BARNES OF JACK HOBBS

OPPOSITE *The front page of the* Daily Sketch, *19 August 1926, showing the crowd rushing across the Oval to cheer in front of the pavilion as the players leave the pitch.*

Unturned, genial, correct, humble, John Berry Hobbs was one of the greatest and most balanced of cricketers. He was the first professional to be knighted for his services to the game. Between 1905 and 1934 he scored 61,237 runs and hit 197 hundreds. One of the 11 offspring of a servant, Hobbs was to score 100 before lunch 20 times, contemporaries saying he could have scored 400 hundreds if he'd put his mind to it. Sometimes he simply didn't bother, especially if his team was on top. His batting was kind not cruel, and greed was foreign to his temperament.

Until the Kaiser's war he was a dasher, after it, already aged 35, he was a ripe old master. Hobbs preferred to be remembered for those youthful years. By 1926 Hobbs' career was, critics imagined, near its end. He was 43 now and slowing down. Nevertheless, England had no hesitation in asking him to open the batting with the immaculate, dogged Yorkshireman Herbert Sutcliffe

as England tried to regain the Ashes that year. With rain spoiling the season, the first four Tests were drawn, and the fifth at The Oval was to be played to a finish.

Upon winning the toss England batted first. Chapman's outfit did not begin well. Hobbs laughed as he missed a simple full toss from Arthur Mailey and was bowled, just as the spinner had dreamed. England spluttered nervously to 280, a total keenly protected by Larwood and Tate who bowled Australia out for 302. With Australia to bat last there was a cigarette paper between the teams. England moved carefully to 49 for no wicket by the end of the second day.

Those first two days had been tense, cricket played on a knife edge. The Oval had been packed, with people sleeping on the pavements outside the ground to be certain of a place next morning.

Beachcomber wrote that 'everybody you meet takes it for granted that there is nothing but cricket on your mind. If you say to a man "What's the time?" he replies mechanically, "432 for nine".' Everyone eagerly awaited the third day which boded well for England, if the openers could continue their marvellous form.

And then overnight thunderstorms broke over South London. It was beyond belief. The pitch was still wet when Hobbs on 28 and Sutcliffe on 20 resumed at 11am. Rubbing their hands gleefully the Australians set about their work, Richardson turning his off-breaks into his leg-trap, Grimmett, the miser, and Mailey, the millionaire, spinning the ball aggressively. To their consternation the Australians found the wicket to be dead at first. Moreover, Sutcliffe was batting with his usual disdainful air, as if the wicket was as placid as could be and the bowling just a lot of tommy-rot. Sutcliffe did not score for 34 minutes but he did not get out either.

Worse for them, Hobbs was pottering

TWO KILLED, 11 INJURED IN AIR LINER CRASH IN FOG

DAILY SKETCH

No. 5,417. Telephones {London—Museum 9841. Manchester—City 6501.}   LONDON, THURSDAY, AUGUST 19, 1926.   [Registered as a Newspaper.]   ONE PENNY.

HOW THE KITCHENER FAKE BEGAN

CROWD'S WILD RUSH AFTER TEST MATCH VICTORY

How the excited crowd at the Oval yesterday rushed across the ground to cheer the English eleven on their great victory over the Australians in the final Test Match. Unprecedented scenes of enthusiasm were witnessed, the crowd for a long time clamouring for speeches from favourite players.

smoothly along and acknowledging applause for a 50 scored in 107 minutes. Then, at last, a hot sun broke through and the wicket became spiteful. Now the balls reared wickedly at the batsmen. Now the fieldsmen hustled, grasping for catches. Unperturbed, Sutcliffe and Hobbs moved on to the back foot and dropped dangerous balls at their toes. Anything missing the stumps was taken on the body or allowed to go through to Oldfield. Their judgement spoke of decades of experience and icy nerves. Moreover, they pinched cheeky singles without so much as bothering to call. There was no need. That series they averaged 118 as a pair. Each man could read his partner's mind. Tip, wink, and off they'd scurry for a single.

Minutes ticked by and turned into hours. Morale soared in the England camp. A dressing room driven to silence by the rain and the pitch now began to chatter again. Grimmett, Mailey and even Charlie Macartney could not dislodge the openers. By lunch they had defied all forecasts by reaching 161 for no wicket. They were cheered as they left the battlefield for everyone knew, now, that the Ashes were England's for the taking. Hobbs had led the way. With all England, apparently, relying upon him, he'd calmly met any difficulty and shown his team-mates what could be done. Nor had he failed to punish the wayward delivery, pulling anything short through the cluster of close fieldsmen, using his feet to kill the spin stone dead. He was a master at work.

After lunch the wicket began to ease. In the second over Hobbs reached his hundred with another sharp single off Gregory and the crowd rose to salute him. Sutcliffe was on 58 and the pair had been at work for nearly three hours and 36 minutes.

Almost at once Hobbs was out, a ball from Gregory touching his off-bail. Hobbs' hundred, his 11th against Australia, was chanceless and included ten boundaries. Sportingly Herbie Collins and his men joined in the stirring ovation which took Hobbs back to the pavilion on this, his home ground. Jack Fingleton described Hobbs and Sutcliffe as 'the outstanding opening partnership in history'. They'd added 112 in less than 2½ hours before lunch against desperate opponents and on a treacherous pitch.

The issue had been settled. Sutcliffe carried on to 161 whereupon, in the last over of the day, he was bowled by a googly from Mailey. Hobbs watched him as he returned to the dressing room. 'There was Herbert, black and blue and not a hair out of place.' Others chipped in and England led by 414.

Prime Minister Baldwin and half his Cabinet turned up to watch what was to be the last day, for it had rained again. No Australian could summon the strength or the skill to match Hobbs and his partner. They were a beaten side and they knew it. Rhodes and Larwood skittled them for 125 and, amidst unparalleled scenes of excitement, England had regained the Ashes.

GILBERT JESSOP

England v Australia, The Oval, 1902

SCORECARD ON PAGE 173

A Spy cartoon of Jessop from the magazine Vanity Fair. *Between 1877 and 1913, 31 cricketers appeared in the famous* Vanity Fair *series of prominent contemporary figures, most drawn by Spy (Sir Leslie Ward).*

Until 13 August 1902 the Australians didn't think much of Jessop. 'Just a slogger', they used to say. English critics took a different view. Jessop could swing a match. In his career he scored, on average, 80 runs to the hour, far faster than anyone else. Any team in which he played had a chance. The Australians scoffed at his rudimentary ways and went about their work. Battle was joined with Australia already two up as the teams reached The Oval. England were in urgent need of a boost to their morale.

Australia won the toss and batted first in cold, autumnal conditions, and reached a cosy if not frightening 324. England's reply was disappointing, though once more they were caught on a wet pitch. Jessop made 13 in eight minutes and England avoided the follow-on thanks to some tail-end hitting and a dropped catch or two. Nevertheless, a deficit of 141 was towering.

In their turn Australia collapsed on a pitch drying slowly. Trumper was run out by Jessop and the rest were bombarded by Lockwood and Braund. To win England needed to score 263, a formidable task.

Alas, rain fell that night. The big crowd gathered at The Oval more in hope than expectation. At once their worst fears were confirmed. Trumble, who was to bowl throughout both innings, ambled up once more in his inoffensive way and began with an uneventful over. Saunders, whose renown lay as much with his trick of running up behind the umpire as with his left-arm twirlers, took the second over. This time the umpire did not stand ten yards back to give the batsman a sight of the advancing bowler. In the event MacLaren played on third ball, whereupon Tyldesley was beaten first ball and comprehensively bowled second. Saunders next bowled Palairet. At 10 for three, the position was nearly hopeless.

Adding insult to injury, further rain fell causing a stoppage for 35 minutes. Then Hayward was caught behind off Saunders: 31 for four. Seventeen runs later and rather unluckily, Braund was caught by Kelly, who grasped the ball to his body as he fell. England 48 for five. This, certainly, was the end.

Jackson, with true Yorkshire grit, hung on and was joined, now, by the broad-shouldered Jessop whose walk to the crease was rapid as if to say: 'Let's get this business over.'

If anyone supposed that Jessop would be inhibited by the dire situation he was in error. Jessop scored off all his first six deliveries. Seven runs were taken off Saunders, and then Trumble was driven high to the pavilion awning. Jessop was hitting straight, forcing himself not to lash across the line against Trumble, whose spin was deadly. Jettisoning his usual smites to leg did not, however, mean playing with cumbersome care. He drove Saunders again and then, on 23, dashing down the pitch, Jessop missed. So did Kelly, the wicket-keeper. Undeterred Jessop hit the next ball over Armstrong at cover, and then hit a skimmer wide of Trumper at long-off. The chance was dropped with the fielder at full pelt. Rather like Marshall Foch ('My flanks are turned, and my centre is surrounded. I shall attack.') Jessop had decided to go forwards.

Lunch was taken after a perilous period of cricket played on a still dodgy pitch. England, 87 for five, with Jackson on 39 and Jessop on 29, now needed 176. Hard, but you never can tell.

Jessop resumed after lunch, as usual without a box. He never felt the need for protection. At the crease he crouched over his bat like a great cat about to pounce, all the while working his hands around the handle. As a boy he stood tall but in maturity he'd adopted this crouch because he was eager to dash down the pitch .

Trumble bowled magnificently, Saunders buckled under the pressure. Capable of bowling a dangerous ball, he was broken by the ferocity of Jessop's charge. Once Jessop cut Trumble to the distant Vauxhall boundary and ran five.

Soon he was pulling Saunders to leg with calculated power. Now the crowd could scarcely contain itself, and when he outdid all his previous efforts by hitting four consecutive boundaries off wild deliveries from Saunders to the square-leg wall, thousands of spectators stood and cheered.

Then Jackson fell. Stuck on 49 for 10 minutes, he was caught and bowled by Trumble who had gigantic hands and never missed anything off his own bowling. The contrasting pair had added 109 in 67 minutes.

Hirst arrived and at once survived a loud shout for lbw. It looked plumb. Hirst attacked Saunders, who'd been bowling too long. Finally Armstrong was called upon to bowl his slow leg-breaks. Jessop found timing difficult – it is often wise to bowl slower to someone steaming onwards – but he played some enormous drives off Trumble, one of which cleared the pavilion. He smote again, and again cleared the boundary. This took him to 96 whereupon he sent Armstrong to the fence to reach his hundred amidst an ovation scarcely ever matched in cricketing history. He'd been batting for 75 minutes, easily the fastest ton ever scored in Anglo-Australian Test cricket.

After one more boundary, Jessop swept half-heartedly at Armstrong and popped the ball to Noble at square-leg. It had been hitting of a kind rarely seen.

But the game wasn't over. Lockwood fell lamely and 49 were wanted with two wickets to fall. Lilley and Hirst played carefully, collecting runs till Lilley was caught at mid-off. Fifteen to win, Yorkshiremen Hirst and Rhodes in partnership. It's an old story. Nerves were tight. Darling shifted his field nearly every ball. The crowd of 22,000 hardly dared to breathe. Did Hirst say: 'We'll get 'em in singles, Wilfred'? People could hardly watch. Rhodes edged a four through the slips. After this every run was a single, though an overthrow was added to one. Finally, finally the scores were level. A clergyman who thought it was won ran on the field. He didn't notice his mistake till he was near the middle with a policeman in hot pursuit. Then Rhodes hit Trumble past

ABOVE *The Gerry Wright painting of Gilbert Jessop, wearing an England blazer.*

RIGHT *A contemporary coloured post card of Jessop, playing to leg.*

MR G. L. JESSOP (GLOSTER.)

mid-on and everyone ran. The noise and cheering lasted for an hour or more.

England had won and, despite Hirst's heroic efforts, it was Jessop's match. Silent and still at the crease, flashing into his shots, his batting had been a glorious yet calculated gamble. Until Botham, perhaps, in 1981 it is hard to imagine that a more inspiring innings could ever light up the relentless world of Test match cricket.

ARTHUR SHREWSBURY

England v Australia, Lord's, 1886
SCORECARD ON PAGE 174

On 19 May 1903 Arthur Shrewsbury, the famous Nottinghamshire batsman, picked up his five-chambered revolver and shot himself. One bullet penetrated the left side of his chest. This not being effective, he turned the weapon to his right temple and shot again. Death was instantaneous. Shrewsbury had been having treatment for an old internal disorder which he thought, wrongly according to his doctor, would stop him playing county cricket again. So ended the life of England's outstanding professional batsman of the last century. Upon being asked to name his Test side, W. G. Grace used to mutter: 'Give me Arthur.' It did not matter, apparently, who made up the rest of the team.

Shrewsbury was an innovator. His want of height and robustness forced him to adapt a technique far in advance of his period. Not for him the forward plunge and elegant drive through the covers. Not for him the move away from the ball to allow a full and free swing of the bat as recommended by the amateur stylists. Shrewsbury played forward only when he could easily reach the ball. Otherwise he used his pads to protect his wicket; which many amateurs regarded as not playing the game, and relied upon concentration and hard work to bring him runs. Lockwood, the great Surrey bowler, once expressed the frustration felt by endless opponents faced with the unbending tenacity of Shrewsbury's defence. Lockwood was not quite so cerebral a character as the Notts opener, who was also a Sunday school teacher. When Shrewsbury marched out to bat, Lockwood would say: ''Ere 'e comes singin' 'is ruddy 'ymns.'

One day at the Oval, Lockwood bowled for hours in rain to Shrewsbury until, in mid-afternoon, and quite out of the blue, a ball spat up from the wicket. Shrewsbury, a hundred or so not out by now, scrutinised the pitch minutely, prodded and poked it. This was too much for Lockwood. 'That ruddy gasometer 'as bin up an' it's bin down, an' it's ruddy well goin' up again, while 'e's bin 'ere. An' ah've never seen ruddy sight of 'is stumps. An' 'e's pattin' ruddy pitch.' Hereabouts, according to Neville Cardus, words failed him.

The greatest professional batsman of his day, Arthur Shrewsbury.

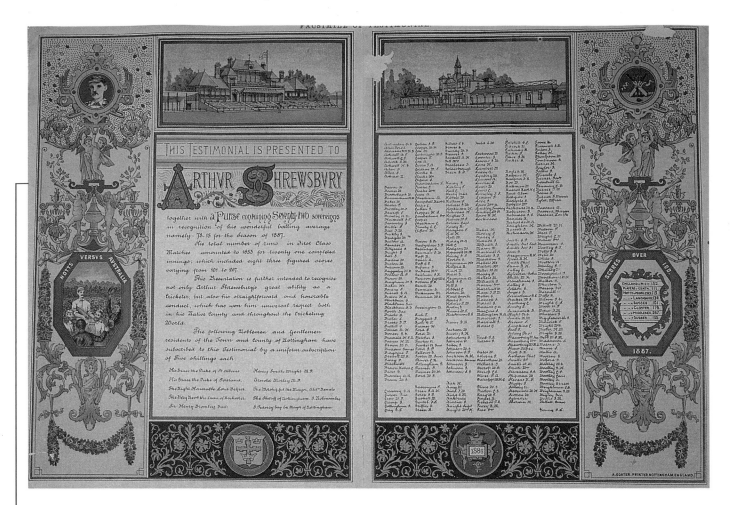

The illuminated address presented to Arthur Shrewsbury in 1888 by the Mayor of Nottingham in recognition of his average of 78.15 in 1887. Shrewsbury wanted the presentation in the Trent Bridge pavilion and was embarrassed by having to make a speech bareheaded in the Town Hall. He was so sensitive about his premature baldness that even in the dressing room he could switch from ordinary headgear to cap and back without revealing his bald head.

Shrewsbury was the first man to reach a thousand in Test cricket. Patient, reverent, he was the last professional to captain England before Len Hutton in 1952. He led England in Australia in 1884–85, winning a series thanks largely to his own masterly unbeaten hundred against Spofforth, Trumble and Giffen in the deciding Test on the Melbourne cricket ground. But this brave hundred was not Shrewsbury's masterpiece. This plaudit is reserved for his magnificent 164 at Lord's a year or so later.

He strode out at 12.20pm on the first day, W. G. Grace having lost his wicket, to encounter a sticky enough dog to stretch even his monumental concentration and wristy back-play. No sooner had he taken guard at 27 for one when rain fell. Play was not resumed until 1.47pm. At once Shrewsbury gave a difficult chance to slip off T. W. Garrett. Australia knew when the ball touched the turf that a priceless opportunity to move the immovable had been missed.

Lunch was taken at 2.00pm with Shrewsbury 7 not out. After lunch the pitch deteriorated further. It was to change during the ensuing seven hours from fiery, to slow, to sticky. Only in the short middle period was batting a remotely comfortable task. In Spofforth, too, Australia had the greatest bowler of the era. Breaking the ball back from off-stump, cutting his pace a yard or so to concentrate his threat, varying his pace devilishly, Spofforth pounded on with his whirlwind action. Tall and agile, his hostility was unceasing, and his eye never less than satanic.

Scotton, Read and Steel fell and W. Barnes joined Shrewsbury with the score on 119 for four. It was now 4.44pm and the wicket was at its worst. Shrewsbury finally reached his 50, still grimly resisting the aggressive but increasingly irritated Australians. They could not drag him forward. Continually he moved back and dropped his wrists on the ball, taking the sting out of it, smoothing it short of the grasping short-legs around him. Watching the ball with prodigious care, Shrewsbury's concentration never wavered.

Shrewsbury's powers of concentration were phenomenal. Back home at Trent Bridge, if he were unbeaten at lunch, he would ask an attendant to bring out a cup of tea for him at 4.30. He

Lord Sheffield's XI in 1886, a couple of months before Shrewsbury's great innings at Lord's. From left, back: Farrands (umpire), Bates (scorer), Flowers, Barnes, Ulyett, Salter (scorer), Thoms (umpire). Seated: Shaw, W. Newham, W. G. Grace, W. W. Read, Shrewsbury. Sitting on ground: Phillips, Bates, Scotton.

never doubted he would still be in.

At the close of that critical first day the great professional batsman stood on 91 not out, culled from a score of 202 for four. Of course his innings had not been chanceless. In such conditions it was not possible to bat so long without being occasionally in danger. On 35 he might have been stumped off Giffen, and on 55 he might have been taken at short-leg off the same bowler, but the ball eluded diving hands.

Play resumed at 11.35am next morning. Shrewsbury's practical approach to batting continued to torment his opponents. He could not pick leg-spinners – suspiciously he prodded them, mistrustful of the wristy energy upon the ball. He did not like unpredictability. He would bide his time, certain that a bad ball would arrive sooner or later.

At 11.56am he reached his hundred. Spectators and opponents clapped, recognising that a battle had been won by a game warrior. When Barnes was out for 58, the pair had added 161 runs. The Australians were never to be the same again on that tour. Shrewsbury had confirmed his reputation as the greatest sticky wicket batsman of all.

At lunch Shrewsbury had advanced to 152 and when, finally, he was caught at slip off the mighty Trumble he had been at the crease for six hours and 51 minutes and had hit 16 boundaries. His 164 was the highest score for England (W. G. Grace passed it within a month).

To The Times this innings was a 'masterpiece'. Shrewsbury's judgement of length and strong back play were noticed and yet many, not least the Australians, would have been pleased if he'd set elegance higher and effectiveness lower. By using his pads, by hitting to leg, by emphasising defence rather than offence, Shrewsbury had adopted tactics rather in advance of his time. Accordingly he was to stand blamed when others found this route to run-scoring.

This was his greatest hour. Australia lost heavily and did not regain the Ashes until 1897–98. Shrewsbury battled on until 1902, when he scored two hundred in a game for the first time. He tormented bowlers and perhaps himself besides. In the end he could not sufficiently distinguish batting from living. When he could not any longer do the first he would not, any longer, do the second.

GARY SOBERS

West Indies v England, Kingston, 1967—68
SCORECARD ON PAGE 174

❝ *He was never in trouble, never hit. He even middled balls leaping at his body. When he was facing it seemed as if the ball wasn't doing anything.* ❞
RIVAL CAPTAIN COWDREY ON SOBERS' INNINGS.

Gary Sobers square-drives for West Indies on the tour of England in 1973.

OPPOSITE *Sobers drives through the covers at Lord's in 1973. Sobers was the greatest of all all-rounders. There was nothing on the cricket field he couldn't do.*

Sir Garfield St Aubrun Sobers was cricket's eighth knight and probably its greatest ever player. Sleek, graceful and yet walking in a strange hiccuppy way, chin jutting forward rather like the pink panther, Sobers was a cricketer who combined versatility with a classically correct technique. He was, too, a man of laughter who, while fiercely competitive could never consider cricket to be anything more than a game. To do anything ugly or unfair was foreign to his nature. A genius of inspired orthodoxy, and a man who lived life to the full, he was a cricketer's cricketer.

Born the fifth child of a merchant seaman who died when his ship was torpedoed by a German U-boat, born therefore into a humble family, Sobers was, from the start, an outstanding sportsman. He represented Barbados in golf, basketball and soccer and by 17 was playing for the West Indies against England, bowling his spinners.

For a time flashes of genius were interspersed with horrendous mistakes so that Sobers' game remained an enigma. And then, magnificently, Sobers broke through scoring his first 100 at Sabina Park in 1958 and continuing to reach an immaculate and unbeaten 365. No one again doubted his greatness.

To my mind Sobers' greatest innings among many was played in the second Test against England at Sabina Park, Jamaica, in 1968, where both teams were horrified to discover that a thunderstorm had left the pitch wet. Cowdrey's decision to bat first gave England, who had dominated the first Test, the use of it before it turned from torpor to treachery, and England reached 376. When the West Indians were all out after 48 overs for 143, Cowdrey enforced the follow-on. Snow's spell of seven for 49 was one of the most terrifying in Test history. Kanhai fell to a kicking leg cutter and Sobers leg before first ball to a shooter that would have got anybody.

Determined to show his mettle, Cowdrey forbade golf and fishing on the Sunday, ordering his players to rest which they did by the pool, in some cases for rather too long. The fast bowlers did not regain their sting when play resumed, but when Sobers entered on a king pair at 174 for four his first ball from Brown jumped from a crevice and lobbed from the captain's bat over Titmus' head at short leg. Soon two awkward cutters found the edge, one falling short of Graveney and the second being dropped by D'Oliveira, standing at slip while Graveney attended to tummy trouble in the dressing room. Sobers had scored seven.

Till now the Sabina Park crowd had endured the disasters of their team without anger. Then Basil Butcher glanced D'Oliveira and Jim Parks took a low catch. Umpire Sang Hue, a Jamaican, correctly gave Butcher out.

As Holford walked out to bat cries of dissent were heard from the cheapest sectors of the ground and soon a bottle sailed over the wire mesh fence. This started a hail and led to baton-swinging policemen storming into the crowd, doubling their fury.

Cowdrey and Sobers appealed for peace and Jones and Brown began clearing the ground, using their hats to collect rubbish. Unfortunately the police chose this moment to charge and to throw canisters of tear gas, whereupon a stampede began as the gas blew across the field and into the pavilion. Women screamed, children cried and people were trampled underfoot.

It was 90 minutes before play resumed. Sobers and his board apologised profusely but dared not abandon play for no-one had gone home. They offered to play the lost time on a sixth morning and so it was agreed.

Probably alone of the West Indians Sobers was convinced all was not lost.

Sobers' great innings at Sabina Park was interrupted by a crowd unhappy at the dismissal of Basil Butcher. A frowning Sobers goes out to appeal against the bottle-throwing demonstrations. England's captain Cowdrey looks stern as he accompanies him. On the right is R. C. Marley, President of the Jamaican Cricket Association.

had reached his 50 in two hours and the West Indians were 81 in front.

Holford fell immediately after lunch and now Sobers took command, striking 16 off one Titmus over, hitting a glorious straight six over the wall that serves as a sight screen in Sabina Park. By the time Murray fell to a grubber 37 had been added in 30 minutes.

Cowdrey was on the defensive and Sobers moved through the 90s single by single, his second 50 taking nearly four hours. From so dazzling a player, so instinctive an aggressor, it had been a masterpiece of defence. Sobers' technique was simply too good.

Charlie Griffith stayed for 77 minutes, frustrating an increasingly woebegone attack. Then Jones trapped him and beat Wes Hall first ball whereupon Sobers audaciously declared, asking England to score 159 runs in 155 minutes.

His gamble nearly worked. Had not 40 minutes been lost to bad light that night England would have lost. As it was they slid to 19 for four overnight, Sobers taking two wickets. David Holford dropped two catches next morning and D'Oliveira held on until the umpires, rather controversially, pulled up the stumps and walked off, leaving the field to a posse of policemen.

Few innings can have been as skilful as this one by Sobers. No batsman had a greater range, for Sobers could be savage or cautious, depending upon his team's need. He made runs on pitches good and dreadful and in situations happy and grim.

England won the series, Sobers trying one daring declaration too many in Trinidad. Pilloried by fickle supporters Sobers urgently tried to rectify his loss in the final Test, scoring 152 and 95 not out and taking six wickets in a doomed crusade. He could save a game off his own bat on any pitch and against any bowling but could not quite beat all England on his own.

Seldom can any judgement have been so supported by events. Upon the resumption Sobers played what Keith Miller regarded as his greatest innings while Brian Close called it unbelievable. Later Sobers simply said: 'I was lucky. You need it on that wicket.' He was right for the pitch was a lottery. Jim Parks conceded 33 byes, few of them his fault as the ball leapt over his head.

Sobers hardly missed a delivery. So intense was his concentration that his eyes appeared to pop out of their sockets as the bowler ran in. With Holford offering stout support Sobers worked towards his hundred and by lunch next day the pair had added 56 runs to the overnight score of 258 for five. Sobers

HERBERT SUTCLIFFE

England v Australia, Melbourne, 1928–29

SCORECARD ON PAGE 175

Herbert Sutcliffe, from the 1934 series of cricketers on Players' cigarette cards.

❧ *If he is bowled he appears to regard the event less as a human miscalculation than some temporary, and reprehensible, lapse of natural laws. There has been a blunder, to which he is unwillingly privy and liable. The effects of this blunder will be entered, with other blunders, in a score book, and the world may read of it in due time. He does not regret that it has occurred, for he is never sorry for himself, but he is sorry that Nature should have forgotten herself.* ❧

R. C. ROBERTSON - GLASGOW

Australian crowds were, by 1928–29, used to Hobbs and Sutcliffe batting, apparently, for ever. Four years earlier they'd twice added over 100 for the first wicket in Sydney. Then they added 283 in Melbourne. Yabber, the celebrated Hill barracker had yelled: 'Send for Nurse Bland, she'll get the bastards out.' Nurse Bland was a well-known midwife who, shortly before the Tests, had been in the news following an abortion scandal.

Sutcliffe stayed in all day in four Tests that winter of 1928–29 and was out in the last over in another. He was at his best against Australia because he loved a dog-fight: Herbert was not a classical player. Picking his bat up towards third slip, standing open-chested and with his weight on the left leg, using his pads in defence, his batting was not the stuff of poetry but of facts and figures. A supreme judge of a single, Sutcliffe was never flustered at the crease, so much so that the more democratic Australians disliked him. He was just the sort of aloof, autocratic Pom to rub them up the wrong way.

He was a tough cricketer whose game rose to a challenge. Sutcliffe had big-match temperament in abundance. Barracking him was a waste of time. The fact that he'd missed five outswingers in a row was an absolute irrelevance – without so much as a blink he'd steel himself for the next ball.

England won the first two Tests of the 1928–29 tour but as play resumed on the sixth morning of the following contest played in Melbourne, nothing appeared more certain than that the Australians would pull one back, for that night it had rained hard. A bright morning promised an old-fashioned Australian sticky, worse even than its English counterpart. After a close contest England needed 332 to win.

Play could not begin on time, the outfield being too wet. Friends commiserated with the Englishmen as they waited in the pavilion. Hughie Trumble told Hobbs that 70 would be a good score. Noble, Armstrong, Mailey and Macartney said England would do well to reach 80. No one thought Chapman's team had the remotest chance.

Play began just before lunch, after the captains had disagreed and the umpires ruled in favour of the Aussie captain, Jack Ryder. Australia still had two wickets left but in spite of the ball being like a bar of soap only a handful of runs were added. Naturally these tail-enders did not pat down the chinks raised by each ball on the wicket.

Between innings the groundsman did not roll the pitch for the allotted seven minutes. Upon being asked why he said that the roller was beginning to lift bits off the top of the wicket. England had to bat for ten minutes before lunch, a rotten time for the openers. Hobbs and Sutcliffe hung on grimly, and scored one run in this fraught period. As the Australians trooped from the field, Hobbs and Sutcliffe remained, carefully patting down the dislodged turf, flattening the pitch as much as possible.

Trumble forecast: 'It'll be over by tea time.' After lunch the pitch began to misbehave alarmingly. By now the ground was rapidly filling. A local said: 'Look at them hurrying up to be in at the death.'

Still Hobbs and Sutcliffe were not parted, though both took many blows to the body. Blackie bowled with only three men on the off-side and most of the rest huddled around the bat. The pair had bluffed Collins, Richardson and their colleagues at The Oval in 1926 and now they did it again. Hobbs was dropped by Stork Hendry at slip. This apart, they advanced with aplomb, taking a chance on anything short, forcing the square-legs to retreat to a respectful distance so that glanced catches could not so readily be snapped up.

TOP *The final scoreboard at Melbourne after the third Test of 1928–29 showing Sutcliffe 135 in a winning total of 332 for seven.*

ABOVE *Hobbs and Sutcliffe walking out to bat. Australian opener Jack Fingleton called them 'the outstanding opening partnership in history'.*

An hour passed and no wicket had fallen. Trumble could not believe his eyes. Hobbs met the ball with the middle of the bat while Sutcliffe protected his wicket with his pads and took countless balls upon his ribs.

Hobbs waved to the pavilion for a new bat. Jardine took one out. Hobbs had a message to impart: 'I want you to bat next', he told Jardine. Hobbs wasn't captain but Chapman was too wise to ignore his senior lieutenant. If England could last the rest of the day without losing too many good wickets all was not lost. And Jardine's defensive skills and bravery were universally respected.

Eventually the first hundred was hoisted, still without a wicket being lost. Then Hobbs was out, leg before to Blackie for 49. Again the game was in the balance. Jardine pushed forward to his first two deliveries which were pitched well up. Both hit him on the solar plexus. He lashed out at Grimmett in an effort to scatter his short-legs. Jardine was surviving by the skin of his teeth. His 33, Sutcliffe later wrote, was worth 120. Through it all Sutcliffe was utterly unmoved. He simply endured. Only dynamite could have shifted him before the close of play. England lost just one wicket that day.

Next morning the wicket was dry and England, with nine wickets left, had to make another 160 runs, a task which was completed more easily than the three-wicket margin indicated, for England were, at one point, 318 for three before wickets were lost carelessly. Sutcliffe made 135 in an innings he regarded as his greatest. Perhaps still more significantly, Jardine thought his 33 to be his finest effort. Later he was to write: 'Without Hobbs and Sutcliffe, the remaining nine Englishmen could have been bowled out twice on such a wicket for half the runs.' Ryder's men were shattered and the Ashes were bound for the old country.

VICTOR TRUMPER

Australia v England, Old Trafford, 1902

SCORECARD ON PAGE 175

Victor Trumper as portrayed on a post card around the turn of the century.

Victor Trumper was a scruffy genius. He wore crumpled shirts on the field, and ill-ironed creams plucked from a cricket bag held together by a belt at each end, a bag fit to bursting with the ragtags and bobtails of a cricketer. At school he was short, spare and narrow-shouldered, not at all the sort of boy you'd pick as an athlete. Few imagined, then, that this humble, frail creature would bewitch spectators with batting of a versatility and a dash unequalled in the history of the game.

Contemporaries unanimously were in awe of him. 'No one', said Charlie Macartney, 'was as good as Vic. You only had to see his walk.' And Braund used to say that 'it didn't matter where I pitched a ball Vic could hit it to three different places'. Joe Darling, his captain in England in 1902, used to demand absolute punctuality. He'd board the charabanc at the appointed hour, call out 'is Vic here?' and if he was they'd be off, no matter who else was absent. Trumper was allowed a little leeway. After all, he defied orthodoxy on the field too.

England had toured Australia in 1901–02 and lost heavily, though Trumper's form was poor. Few expected him to redeem his reputation in England the following season. He did so, and in style.

For Trumper, the wet, miserable northern summer of 1902 was a triumph. He scored 11 hundreds and 2,570 runs all told. Colleagues say that had he been greedy he'd have made 4,000. One critic wrote that those fortunate enough 'to witness his amazing brilliance will never be able to forget the unrivalled skill and resource he displayed. On sticky wickets he hit with freedom while everyone else paddled about.' M. A. Noble, school-mate, teammate and fine cricketer, compared Trumper to a great orator. 'You follow the discourse, even anticipate correctly the words he is going to say. It all seems

so natural, yet if you try to do it yourself you fail miserably.'

Trumper's outstanding innings of the year was played in the gripping and decisive Test at Manchester. Australia were already one up, having escaped from Wilfred Rhodes' (seven for 17) clutches in Birmingham thanks to rain. They were rained off at Lord's too, and won handsomely at Leeds.

Old Trafford gave Archie MacLaren a chance to level the series. Once again the pitch was soft, too soft for fast bowlers to begin with. They could not bowl for fear of a slip and an injury. For this reason Joe Darling decided to bat upon winning the toss. Both captains knew the pitch would be spiteful after lunch when the ground had dried enough for the bowlers to bowl at their fastest. Everything depended upon the play before lunch. In the England dressing room MacLaren told his men that if they could keep Vic quiet for two hours the game was theirs. They tried hard, and failed miserably.

At the appointed hour Trumper, wan and drawn of face, delicate of health, glided to the wicket with Duff, his partner. Neither man used a rubber on his bat handle. They used to rub the string with a piece of glass and apply powdered resin. Trumper disliked leather and rubber because they interfered with the instinctive movements of the hands. To him the bat was a wand and sensitivity was everything.

Taking guard quickly, Trumper at once began to divert the ball in every conceivable direction. His driving was scintillating and his late cuts past Braund at slip defied the eye. Rhodes, Jackson, Fred Tate and Braund could not contain him.

Despite MacLaren's desperate manœuvrings, Australia reached 100 in 57 minutes, still the fastest Ashes opening stand of 100. At last Lockwood could bowl, if gingerly. In his first over Duff

THE GREAT INTERNATIONAL CRICKET MATCH
When Australia Beat England by Three Runs.

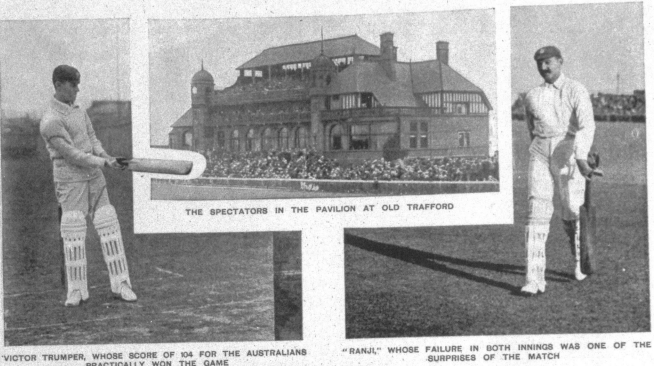

VICTOR TRUMPER, WHOSE SCORE OF 104 FOR THE AUSTRALIANS PRACTICALLY WON THE GAME

THE SPECTATORS IN THE PAVILION AT OLD TRAFFORD

"RANJI," WHOSE FAILURE IN BOTH INNINGS WAS ONE OF THE SURPRISES OF THE MATCH

A. C. MACLAREN LEADING ENGLAND INTO THE FIELD

The players directly behind him are Ranji and Palairet

H. TRUMBLE, J. DARLING, AND S. GREGORY COMING OUT TO FIELD

THE END OF AUSTRALIA'S SECOND INNINGS—A. C. MACLAREN AND H. TRUMBLE

OPPOSITE *A page from* The Tatler, *30 July 1902, on 'The Great Cricket Match'.*

✐ Oh! he's just a dashing batsman,
He's a Rajah, he's a toff,
Without any fancy feeling
For the 'on' or for the 'off.'
He just takes his bat and thin
With one apologetic cough,
Sets to work to play the devil
With the bowlin'. ✐
OLD BUSH BALLAD

A back view of Trumper jumping out to drive.

was caught behind the wicket. With Trumper he had added 135 in 78 minutes. Trumper had already scored 80. With five minutes to go to lunch Trumper was on 92. Promptly he pulled and hooked Lockwood for two more boundaries to reach his hundred out of 168, the first batsman ever to score three figures before lunch in a Test. Two other Australians, Macartney (1926) and Bradman (1930) eventually followed suit, though in friendlier circumstances. Trumper had cut and hooked at will. Once he lifted his bat fast to a yorker and jabbed down on the ball at the final moment with his bat at an angle and sped it away to the boundary. This cannot be done! And this on the first morning of a Test!

Lunch, taken at 173 for one, broke the spell. Trumper was caught behind off Rhodes immediately upon the resumption. Lockwood took six for 48, Jackson hit a vigorous hundred, Lockwood bowled Australia out a second time and England were left to score 124 to win. They reached 68 for one but, alas, they lost their nerve in a misguided attempt to beat the weather and their opponents. Poor Fred Tate was last man out, smiting fervently at Saunders, leaving Wilfred Rhodes high and dry at the bowling end. Australia had retained the Ashes.

Trumper was to play many more extraordinary innings. Some will argue that his unbeaten 185 in Sydney in 1903 after England had led by 292 on first innings was even better. Perhaps. He scored at 49 an hour while seven wickets fell for 95 at the other end, yet Australia lost by five wickets. His innings in Invercargill in 1914 was reckoned to be the best ever played in New Zealand. Yet I like this effort in Manchester, if only because of the way it utterly confounded the best-laid plans of an England captain.

Beloved by his people, gentle Victor Trumper was to die young and in great pain at his home in Chatswood of Bright's disease. He was 37 years old. His funeral was profoundly moving and highly attended, as befitted a man who had touched hearts.

THE SCORECARDS

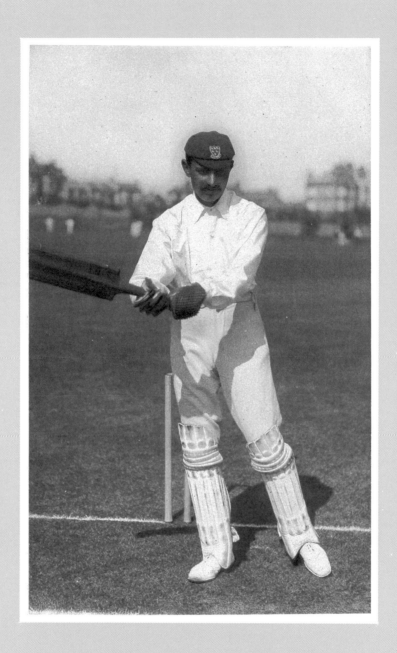

Prince Ranjitsinhji as photographed by Hawkins of Brighton. Ranji made the leg-glance famous, but the photography of the day could not capture his wristy stroke and had to settle for posed, static representations like this.

IAN BOTHAM
England v Australia, Headingley, 16, 17, 18, 20, 21 July 1981

AUSTRALIA

J. Dyson	b Dilley	102	c Taylor b Willis	34
G. M. Wood	lbw b Botham	34	c Taylor b Botham	10
T. M. Chappell	c Taylor b Willey	27	c Taylor b Willis	8
*K. J. Hughes	c and b Botham	89	c Botham b Willis	0
R. J. Bright	b Dilley	7	(8) b Willis	19
G. N. Yallop	c Taylor b Botham	58	(5) c Gatting b Willis	0
A. R. Border	lbw b Botham	8	(6) b Old	0
†R. W. Marsh	b Botham	28	(7) c Dilley b Willis	4
G. F. Lawson	c Taylor b Botham	13	c Taylor b Willis	1
D. K. Lillee	not out	3	c Gatting b Willis	17
T. M. Alderman	not out	0	not out	0
Extras	(b 4, lb 13, w 3, nb 12)	32	(lb 3, w 1, nb 14)	18
	(9 wickets declared)	**401**		**111**

ENGLAND

G. A. Gooch	lbw b Alderman	2	c Alderman b Lillee	0
G. Boycott	b Lawson	12	lbw b Alderman	46
*J. M. Brearley	c Marsh b Alderman	10	c Alderman b Lillee	14
D. I. Gower	c Marsh b Lawson	24	c Border b·Alderman	9
M. W. Gatting	lbw b Lillee	15	lbw b Alderman	1
P. Willey	b Lawson	8	c Dyson b Lillee	33
I. T. Botham	c Marsh b Lillee	50	not out	149
†R. W. Taylor	c Marsh b Lillee	5	c Bright b Alderman	1
G. R. Dilley	c and b Lillee	13	b Alderman	56
C. M. Old	c Border b Alderman	0	b Lawson	29
R. G. D. Willis	not out	1	c Border b Alderman	2
Extras	(b 6, lb 11, w 6, nb 11)	34	(b 5, lb 3, w 3, nb5)	16
		174		**356**

ENGLAND

	O	M	R	W	O	M	R	W
Willis	30	8	72	0	15.1	3	43	8
Old	43	14	91	0	9	1	21	1
Dilley	27	4	78	2	2	0	11	0
Botham	39.2	11	95	6	7	3	14	1
Willey	13	2	31	1	3	1	4	0
Boycott	3	2	2	0				

FALL OF WICKETS

First innings: 55, 149, 196, 220, 332, 354, 357, 396, 401
Second innings: 13, 56, 58, 58, 65, 68, 74, 75, 110, 111

AUSTRALIA

	O	M	R	W	O	M	R	W
Lillee	18.5	7	49	4	25	6	94	3
Alderman	19	4	59	3	35.3	6	135	6
Lawson	13	3	32	3	23	4	96	1
Bright					4	0	15	0

FALL OF WICKETS

First innings: 12, 40, 42, 54, 87, 112, 148, 166, 167, 174
Second innings: 0, 18, 37, 41, 105, 133, 135, 252, 319, 356

IAN CHAPPELL
Australia v England, The Oval, 10, 11, 12, 14, 15, 16 August 1972

ENGLAND

B. Wood	c Marsh b Watson	26	lbw b Massie	90
J. H. Edrich	lbw b Lillee	8	b Lillee	18
P. H. Parfitt	b Lillee	51	b Lillee	18
J. H. Hampshire	c Inverarity b Mallett	42	c I. M. Chappell b Watson	20
B. L. D'Oliveira	c G. S. Chappell b Mallett	4	c I. M. Chappell b Massie	43
A. W. Greig	c Stackpole b Mallett	16	c Marsh b Lillee	29
*R. Illingworth	c G. S. Chappell b Lillee	0	lbw b Lillee	31
†A. P. E. Knott	c Marsh b Lillee	92	b Lillee	63
J. A. Snow	c Marsh b Lillee	3	c Stackpole b Mallett	14
G. G. Arnold	b Inverarity	22	lbw b Mallett	4
D. L. Underwood	not out	3	not out	0
Extras	(lb 8, w 1, nb 8)	17	(b 11, lb 8, nb 7)	26
		284		**356**

AUSTRALIA

G. D. Watson	c Knott b Arnold	13	lbw b Arnold	6
K. R. Stackpole	b Snow	18	c Knott b Greig	79
*I. M. Chappell	c Snow b Arnold	118	c sub (R. G. D. Willis) b Underwood	37
G. S. Chappell	c Greig b Illingworth	113	lbw b Underwood	16
R. Edwards	b Underwood	79	lbw b Greig	1
A. P. Sheahan	c Hampshire b Underwood	5	not out	44
†R. W. Marsh	b Underwood	0	not out	43
R. J. Inverarity	c Greig b Underwood	28		
A. A. Mallett	run out	5		
R. A. L. Massie	b Arnold	4		
D. K. Lillee	not out	0		
Extras	(lb 8, w 1, nb 7)	16	(lb 6, nb 10)	16
		399		**242**

AUSTRALIA

	O	M	R	W	O	M	R	W
Lillee	24.2	7	58	5	32.2	8	123	5
Massie	27	5	69	0	32	10	77	2
Watson	12	4	23	1	19	8	32	1
Mallett	23	4	80	3	23	7	66	2
G. S. Chappell	2	0	18	0				
Inverarity	4	0	19	1	15	4	32	0

FALL OF WICKETS

First innings: 25, 50, 133, 142, 145, 145, 159, 181, 262, 284
Second innings: 56, 81, 114, 194, 205, 270, 271, 333, 356, 356

ENGLAND

	O	M	R	W	O	M	R	W
Arnold	35	11	87	3	15	5	26	1
Snow	34.5	5	111	1	6	1	21	0
Greig	18	9	25	0	25.3	10	49	2
D'Oliveira	9	4	17	0				
Underwood	38	16	90	4	35	11	94	2
Illingworth	17	4	53	1	8.5	2	26	0
Parfitt					2	0	10	0

FALL OF WICKETS

First innings: 24, 34, 235, 296, 310, 310, 383, 387, 399, 399
Second innings: 16, 132, 136, 137, 171

* Captain   † Wicket-keeper

LEARIE CONSTANTINE
West Indies v Middlesex, Lord's, 9, 11, 12 June 1928

MIDDLESEX

Batsman	1st innings		2nd innings	
N. Haig	b Small	119	b Constantine	5
H. W. Lee	c Martin b Constantine	7	b Constantine	15
J. W. Hearne	c Nunes b Roach	75	lbw Small	28
E. Hendren	not out	100	c Francis b Constantine	52
E. T. Killick	b Francis	6	c Francis b Constantine	4
G. O. Allen	run out	4	c and b Francis	7
F. T. Mann	b Francis	32	b Small	4
I. A. R. Peebles	not out	0	b Constantine	0
T. J. Durston			not out	9
W. F. Price			b Constantine	3
J. A. Powell			b Constantine	1
Extras	(b 2, lb 4, nb 3)	9	(b 3, lb 2, nb 3)	8
	(6 wickets declared)	352		136

WEST INDIANS	O	M	R	W	O	M	R	W
Francis	35.5	4	107	2	10	3	30	1
Constantine	20	1	77	1	14.3	1	57	7
Browne	11	2	21	0				
Small	29	5	72	1	11	3	36	2
Martin	13	0	30	0	3	0	5	0
Roach	7	0	36	1				

FALL OF WICKETS
First innings: 16, 169, 227, 240, 258, 307
Second innings: 26, 26, 98, 107, 116, 121, 121, 124, 134, 136

WEST INDIANS

Batsman	1st innings		2nd innings	
G. Challenor	c Hendren b Durston	23	b Haig	33
C. A. Roach	c Lee b Durston	0	run out	10
M. P. Fernandez	c Hearne b Allen	29	c Allen b Haig	54
W. H. St. Hill	c Hendren b Peebles	5	b Durston	5
E. L. Bartlett	st Price b Powell	13	lbw Hearne	26
F. R. Martin	not out	26	not out	1
L. N. Constantine	b Peebles	86	c Haig b Lee	103
J. A. Small	c Hendren b Haig	7	c and b Peebles	5
R. K. Nunes	b Durston	17		
C. R. Browne	c Allen b Durston	0	not out	4
G. N. Francis	lbw Haig	1		
Extras	(b 18, lb 3, nb 2)	23	(b 18)	18
		230	(7 wickets)	259

MIDDLESEX	O	M	R	W	O	M	R	W
Durston	21	10	16	4	15	3	32	1
Haig	24.4	7	32	2	22	5	80	2
Hearne	11	4	25	0	15	3	51	1
Peebles	18	2	51	2	11	2	45	1
Allen	8	2	43	1				
Powell	7	1	40	1				
Lee					4.4	0	27	1

FALL OF WICKETS
First innings: 2, 39, 51, 77, 79, 186, 199, 223, 223, 230
Second innings: 28, 63, 70, 106, 121, 254, 254

COLIN COWDREY
England v Australia, Melbourne, 31 December 1954, 1, 3, 4, 5 January 1955

ENGLAND

Batsman	1st innings		2nd innings	
*L. Hutton	c Hole b Miller	12	lbw b Archer	42
W. J. Edrich	c Lindwall b Miller	4	b Johnston	13
P. B. H. May	c Benaud b Lindwall	0	b Johnston	91
M. C. Cowdrey	b Johnson	102	b Benaud	7
D. C. S. Compton	c Harvey b Miller	4	c Maddocks b Archer	23
T. E. Bailey	c Maddocks b Johnston	30	not out	24
†T. G. Evans	lbw b Archer	20	c Maddocks b Miller	22
J. H. Wardle	b Archer	0	b Johnson	38
F. H. Tyson	b Archer	6	c Harvey b Johnston	6
J. B. Statham	b Archer	3	c Favell b Johnston	0
R. Appleyard	not out	1	b Johnston	6
Extras	(b 9)	9	(b 2, lb 4, w 1)	7
		191		279

AUSTRALIA	O	M	R	W	O	M	R	W
Lindwall	13	0	59	1	18	3	52	0
Miller	11	8	14	3	18	6	35	1
Archer	13.6	4	33	4	24	7	50	2
Benaud	7	0	30	0	8	2	25	1
Johnston	12	6	26	1	24.5	2	85	5
Johnson	11	3	20	1	8	2	25	1

FALL OF WICKETS
First innings: 14, 21, 29, 41, 115, 169, 181, 181, 190, 191
Second innings: 40, 96, 128, 173, 185, 211, 257, 273, 273, 279

AUSTRALIA

Batsman	1st innings		2nd innings	
L. E. Favell	lbw b Statham	25	b Appleyard	30
A. R. Morris	lbw b Tyson	3	c Cowdrey b Tyson	4
K. R. Miller	c Evans b Statham	7	(5) c Edrich b Tyson	6
R. N. Harvey	b Appleyard	31	c Evans b Tyson	11
G. B. Hole	b Tyson	11	(6) c Evans b Statham	5
R. Benaud	c sub (J. V. Wilson) b Appleyard	15	(3) b Tyson	22
R. G. Archer	b Wardle	23	b Statham	15
†L. V. Maddocks	c Evans b Statham	47	b Tyson	0
R. R. Lindwall	b Statham	13	lbw b Tyson	0
*I. W. Johnson	not out	33	not out	4
W. A. Johnston	b Statham	11	c Evans b Tyson	0
Extras	(b 7, lb 3, nb 2)	12	(b 1, lb 13)	14
		231		111

ENGLAND	O	M	R	W	O	M	R	W
Tyson	21	2	68	2	12.3	1	27	7
Statham	16.3	0	60	5	11	1	38	2
Bailey	9	1	33	0	3	0	14	0
Appleyard	11	3	38	2	4	1	17	1
Wardle	6	0	20	1	1	0	1	0

FALL OF WICKETS
First innings: 15, 38, 43, 65, 92, 115, 134, 151, 205, 231
Second innings: 23, 57, 77, 86, 87, 97, 98, 98, 110, 111

---

* Captain † Wicket-keeper

SUNIL GAVASKAR
India v England, Old Trafford, 6, 7, 8, 10, 11 June 1974

ENGLAND

G. Boycott	lbw b Abid Ali	10		c Engineer b Solkar	6
D. L. Amiss	c Madan Lal b Chandrasekhar	56		c Gavaskar b Bedi	47
J. H. Edrich	b Abid Ali	7	(4)	not out	100
*M. H. Denness	b Bedi	26	(5)	not out	45
K. W. R. Fletcher	not out	123			
D. L. Underwood	c Solkar b Bedi	7	(3)	c Engineer b Abid Ali	9
A. W. Greig	c Engineer b Madan Lal	53			
†A. P. E. Knott	lbw b Madan Lal	0			
C. M. Old	c Engineer b Chandrasekhar	12			
R. G. D. Willis	lbw b Abid Ali	24			
M. Hendrick					
Extras	(b 1, lb 7, w 1, nb 1)	10		(b 4, lb 2)	6
	(9 wickets declared)	**328**		(3 wickets declared)	**213**

INDIA

S. M. Gavaskar	run out	101		c Hendrick b Old	58
E. D. Solkar	c Willis b Hendrick	7		c Hendrick b Underwood	19
S. Venkataraghavan	b Willis	3	(9)	not out	5
*A. L. Wadekar	c Hendrick b Old	6	(3)	c Knott b Greig	14
G. R. Viswanath	b Underwood	40	(4)	c Knott b Old	50
B. P. Patel	c Knott b Willis	5	(5)	c Knott b Old	3
†F. M. Engineer	b Willis	0	(6)	c Knott b Hendrick	12
Madan Lal	b Hendrick	2	(7)	hit wkt b Willis	7
S. Abid Ali	c Knott b Hendrick	71	(8)	c Boycott b Greig	4
B. S. Bedi	b Willis	0		b Old	0
B. S. Chandrasekhar	not out	0		st Knott b Greig	0
Extras	(b 3, lb 3, nb 5)	11		(b 1, lb 2, nb 7)	10
		264			**182**

INDIA	O	M	R	W	O	M	R	W
Abid Ali	30.3	6	79	3	11	2	31	1
Solkar	13	4	33	0	7	0	24	1
Madan Lal	31	11	56	2	12	2	39	0
Venkataraghavan	5	1	8	0	9	1	17	0
Bedi	43	14	87	2	20	2	58	1
Chandrasekhar	21	4	55	2	11	2	38	0

FALL OF WICKETS

First innings: 18, 28, 90, 104, 127, 231, 231, 265, 328
Second innings: 13, 30, 104

ENGLAND	O	M	R	W	O	M	R	W
Willis	24	3	64	4	12	5	33	1
Old	16	0	46	1	16	7	20	4
Hendrick	20	4	57	3	17	1	39	1
Underwood	19	7	50	1	15	4	45	1
Greig	5	1	18	0	25.1	8	35	3

FALL OF WICKETS

First innings: 22, 25, 32, 105, 129, 135, 143, 228, 228, 246
Second innings: 32, 68, 103, 111, 139, 157, 165, 180, 180, 182

DAVID GOWER
England v Pakistan, Faisalabad, 12, 13, 14 16, 17 March 1984

PAKISTAN

Mohsin Khan	c Lamb b Dilley	20		b Dilley	2
Mudassar Nazar	c Gatting b Cook	12		lbw b Foster	4
Qasim Omar	c Gatting b Foster	16		c Taylor b Dilley	17
Salim Malik	c Lamb b Cook	116		c sub b Marks	76
*Zaheer Abbas	lbw b Gatting	68		not out	32
Wasim Raja	b Marks	112		not out	5
Abdul Qadir	c Foster b Dilley	50			
†Anil Dalpat	lbw b Dilley	8			
Sarfraz Nawaz	not out	16			
Tausif Ahmed	not out	1			
Azeem Hafeez					
Extras	(lb 11, w 2, nb 17)	30		(lb 1)	1
	(8 wickets declared)	**449**		(4 wickets)	**137**

ENGLAND

C. L. Smith	b Sarfraz	66
M. W. Gatting	c Salim b Tausif	75
D. W. Randall	b Sarfraz	65
A. J. Lamb	c Anil b Azeem	19
*D. I. Gower	st Anil b Mudassar	152
G. Fowler	c Omar b Wasim	57
†R. W. Taylor	c Salim b Qadir	0
V. J. Marks	b Sarfraz	83
G. R. Dilley	not out	2
N. G. B. Cook	not out	1
N. A. Foster	did not bat	
Extras	(b 10, lb 4, nb 12)	26
	(8 wickets declared)	**546**

ENGLAND	O	M	R	W	O	M	R	W
Foster	30	7	109	1	5	1	10	1
Dilley	28	6	101	3	9	0	41	2
Cook	54	14	133	2	16	6	38	0
Marks	27	9	59	1	8	2	26	1
Gatting	3	0	17	1	2	0	18	0
Fowler					1	0	3	0

FALL OF WICKETS

First innings: 35, 53, 70, 200, 323, 416, 430, 433
Second innings: 6, 6, 56, 123

PAKISTAN	O	M	R	W
Azeem	19	3	71	1
Sarfraz	50	11	129	3
Wasim	26	6	61	1
Qadir	51	14	124	1
Tausif	30	8	96	1
Mudassar	13	1	39	1

FALL OF WICKETS

First innings: 127, 163, 214, 245, 361, 361, 528, 545

GORDON GREENIDGE
West Indies v England, Lord's, 28, 29, 30 June, 2, 3 July 1984

ENGLAND

G. Fowler	c Harper b Baptiste	106	lbw b Small	11
B. C. Broad	c Dujon b Marshall	55	c Harper b Garner	0
*D. I. Gower	lbw b Marshall	3	c Lloyd b Small	21
A. J. Lamb	lbw b Marshall	23	c Dujon b Marshall	110
M. W. Gatting	lbw b Marshall	1	lbw b Marshall	29
I. T. Botham	c Richards b Baptiste	30	lbw b Garner	81
§P. R. Downton	not out	23	lbw b Small	4
G. Miller	run out	0	b Harper	9
D. R. Pringle	lbw b Garner	2	lbw b Garner	8
N. A. Foster	c Harper b Marshall	6	not out	9
R. G. D. Willis	b Marshall	2		
Extras	(b 4, lb 14, w 2, nb 15)	35	(b 4, lb 7, w 1, nb 6)	18
		286	(9 wkts dec)	**300**

WEST INDIES

C. G. Greenidge	c Miller b Botham	1	not out	214
D. L. Haynes	lbw b Botham	12	run out	17
H. A. Gomes	c Gatting b Botham	10	not out	92
I. V. A. Richards	lbw b Botham	72		
*C. H. Lloyd	lbw b Botham	39		
§P. J. Dujon	c Fowler b Botham	8		
M. D. Marshall	c Pringle b Willis	29		
E. A. E. Baptiste	c Downton b Willis	44		
R. A. Harper	c Gatting b Botham	8		
J. Garner	c Downton b Botham	6		
M. A. Small	not out	3		
Extras	(lb 5, w 1, nb 7)	13	(b 4, lb 4, nb 13)	21
		245	(1 wkt)	**344**

WEST INDIES	O	M	R	W	O	M	R	W
Garner	32	10	67	1	30.4	3	91	3
Small	9	0	38	0	12	2	40	3
Marshall	36.5	10	85	6	22	6	85	2
Baptiste	20	6	36	2	26	8	48	0
Harper	8	0	25	0	8	1	18	1

FALL OF WICKETS

First innings: 101, 106, 183, 185, 243, 248, 251, 255, 264, 286

Second innings: 5, 33, 36, 88, 216, 230, 273, 290, 300

ENGLAND	O	M	R	W	O	M	R	W
Willis	19	5	48	2	15	5	48	0
Botham	27.4	6	103	8	20.1	2	117	0
Pringle	11	0	54	0	8	0	44	0
Foster	6	2	13	0	12	0	69	0
Miller	2	0	14	0	11	0	45	0

FALL OF WICKETS

First innings: 1, 18, 35, 138, 147, 173, 213, 231, 241, 245

Second innings: 57

TONY GREIG
England v India, Calcutta, 1, 2, 3, 5, 6 January 1977

INDIA

S. M. Gavaskar	c Old b Willis	0	b Underwood	18
A. D. Gaekwad	b Lever	32	c Tolchard b Greig	8
P. Sharma	c Greig b Lever	9	c Knott b Willis	20
G. R. Viswanath	c Tolchard b Underwood	35	c Lever b Greig	3
B. P. Patel	hit wkt b Willis	21	lbw b Old	56
E. D. Solkar	c Greig b Willis	2	c Knott b Willis	3
Madan Lal	c Knott b Old	17	c Brearley b Old	16
†S. M. H. Kirmani	not out	25	b Old	0
E. A. S. Prasanna	b Willis	2	c Brearley b Underwood	13
*B. S. Bedi	c Lever b Old	1	b Underwood	18
B. S. Chandrasekhar	b Willis	1	not out	4
Extras	(lb 2, nb 8)	10	(b 2, lb 4, nb 16)	22
		155		**181**

ENGLAND

D. L. Amiss	c Kirmani b Prasanna	35	not out	7
G. D. Barlow	c Kirmani b Madan Lal	4	not out	7
J. M. Brearley	c Solkar b Bedi	5		
D. W. Randall	lbw b Prasanna	37		
R. W. Tolchard	b Bedi	67		
*A. W. Greig	lbw b Prasanna	103		
†A. P. E. Knott	c Gavaskar b Bedi	2		
C. M. Old	c Madan Lal b Prasanna	52		
J. K. Lever	c Gavaskar b Bedi	2		
D. L. Underwood	c Gavaskar b Bedi	4		
R. G. D. Willis	not out	0		
Extras	(b 5, lb 5)	10	(lb 1, nb 1)	2
		321	(0 wickets)	**16**

ENGLAND	O	M	R	W	O	M	R	W
Willis	20	3	27	5	13	1	32	2
Lever	22	2	57	2	3	0	12	0
Underwood	13	5	24	1	32.5	18	50	3
Old	20	5	37	2	12	4	38	3
Greig					10	0	27	2

FALL OF WICKETS

First innings: 1, 23, 65, 92, 99, 106, 136, 147, 149, 155

Second innings: 31, 33, 36, 60, 70, 97, 97, 146, 171, 181

INDIA	O	M	R	W	O	M	R	W
Madan Lal	17	4	25	1	1	0	3	0
Solkar	6	1	15	0				
Bedi	64	25	110	5	1.4	0	6	0
Chandrasekhar	33	9	66	0				
Prasanna	57.4	16	93	4	1	0	5	0
Sharma	1	0	2	0				

FALL OF WICKETS

First innings: 7, 14, 81, 90, 232, 234, 298, 307, 321, 321

---

* Captain   † Wicket-keeper

Neil Harvey
Australia v South Africa, Durban, 20, 21, 23, 24 January 1950

SOUTH AFRICA

E. A. B. Rowan	c Johnston b Miller	143	c Saggers b Lindwall	4
O. E. Wynne	b Johnston	18	b Johnson	29
J. D. Nel	c and b Johnson	14	lbw b Johnston	20
*A. D. Nourse	c Saggers b Johnston	66	c McCool b Johnson	27
†W. W. Wade	b Lindwall	24	b Johnston	0
N. B. F. Mann	b Johnston	9	(9) lbw b Johnson	0
J. E. Cheetham	c Hassett b Johnston	4	(6) c Hassett b Johnson	1
J. C. Watkins	b Lindwall	5	(7) st Saggers b Johnson	2
H. J. Tayfield	run out	15	(8) b Johnston	3
V. I. Smith	b Lindwall	1	b Johnston	4
C. N. McCarthy	not out	0	not out	2
Extras	(b 3, lb 7, nb 2)	12	(b 5, lb 1, nb 1)	7
		311		**99**

AUSTRALIA

A. R. Morris	c Smith b Tayfield	25	hit wkt b Tayfield	44
J. Moroney	b Tayfield	10	lbw b Tayfield	10
I. W. Johnson	lbw b Tayfield	2		
K. R. Miller	b Tayfield	2	(3) lbw b Mann	10
*A. L. Hassett	lbw b Tayfield	2	(4) lbw b Mann	11
†R. A. Saggers	c Cheetham b Mann	2		
C. L. McCool	lbw b Mann	1	not out	39
R. R. Lindwall	b Mann	7		
R. N. Harvey	c and b Tayfield	2	(5) not out	151
S. J. E. Loxton	c Cheetham b Tayfield	16	(6) b Mann	54
W. A. Johnston	not out	2		
Extras	(b 3, lb 1)	4	(b 7, lb 9, nb 1)	17
		75	(5 wickets)	**336**

AUSTRALIA

	O	M	R	W	O	M	R	W
Lindwall	19	3	47	3	4	1	7	1
Miller	24	5	73	1	7	0	12	0
McCool	13	3	35	0				
Johnston	31.2	5	75	4	18.2	6	39	4
Loxton	6	1	31	0				
Johnson	16	5	38	1	17	2	34	5

FALL OF WICKETS
First innings: 32, 75, 242, 264, 283, 289, 293, 304, 308, 311
Second innings: 9, 51, 85, 85, 88, 90, 93, 93, 93, 99

SOUTH AFRICA

	O	M	R	W	O	M	R	W
McCarthy	6	2	8	0	12	3	32	0
Watkins	4	1	9	0	6	2	10	0
Mann	10	1	31	3	51.6	13	101	3
Tayfield	8.4	1	23	7	49	5	144	2
Smith					5	0	32	0

FALL OF WICKETS
First innings: 31, 35, 37, 39, 42, 45, 46, 53, 63, 75
Second innings: 14, 33, 59, 95, 230

Graeme Hick
Worcestershire v Somerset, Worcester, 24, 25, 26, 27 August 1989

SOMERSET

S. J. Cook	lbw b Lampitt	10	b Lampitt	3
P. M. Roebuck	c Illingworth b Lampitt	22		
R. J. Harden	lbw b McEwan	27	(4) b McEwan	0
C. J. Tavare	c D'Oliveira b McEwan	89	(5) b McEwan	62
N. J. Pringle	c Rhodes b Weston	4	(2) lbw b Lampitt	0
J. C. M. Atkinson	c and b Hick	46	c Rhodes b McEwan	6
†N. D. Burns	c Illingworth b Lampitt	5	(3) c Rhodes b Tolley	38
*V. J. Marks	c Rhodes b McEwan	45	(7) not out	24
G. D. Rose	not out	50	(8) not out	19
N. A. Mallender	b McEwan	20		
A. N. Jones	b Lampitt	13		
Extras	(lb 4, nb 3)	7	(lb 7, w 1, nb 1)	9
		338	(6 wkts dec)	**161**

WORCESTERSHIRE

T. S. Curtis	b Mallender	1	b Rose	84
P. Bent	lbw b Mallender	0	run out	25
G. A. Hick	c Rose b Jones	86	not out	136
D. B. D'Oliveira	c Burns b Jones	63	c Pringle b Rose	0
*P. A. Neale	c Burns b Jones	4	c Pringle b Marks	25
M. J. Weston	not out	11	c Burns b Jones	8
†S. J. Rhodes	not out	7	not out	13
S. R. Lampitt				
C. M. Tolley				
R. K. Illingworth				
S. M. McEwan				
Extras	(b 11, lb 8, w 2, nb 7)	28	(lb 10, w 1)	11
	(5 wkts dec)	**200**	(5 wkts)	**302**

WORCESTERSHIRE

	O	M	R	W	O	M	R	W
McEwan	38	4	111	4	16	5	46	3
Lampitt	36.5	8	89	4	16	3	48	2
Tolley	27	8	59	0	6	0	21	1
Illingworth	20	11	22	0				
Weston	11	4	32	1	5	0	26	0
Hick	13	5	21	1				
Neale					1	0	8	0

FALL OF WICKETS
First innings: 13, 42, 73, 78, 162, 173, 249, 254, 309, 338
Second innings: 3, 8, 11, 84, 116, 117

SOMERSET

	O	M	R	W	O	M	R	W
Jones	15	1	55	3	14.1	1	77	1
Mallender	15	4	18	2	9	1	47	0
Rose	15	2	51	0	15	1	69	2
Atkinson	2	0	3	0				
Marks	11.2	2	42	0	18	1	99	1
Pringle	3	0	12	0				

FALL OF WICKETS
First innings: 6, 16, 169, 170, 176
Second innings: 51, 179, 179, 254, 287

* Captain   † Wicket-keeper

Archie Jackson
Australia v England, Adelaide, 1, 2, 4, 5, 6, 7, 8 February 1929

ENGLAND

J. B. Hobbs	c Ryder b Hendry	74	c Oldfield b Hendry		1
H. Sutcliffe	st Oldfield b Grimmett	64	c Oldfield b A'Beckett		17
W. R. Hammond	not out	119	c and b Ryder		177
D. R. Jardine	lbw b Grimmett	1	c Woodfull b Oxenham		98
E. H. Hendren	b Blackie	13	c Bradman b Blackie		11
*A. P. F. Chapman	c A'Beckett b Ryder	39	c Woodfull b Blackie		0
†G. Duckworth	c Ryder b Grimmett	5	(11) lbw b Oxenham		1
H. Larwood	b Hendry	3	(7) lbw b Oxenham		5
G. Geary	run out	3	(8) c and b Grimmett		6
M. W. Tate	b Grimmett	2	(9) lbw b Oxenham		47
J. C. White	c Ryder b Grimmett	0	(10) not out		4
Extras	(b 3, lb 7, w 1)	11	(b 6, lb 10)		16
		334			**383**

AUSTRALIA

W. M. Woodfull	c Duckworth b Tate	1	c Geary b White		30
A. A. Jackson	lbw b White	164	c Duckworth b Geary		36
H. S. T. L. Hendry	c Duckworth b Larwood	2	c Tate b White		5
A. F. Kippax	b White	3	c Hendren b White		51
*J. Ryder	lbw b White	63	c and b White		87
D. G. Bradman	c Larwood b Tate	40	run out		58
E. L. a'Beckett	hit wkt b White	36	c Hammond b White		21
R. K. Oxenham	c Chapman b White	15	c Chapman b White		12
†W. A. S. Oldfield	b Tate	32	not out		15
C. V. Grimmett	b Tate	4	c Tate b White		9
D. D. Blackie	not out	3	c Larwood b White		0
Extras	(lb 5, w 1)	6	(b 9, lb 3)		12
		369			**336**

AUSTRALIA	O	M	R	W	O	M	R	W
A'Beckett	31	8	44	0	27	9	41	1
Hendry	31	14	49	2	28	11	56	1
Grimmett	52.1	12	102	5	52	15	117	1
Oxenham	35	14	51	0	47.4	21	67	4
Blackie	29	6	57	1	39	11	70	2
Ryder	5	1	20	1	5	1	13	1
Kippax					2	0	3	0

FALL OF WICKETS

First innings: 143, 143, 149, 179, 246, 263 270, 308, 312, 334

Second innings: 1, 21, 283, 296, 297, 302, 327, 337, 381, 383

ENGLAND	O	M	R	W	O	M	R	W
Larwood	37	6	92	1	20	4	60	0
Tate	42	10	77	4	37	9	75	0
White	60	16	130	5	64.5	21	126	8
Geary	12	3	32	0	16	2	42	1
Hammond	9	1	32	0	14	3	21	0

FALL OF WICKETS

First innings: 1, 6, 19, 145, 227, 287, 323, 336, 365, 369

Second innings: 65, 71, 74, 211, 224, 258, 308, 320, 336, 336

Kapil Dev
India v Zimbabwe, Tunbridge Wells, 18 June 1983

INDIA

S. M. Gavaskar	lbw b Rawson	0
K. Srikkanth	c Butchart b Curran	0
M. Amarnath	c Houghton b Rawson	5
S. M. Patil	c Houghton b Curran	1
Yashpal Sharma	c Houghton b Rawson	9
*Kapil Dev	not out	175
R. M. H. Binny	lbw b Traicos	22
R. J. Shastri	c Pycroft b Fletcher	1
Madan Lal	c Houghton b Curran	17
†S. M. H. Kirmani	not out	24
B. S. Sandhu		
Extras	(lb 9, w 3)	12
	(60 overs – 8 wickets)	**266**

ZIMBABWE	O	M	R	W
Rawson	12	4	47	3
Curran	12	1	65	3
Butchart	12	2	38	0
Fletcher	12	2	59	1
Traicos	12	0	45	1

FALL OF WICKETS

0, 6, 6, 9, 17, 77, 78, 140

ZIMBABWE

R. D. Brown	run out	35
G. A. Patterson	lbw b Binny	23
J. G. Heron	run out	3
A. J. Pycroft	c Kirmani b Sandhu	6
†D. L. Houghton	lbw b Madan Lal	17
*D. A. G. Fletcher	c Kapil Dev b Amarnath	13
K. M. Curran	c Shastri b Madan Lal	73
I. P. Butchart	b Binny	18
G. E. Peckover	c Yashpal b Madan Lal	14
P. W. E. Rawson	not out	2
A. J. Traicos	c and b Kapil Dev	3
Extras	(lb 17, w 7, nb 4)	28
	(57 overs)	**235**

INDIA	O	M	R	W
Kapil Dev	11	1	32	1
Sandhu	11	2	44	1
Binny	11	2	45	2
Madan Lal	11	2	42	3
Amarnath	12	1	37	1
Shastri	1	0	7	0

FALL OF WICKETS

44, 48, 61, 86, 103, 113, 168, 189, 230, 235

---

* Captain   † Wicket-keeper

CLIVE LLOYD
West Indies v Australia, World Cup Final, Lord's, 21 June 1975

WEST INDIES

R. C. Fredericks	hit wicket b Lillee	7
C. G. Greenidge	c Marsh b Thomson	13
A. I. Kallicharran	c Marsh b Gilmour	12
R. B. Kanhai	b Gilmour	55
*C. H. Lloyd	c Marsh b Gilmour	102
I. V. A. Richards	b Gilmour	5
K. D. Boyce	c G. S. Chappell b Thomson	34
B. D. Julien	not out	26
†D. L. Murray	c and b Gilmour	14
V. A. Holder	not out	6
A. M. E. Roberts		
Extras	(lb 6, nb 11)	17
	(60 overs – 8 wickets)	**291**

AUSTRALIA

	O	M	R	W
Lillee	12	1	55	1
Gilmour	12	2	48	5
Thomson	12	1	44	2
Walker	12	1	71	0
G. S. Chappell	7	0	33	0
Walters	5	0	23	0

FALL OF WICKETS

12, 27, 50, 199, 206, 209, 261, 285

AUSTRALIA

R. B. McCosker	c Kallicharran b Boyce	7
A. Turner	run out	40
*I. M. Chappell	run out	62
G. S. Chappell	run out	15
K. D. Walters	b Lloyd	35
†R. W. Marsh	b Boyce	11
R. Edwards	c Fredericks b Boyce	28
G. J. Gilmour	c Kanhai b Boyce	14
M. H. N. Walker	run out	7
J. R. Thomson	run out	21
D. K. Lillee	not out	16
Extras	(b 2, lb 9, nb 7)	18
	(58.4 overs)	**274**

WEST INDIES

	O	M	R	W
Julien	12	0	58	0
Roberts	11	1	45	0
Boyce	12	0	50	4
Holder	11.4	1	65	0
Lloyd	12	1	38	1

FALL OF WICKETS

25, 81, 115, 162, 170, 195, 221, 231, 233, 274

COLIN MILBURN
Western Australia v Queensland, Brisbane, 22, 23, 24, 25 November 1968

WESTERN AUSTRALIA

C. Milburn	c and b Morgan	243
D. Chadwick	st Maclean b Paulsen	91
R. J. Inverarity	c Morgan b Dudgeon	108
†G. C. Becker	c Surti b Dudgeon	112
J. T. Irvine	not out	26
R. W. Marsh	c Surti b Paulsen	19
R. Edwards	not out	3
G. D. McKenzie		
G. A. R. Lock		
L. C. Mayne		
J. D. Gannon		
Extras	(lb 8, w 1, nb 4)	13
	(5 wkts, dec)	**615**

QUEENSLAND

	O	M	R	W
Allan	21	1	86	0
Duncan	21	1	129	0
Morgan	25	3	107	1
Surti	21	4	124	0
Paulsen	15	0	114	2
Dudgeon	12	2	42	2

FALL OF WICKETS

First innings: 328, 376, 563, 580, 612

QUEENSLAND

J. F. C. Loxton	hit wkt b Gannon	40	st Becker b Lock	20
G. T. Gray	c Chadwick b Lock	43	b Lock	15
M. J. Lucas	c Mayne b Gannon	9	b Mayne	1
R. F. Surti	c Milburn b Mayne	77	run out	49
K. D. Dudgeon	b McKenzie	44	c Chadwick b Lock	3
R. E. Parker	c Gannon b Lock	5	c Irvine b Lock	87
†J. A. Maclean	c Inverarity b Mayne	4	lbw b Lock	27
O. J. Morgan	c Becker b Mayne	16	c Becker b Mayne	21
R. G. Paulsen	not out	18	c McKenzie b Lock	9
*P. J. Allan	c Gannon b Lock	5	b Lock	12
J. R. F. Duncan	c Milburn b Lock	0	not out	7
Extras	(b 10, lb 7, nb 4)	21	(b 3, nb 4)	7
		282		**258**

WESTERN AUSTRALIA

	O	M	R	W	O	M	R	W
McKenzie	18	7	41	1	13	1	49	0
Mayne	23	2	114	3	11	0	66	2
Lock	27.7	6	70	4	21.7	6	61	7
Gannon	8	1	25	2	2	1	2	0
Milburn	1	0	11	0	7	2	33	0
Inverarity					7	0	40	0

FALL OF WICKETS

First innings: 50, 64, 184, 190, 199, 215, 241, 265, 281, 282

Second innings: 1, 70, 73, 80, 97, 124, 130, 223, 245, 258

GRAEME POLLOCK
South Africa v Australia, Durban, 5, 6, 7, 9 February 1970

SOUTH AFRICA

B. A. Richards	b Freeman	140
J. L. Goddard	c Lawry b Gleeson	17
*A. Bacher	b Connolly	9
R. G. Pollock	c and b Stackpole	274
E. J. Barlow	lbw b Freeman	1
B. L. Irvine	b Gleeson	13
H. R. Lance	st Taber b Gleeson	61
M. J. Procter	c Connolly b Stackpole	32
†D. Gamsy	lbw b Connolly	7
P. M. Pollock	not out	36
A. J. Traicos	not out	5
Extras	(b 1, lb 3, nb 23)	27
	(9 wickets declared)	**622**

AUSTRALIA

K. R. Stackpole	c Gamsy b Goddard	27	lbw b Traicos	71
*W. M. Lawry	lbw b Barlow	15	c Gamsy b Goddard	14
I. M. Chappell	c Gamsy b Barlow	0	c Gamsy b P. M. Pollock	14
K. D. Walters	c Traicos b Barlow	4	c R. G. Pollock b Traicos	74
I. R. Redpath	c Richards b Procter	4	not out	74
A. F. Sheahan	c Traicos b Goddard	62	c Barlow b Procter	4
E. W. Freeman	c Traicos b P. M. Pollock	5	b Barlow	18
†H. B. Taber	c and b P. M. Pollock	6	c Lance b Barlow	0
G. D. McKenzie	c Traicos b Procter	1	lbw b Barlow	4
J. W. Gleeson	not out	4	c Gamsy b Procter	24
H. N. Connolly	c Bacher b Traicos	14	lbw b Procter	0
Extras	(lb 5, nb 10)	15	(b 9, lb 8, nb 22)	39
		157		**336**

AUSTRALIA

	O	M	R	W
McKenzie	25.5	3	92	0
Connolly	33	7	104	2
Freeman	28	4	120	2
Gleeson	51	9	160	3
Walters	9	0	44	0
Stackpole	21	2	75	2

FALL OF WICKETS

First innings: 88, 126, 229, 231, 281, 481, 558, 575, 580

SOUTH AFRICA

	O	M	R	W	O	M	R	W
Procter	11	2	39	2	18.5	5	62	3
P. M. Pollock	10	3	31	2	21.3	4	45	1
Goddard	7	4	10	2	17	7	30	1
Barlow	10	3	24	3	31	10	63	3
Traicos	8.2	3	27	1	30	8	70	2
Lance	2	0	11	0	7	4	11	0
Richards					3	1	8	0
G. M. Pollock					3	1	8	0

FALL OF WICKETS

First innings: 44, 44, 44, 48, 56, 79, 100, 114, 139, 157
Second innings: 65, 83, 151, 208, 222, 264, 264, 268, 336, 336

DEREK RANDALL
England v Australia, Melbourne, 12, 13, 14, 16, 17 March 1977

AUSTRALIA

I. C. Davis	lbw b Lever	5		c Knott b Greig	68
R. B. McCosker	b Willis	4	(10)	c Greig b Old	25
G. J. Cosier	c Fletcher b Lever	10	(4)	c Knott b Lever	4
*G. S. Chappell	b Underwood	40	(3)	b Old	2
D. W. Hookes	c Greig b Old	17	(6)	c Fletcher b Underwood	56
K. D. Walters	c Greig b Willis	4	(5)	c Knott b Greig	66
†R. W. Marsh	c Knott b Old	28		not out	110
G. J. Gilmour	c Greig B Old	4		b Lever	16
K. J. O'Keeffe	c Brearley b Underwood	0	(2)	c Willis b Old	14
D. K. Lillee	not out	10	(9)	c Amiss b Old	25
M. H. N. Walker	b Underwood	2		not out	8
Extras	(b 4, lb 2, nb 8)	14		(lb 10, nb 15)	25
		138		(9 wickets declared)	**419**

ENGLAND

R. A. Woolmer	c Chappell b Lillee	9		lbw b Walker	12
J. M. Brearley	c Hookes b Lillee	12		lbw b Lillee	43
D. L. Underwood	c Chappell b Walker	7	(10)	b Lillee	7
D. W. Randall	c Marsh b Lillee	4	(3)	c Cosier b O'Keeffe	174
D. L. Amiss	c O'Keeffe b Walker	4	(4)	b Chappell	64
K. W. R. Fletcher	c Marsh b Walker	4	(5)	c Marsh b Lillee	1
*A. W. Greig	b Walker	18	(6)	c Cosier b O'Keeffe	41
†A. P. E. Knott	lbw b Lillee	15	(7)	lbw b Lillee	42
C. M. Old	c Marsh b Lillee	3	(8)	c Chappell b Lillee	2
J. K. Lever	c Marsh b Lillee	11	(9)	lbw b O'Keeffe	4
R. G. D. Willis	not out	1		not out	5
Extras	(b 2, lb 2, w 1, nb 2)	7		(b 8, lb 4, w 3, nb 7)	22
		95			**417**

ENGLAND

	O	M	R	W	O	M	R	W
Lever	12	1	36	2	21	1	95	2
Willis	8	0	33	2	22	0	91	0
Old	12	4	39	3	27.6	2	104	4
Underwood	11.6	2	16	3	12	2	38	1
Greig					14	3	66	2

FALL OF WICKETS

First innings: 11, 13, 23, 45, 51, 102, 114, 117, 136, 138
Second innings: 33, 40, 53, 132, 187, 244, 277, 353, 407

AUSTRALIA

	O	M	R	W	O	M	R	W
Lillee	13.3	2	26	6	34.4	7	139	5
Walker	15	3	54	4	22	4	83	1
O'Keeffe	1	0	4	0	33	6	108	3
Gilmour	5	3	4	0	4	0	29	0
Chappell					16	7	29	1
Walters					3	2	7	0

FALL OF WICKETS

First innings: 19, 30, 34, 40, 40, 61, 65, 78, 86, 95
Second innings: 28, 113, 279, 290, 346, 369, 380, 385, 410, 417

---

* Captain   † Wicket-keeper

K. S. Ranjitsinhji
England v Australia, Old Trafford, 16, 17, 18 July 1896

AUSTRALIA

F. A. Iredale	b Briggs	108	b Richardson		11
J. Darling	c Lilley b Richardson	27	c Lilley b Richardson		16
G. Giffen	c and b Richardson	80	c Ranjitsinhji b Richardson		6
*G. H. S. Trott	c Brown b Lilley	53	c Lilley b Richardson		2
S. E. Gregory	c Stoddart b Briggs	25	c Ranjitsinhji b Briggs		33
H. Donnan	b Richardson	12	c Jackson b Richardson		15
C. Hill	c Jackson b Richardson	9	c Lilley b Richardson		14
H. Trumble	b Richardson	24	not out		17
†J. J. Kelly	c Lilley b Richardson	27	not out		8
T. R. McKibbin	not out	28			
E. Jones	b Richardson	4			
Extras	(b 6, lb 8, w 1)	15	(lb 3)		3
		412	(7 wickets)		**125**

ENGLAND

A. E. Stoddart	st Kelly b Trott	15	b McKibbin		41
*W. G. Grace	st Kelly b Trott	2	c Trott b Jones		11
K. S. Ranjitsinhji	c Trott b McKibbin	62	not out		154
R. Abel	c Trumble b McKibbin	26	c McKibbin b Giffen		13
F. S. Jackson	run out	18	c McKibbin b Giffen		1
J. T. Brown	c Kelly b Trumble	22	c Iredale b Jones		19
A. C. MacLaren	c Trumble b McKibbin	0	c Jones b Trumble		15
†A. F. A. Lilley	not out	65	c Trott b Giffen		19
J. Briggs	b Trumble	0	st Kelly b McKibbin		16
J. T. Hearne	c Trumble b Giffen	18	c Kelly b McKibbin		9
T. Richardson	run out	2	c Jones b Trumble		1
Extras	(b 1)	1	(b 2, lb 3, w 1)		6
		231			**305**

ENGLAND	O	M	R	W	O	M	R	W
Richardson	68	23	168	7	42.3	16	76	6
Briggs	40	18	99	2	18	8	24	1
Jackson	16	6	34	0				
Hearne	28	11	53	0	24	13	22	0
Grace	7	3	11	0				
Stoddart	6	2	9	0				
Lilley	5	1	23	1				

FALL OF WICKETS

First innings: 41, 172, 242, 294, 294, 314, 325, 362, 403, 412
Second innings: 20, 26, 28, 45, 79, 95, 100

AUSTRALIA	O	M	R	W	O	M	R	W
Jones	5	2	11	0	17	0	78	2
Trott	10	0	46	2	7	1	17	0
Giffen	19	3	48	1	16	1	65	3
Trumble	37	14	80	2	29.1	12	78	2
McKibbin	19	8	45	3	21	4	61	3

FALL OF WICKETS

First innings: 2, 23, 104, 111, 140, 140, 154, 166, 219, 231
Second innings: 33, 76, 97, 109, 132, 179, 232, 268, 304, 305

VIVIAN RICHARDS
West Indies v England, St John's, 11, 12, 13, 15, 16 April 1986

WEST INDIES

C. G. Greenidge	b Botham	14			
D. L. Haynes	c Gatting b Ellison	131	(1) run out		70
R. B. Richardson	c Slack b Emburey	24	(2) c Robinson b Emburey		31
H. A. Gomes	b Emburey	24			
*I. V. A. Richards	c Gooch b Botham	26	(3) not out		110
†P. J. L. Dujon	b Foster	21			
M. D. Marshall	c Gatting b Gooch	76			
R. A. Harper	c Lamb b Foster	60	(4) not out		19
M. A. Holding	c Gower b Ellison	73			
J. Garner	run out	11			
B. P. Patterson	not out	0			
Extras	(b 2, lb 11, w 1)	14	(b 4, lb 9, w 1, nb 2)		16
		474	(2 wkts dec)		**246**

ENGLAND

G. A. Gooch	lbw b Holding	51	lbw b Holding		51
W. N. Slack	c Greenidge b Patterson	52	b Garner		8
R. T. Robinson	b Marshall	12	run out		3
*D. I. Gower	c Dujon b Marshall	90	(5) c Dujon b Harper		21
A. J. Lamb	c & b Harper	1	(6) b Marshall		1
M. W. Gatting	c Dujon b Garner	15	(7) b Holding		1
I. T. Botham	c Harper b Garner	10	(8) b Harper		13
†P. R. Downton	c Holding b Garner	5	(9) lbw b Marshall		13
R. M. Ellison	c Dujon b Marshall	6	(4) lbw b Garner		16
J. E. Emburey	not out	7	c Richardson b Harper		0
N. A. Foster	c Holding b Garner	10	not out		0
Extras	(b 5, lb 6, nb 40)	51	(b 10, lb 10, w 2, nb 21)		43
		310			**170**

ENGLAND	O	M	R	W	O	M	R	W
Botham	40	6	147	2	15	0	78	0
Foster	28	5	86	2	10	0	40	0
Ellison	24.3	3	114	2	4	0	32	0
Emburey	37	11	93	2	14	0	83	1
Gooch	5	2	21	1				

FALL OF WICKETS

First innings: 23, 63, 137, 178, 232, 291, 351, 401, 450, 474
Second innings: 100, 161

WEST INDIES	O	M	R	W	O	M	R	W
Marshall	24	5	64	3	16.1	6	25	2
Garner	21.4	2	67	4	17	5	38	2
Patterson	14	2	49	1	15	3	29	0
Holding	20	3	71	1	16	3	45	2
Harper	26	7	45	1	12	8	10	3
Richards	2	0	3	0	3	1	3	0

FALL OF WICKETS

First innings: 127, 132, 157, 160, 205, 223, 237, 289, 290, 310
Second innings: 14, 29, 84, 101, 112, 124, 147, 166, 168, 170

Arthur Shrewsbury, the first great professional.

Frank Worrell
West Indies v Australia, Brisbane, 9, 10, 12, 13, 14 December 1960

WEST INDIES

C. C. Hunte	c Benaud b Davidson	24	c Simpson b Mackay	39
C. W. Smith	c Grout b Davidson	7	c O'Neill b Davidson	6
R. B. Kanhai	c Grout b Davidson	15	c Grout b Davidson	54
G. St A. Sobers	c Kline b Meckiff	132	b Davidson	14
*F. M. M. Worrell	c Grout b Davidson	65	c Grout b Davidson	65
J. S. Solomon	hit wkt b Simpson	65	lbw b Simpson	47
P. D. Lashley	c Grout b Kline	19	b Davidson	0
†F. C. M Alexander	c Davidson b Kline	60	b Benaud	5
S. Ramadhin	c Harvey b Davidson	12	c Harvey b Simpson	6
W. W. Hall	st Grout b Kline	50	b Davidson	18
A. L. Valentine	not out	0	not out	7
Extras	(lb 3, w 1)	4	(b 14, lb 7, w 2)	23
		453		**284**

AUSTRALIA

C. C. McDonald	c Hunte b Sobers	57	b Worrell	16
R. B. Simpson	b Ramadhin	92	c sub b Hall	0
R. N. Harvey	b Valentine	15	c Sobers b Hall	5
N. C. O'Neill	c Valentine b Hall	181	c Alexander b Hall	26
L. E. Favell	run out	45	c Solomon b Hall	7
K. D. Mackay	b Sobers	35	b Ramadhin	28
A. K. Davidson	c Alexander b Hall	44	run out	80
*R. Benaud	lbw b Hall	10	c Alexander b Hall	52
†A. T. W. Grout	lbw b Hall	4	run out	2
I. Meckiff	run out	4	run out	2
L. F. Kline	not out	3	not out	0
Extras	(b 2, lb 8, w 1, nb 4)	15	(b 2, lb 9, nb 3)	14
		505		**232**

AUSTRALIA	O	M	R	W	O	M	R	W
Davidson	30	2	135	5	24.6	4	87	6
Meckiff	18	0	129	1	4	1	19	0
Mackay	3	0	15	0	21	7	52	1
Benaud	24	3	93	0	31	6	69	1
Simpson	8	0	25	1	7	2	18	2
Kline	17.6	6	52	3	4	0	14	0
O'Neill					1	0	2	0

FALL OF WICKETS
First innings: 23, 42, 65, 239, 243, 283, 347, 366, 452, 453
Second innings: 13, 88, 114, 127, 210, 210, 241, 250, 253, 284

WEST INDIES	O	M	R	W	O	M	R	W
Hall	29.3	1	140	4	17.7	3	63	5
Worrell	30	0	93	0	16	3	41	1
Sobers	32	0	115	2	8	0	30	0
Valentine	24	6	82	1	10	4	27	0
Ramadhin	15	1	60	1	17	3	57	1

FALL OF WICKETS
First innings: 84, 138, 194, 278, 381, 469, 484, 489, 496 505
Second innings: 1, 7, 49, 49, 57, 92, 226, 228, 232, 232

Dennis Amiss
England v West Indies, Kingston, 16, 17, 19, 20, 21 February 1974

ENGLAND

G. Boycott	c Kanhai b Sobers	68	c Murray b Boyce	5
D. L. Amiss	c Kanhai b Barrett	27	not out	262
J. A. Jameson	st Murray b Gibbs	23	c Rowe b Barrett	38
F. C. Hayes	c Boyce b Sobers	10	run out	0
*M. H. Denness	c Fredericks b Boyce	67	c Rowe b Barrett	28
A. W. Greig	c Fredericks b Barrett	45	b Gibbs	14
†A. P. E. Knott	c Murray b Barrett	39	(8) run out	6
C. M. Old	c Murray b Julien	2	(9) b Barrett	19
D. L. Underwood	c Fredericks b Sobers	24	(7) c Murray b Sobers	12
P. I. Pocock	c Gibbs b Julien	23	c sub b Boyce	4
R. G. D. Willis	not out	6	not out	3
Extras	(lb 7, nb 12)	19	(b 10, lb 11, w 1, nb 19)	41
		353	(9 wickets)	**432**

WEST INDIES

R. C. Fredericks	b Old	94
L. G. Rowe	lbw b Willis	120
A. I. Kallicharran	c Denness b Old	93
C. H. Lloyd	b Jameson	49
*R. B. Kanhai	c Willis b Greig	39
G. St A. Sobers	c Willis b Greig	57
B. D. Julien	c Denness b Greig	66
K. D. Boyce	c Greig b Willis	8
†D. L. Murray	not out	6
A. G. Barrett	lbw b Willis	0
L. R. Gibbs	not out	6
Extras	(b 16, lb 18, nb 11)	45
	(9 wickets declared)	**583**

WEST INDIES	O	M	R	W	O	M	R	W
Boyce	19	2	52	1	21	4	70	2
Julien	18	3	40	2	13	3	36	0
Sobers	33	11	65	3	34	13	73	1
Barrett	39	16	86	3	54	24	87	3
Gibbs	40	16	78	1	44	15	82	1
Fredericks	4	0	11	0	6	1	17	0
Lloyd	4	2	2	0	3	1	5	0
Kanhai					3	1	8	0
Rowe					2	1	1	0
Kallicharran					3	0	12	0

FALL OF WICKETS
First innings: 68, 104, 133, 134, 224, 278, 286, 322, 333, 353
Second innings: 32, 102, 107, 176, 217, 258, 271, 343, 392

ENGLAND	O	M	R	W
Willis	24	5	97	3
Old	23	6	72	2
Pocock	57	14	152	0
Underwood	36	12	98	0
Greig	49	14	102	3
Jameson	7	2	17	1

FALL OF WICKETS
First innings: 206, 226, 338, 401, 439, 551, 563, 567, 574

* Captain   † Wicket-keeper

DON BRADMAN
Australia v England, Lord's, 27, 28, 30 June, 1 July 1930

ENGLAND

J. B. Hobbs	c Oldfield b Fairfax	1	b Grimmett		19
F. E. Woolley	c Wall b Fairfax	41	hit wkt b Grimmett		28
W. R. Hammond	b Grimmett	38	c Fairfax b Grimmett		32
K. S. Duleepsinhji	c Bradman b Grimmett	173	c Oldfield b Hornibrook		48
E. H. Hendren	c McCabe b Fairfax	48	c Richardson b Grimmett		9
*A. P. F. Chapman	c Oldfield b Wall	11	c Oldfield b Fairfax		121
G. O. B. Allen	b Fairfax	3	lbw b Grimmett		57
M. W. Tate	c McCabe b Wall	54	c Ponsford b Grimmett		10
R. W. V. Robins	c Oldfield b Hornibrook	5	not out		11
J. C. White	not out	23	run out		10
†G. Duckworth	c Oldfield b Wall	18	lbw b Fairfax		0
Extras	(b 2, lb 7, nb 1)	10	(b 16, lb 13, w 1)		30
		425			**375**

AUSTRALIA

*W. M. Woodfull	st Duckworth b Robins	155	not out	26
W. H. Ponsford	c Hammond b White	81	b Robins	14
D. G. Bradman	c Chapman b White	254	c Chapman b Tate	1
A. F. Kippax	b White	83	c Duckworth b Robins	3
S. J. McCabe	c Woolley b Hammond	44	not out	25
V. Y. Richardson	c Hobbs b Tate	30		
†W. A. S. Oldfield	not out	43		
A. G. Fairfax	not out	20		
C. V. Grimmett				
P. M. Hornibrook				
T. W. Wall				
Extras	(b 6, lb 8, w 5)	19	(b 1, lb 2)	3
	(6 wickets declared)	**729**	(3 wickets)	**72**

AUSTRALIA	O	M	R	W	O	M	R	W
Wall	29.4	2	118	3	25	2	80	0
Fairfax	31	6	101	4	12.4	2	37	2
Grimmett	33	4	105	2	53	13	167	6
Hornibrook	26	6	62	1	22	6	49	1
McCabe	9	1	29	0	3	1	11	0
Bradman					1	0	1	0

FALL OF WICKETS
First innings: 13, 53, 105, 209, 236, 239, 337, 363, 387, 425
Second innings: 45, 58, 129, 141, 147, 272, 329, 354, 372, 375

ENGLAND	O	M	R	W	O	M	R	W
Allen	34	7	115	0				
Tate	64	16	148	1	13	6	21	1
White	51	7	158	3	2	0	8	0
Robins	42	1	172	1	9	1	34	2
Hammond	35	8	82	1	4.2	1	6	0
Woolley	6	0	35	0				

FALL OF WICKETS
First innings: 162, 393, 585, 588, 643, 672
Second innings: 16, 17, 22

ROY FREDERICKS
West Indies v Australia, Perth, 12, 13, 14, 16 December 1975

AUSTRALIA

R. B. McCosker	lbw b Roberts	0	c Rowe b Roberts	13
A. Turner	c Gibbs b Roberts	23	c Murray b Roberts	0
I. M. Chappell	b Holding	156	c sub b Roberts	20
*G. S. Chappell	c Murray b Julien	13	c Rowe b Roberts	43
I. R. Redpath	c Murray b Julien	33	lbw b Roberts	0
†R. W. Marsh	c Julien b Boyce	23	c Murray b Roberts	39
G. J. Gilmour	c Julien b Gibbs	45	c Fredericks b Roberts	3
M. H. N. Walker	c Richards b Holding	1	c sub b Julien	3
D. K. Lillee	not out	12	c Lloyd b Julien	4
J. R. Thomson	b Holding	0	b Julien	9
A. A. Mallett	b Holding	0	not out	18
Extras	(b 12, lb 5, nb 6)	23	(b 13, lb 2, nb 2)	17
		329		**169**

WEST INDIES

R. C. Fredericks	c G. S. Chappell b Lillee	169
B. D. Julien	c Mallett b Gilmour	25
L. G. Rowe	c Marsh b Thomson	19
A. I. Kallicharran	c I. M. Chappell b Walker	57
I. V. A. Richards	c Gilmour b Thomson	12
*C. H. Lloyd	b Gilmour	149
†D. L. Murray	c Marsh b Lillee	63
M. A. Holding	c Marsh b Thomson	0
K. D. Boyce	not out	49
A. M. E. Roberts	b Walker	0
L. R. Gibbs	run out	13
Extras	(b 2, lb 16, nb 11)	19
		585

WEST INDIES	O	M	R	W	O	M	R	W
Roberts	13	1	65	2	14	3	54	7
Boyce	12	2	53	1	2	0	8	0
Holding	18.7	1	88	4	10.6	1	53	0
Julien	12	0	51	2	10.1	1	32	3
Gibbs	14	4	49	1	3	1	3	0
Fredericks					1	0	2	0

FALL OF WICKETS
First innings: 0, 37, 70, 149, 189, 277, 285, 329, 329, 329
Second innings: 0, 25, 45, 45, 124, 128, 132, 142, 146, 169

AUSTRALIA	O	M	R	W
Lillee	20	0	123	2
Thomson	17	0	128	3
Gilmour	14	0	103	2
Walker	17	1	99	2
Mallett	26	4	103	0
I. M. Chappell	1.4	1	0	0

FALL OF WICKETS
First innings: 91, 134, 258, 297, 461, 461, 522, 548, 548, 585

* Captain   † Wicket-keeper

W. G. Grace
Gloucestershire v Somerset, Bristol, 16, 17, 18 May 1895

SOMERSET

L. C. H. Palairet	c Bracher b Roberts	80	(3) c Board b Murch		1
G. Fowler	st Board b Grace	118	(1) lbw b Townsend		33
J. B. Challen	b Grace	6	(4) c Wrathall b Townsend		16
R. C. N. Palairet	c Board b Murch	26	(5) c Roberts b Murch		23
H. T. Stanley	c Board b Murch	29	(2) b Murch		31
*S. M. J. Woods	c Board b Murch	6	c Painter b Murch		47
D. L. Evans	lbw b Grace	11	c Board b Murch		2
G. B. Nichols	c Board b Grace	0	(10) c Board b Murch		6
E. J. Tyler	c Ferris b Grace	0	not out		17
†Rev. A. P. Wickham	c Thomas b Murch	3	(11) b Murch		0
J. Bucknell	not out	10	(8) b Murch		0
Extras	(b 5, lb 6, w 3)	14	(b 9, w 4)		13
		303			**189**

GLOUCESTERSHIRE

*W. G. Grace	c Tyler b Woods	288			
J. J. Ferris	b Tyler	4			
C. O. H. Sewell	c and b Woods	2			
C. L. Townsend	lbw b Bucknell	95			
J. R. Painter	lbw b Tyler	34			
H. Wrathall	b Fowler	6	(1) not out		6
E. L. Thomas	b Woods	3	(2) lbw b Bucknell		12
F. C. Bracher	b Bucknell	20			
W. Murch	c Stanley b Tyler	5			
†J. H. Board	not out	2	(3) not out		1
F. G. Roberts	c sub b Tyler	9			
Extras	(b 4, lb 2)	6			
		474	(1 wicket)		**19**

GLOUCESTERSHIRE

	O	M	R	W	O	M	R	W
Townsend	11	2	31	0	34	16	63	2
Roberts	29	7	51	1	13	2	29	0
Sewell	7	0	38	0				
Murch	35.2	14	72	4	44	16	68	8
Ferris	2	0	10	0				
Grace	45	16	87	5				
Wrathall					9	2	16	0

FALL OF WICKETS

First innings: 205, 209, –, –, –, 279, 279, 282, 303
Second innings: 46, 47, 64, 96, –, 162, 162, –, 189, 189

SOMERSET

	O	M	R	W	O	M	R	W
Tyler	42.4	7	160	4				
Woods	40	3	145	3				
Nichols	10	4	21	0				
Bucknell	17	2	68	2	4	1	5	1
Fowler	14	2	56	1	3.3	0	14	0
L. C. H. Palairet	4	0	18	0				

FALL OF WICKETS

First innings: 8, 15, 238, 309, 358, 369, 443, 459, 463, 474
Second innings: 17

Walter Hammond
England v Australia, Lord's, 24, 25, 27, 28 June 1938

ENGLAND

C. J. Barnett	c Brown b McCormick	18	c McCabe b McCormick		12
L. Hutton	c Brown b McCormick	4	c McCormick b O'Reilly		5
W. J. Edrich	b McCormick	0	(4) c McCabe b McCormick		10
*W. R. Hammond	b McCormick	240	(6) c sub b McCabe		2
E. Paynter	lbw b O'Reilly	99	run out		43
D. C. S. Compton	lbw b O'Reilly	6	(7) not out		76
†L. E. G. Ames	c McCormick b Fleetwood-Smith	83	(8) c McCabe b O'Reilly		6
H. Verity	b O'Reilly	5	(3) b McCormick		11
A. W. Wellard	c McCormick b O'Reilly	4	b McCabe		38
D. V. P. Wright	b Fleetwood-Smith	6	not out		10
K. Farnes	not out	5			
Extras	(b 1, lb 12, w 1, nb 10)	24	(b 12, lb 12, w 1, nb 4)		29
		494	(8 wickets declared)		**242**

AUSTRALIA

J. H. W. Fingleton	c Hammond b Wright	31	c Hammond b Wellard		4
W. A. Brown	not out	206	b Verity		10
*D. G. Bradman	b Verity	18	not out		102
S. J. McCabe	c Verity b Farnes	38	c Hutton b Verity		21
A. L. Hassett	lbw b Wellard	56	b Wright		42
C. L. Badcock	b Wellard	0	c Wright b Edrich		0
†B. A. Barnett	c Compton b Verity	8	c Paynter b Edrich		14
A. G. Chipperfield	lbw b Verity	1			
W. J. O'Reilly	b Farnes	42			
E. L. McCormick	c Barnett b Farnes	0			
L. O'B. Fleetwood-Smith	c Barnett b Verity	7			
Extras	(b 1, lb 8, nb 6)	15	(b 5, lb 3, w 2, nb 1)		11
		422	(6 wickets)		**204**

AUSTRALIA

	O	M	R	W	O	M	R	W
McCormick	27	1	101	4	24	5	72	3
McCabe	31	4	86	0	12	1	58	2
Fleetwood-Smith	33.5	2	139	2	7	1	30	0
O'Reilly	37	6	93	4	29	10	53	2
Chipperfield	8.4	0	51	0				

FALL OF WICKETS

First innings: 12, 20, 31, 253, 271, 457, 472, 476, 483, 494
Second innings: 25, 28, 43, 64, 76, 128, 142, 216

ENGLAND

	O	M	R	W	O	M	R	W
Farnes	43	6	135	3	13	3	51	0
Wellard	23	2	96	2	9	1	30	1
Wright	16	2	68	1	8	0	56	1
Verity	35.4	9	103	4	13	5	29	2
Edrich	4	2	5	0	5.2	0	27	2

FALL OF WICKETS

First innings: 69, 101, 152, 276, 276, 307, 308, 393, 393, 422
Second innings: 8, 71, 111, 175, 180, 204

* Captain   † Wicket-keeper

MAY '78

HANIF MOHAMMAD
Pakistan v West Indies, Barbados, 17, 18, 20, 21, 22, 23 January 1958

WEST INDIES

C. C. Hunte	c Imtiaz b Fazal	142	not out	11
R. B. Kanhai	c Mathias b Fazal	27	not out	17
G. St A. Sobers	c Mathias b Mahmood	52		
R. de C. Weekes	c Imtiaz b Mahmood	197		
C. L. Walcott	c Mathias b Kardar	43		
O. G. Smith	c Mathias b Alimuddin	78		
D. St E. Atkinson	b Mahmood	4		
E. St E. Atkinson	b Fazal	0		
*†F. C. M. Alexander	b Mahmood	9		
A. L. Valentine	not out	5		
R. Gilchrist				
Extras	(b 9, lb 4, w 3, nb 6)	22		
	(9 wickets declared)	**579**	(0 wickets)	**28**

PAKISTAN

Hanif Mohammad	b E. St E. Atkinson	17	c Alexander b D. St E. Atkinson	337
†Imtiaz Ahmed	lbw b Gilchrist	20	lbw b Gilchrist	91
Alimuddin	c Weekes b Gilchrist	3	c Alexander b Sobers	37
Saeed Ahmed	st Alexander b Smith	13	c Alexander b Smith	65
Wazir Mohammad	lbw b Valentine	4	c Alexander b E. St E. Atkinson	35
W. Mathias	c Alexander b Smith	17	lbw b E. St E. Atkinson	17
*A. H. Kardar	c D. St E. Atkinson b Smith	4	not out	23
Fazal Mahmood	b Gilchrist	4	b Valentine	19
Nasim-ul-Ghani	run out	11	b Valentine	0
Mahmood Hussain	b Gilchrist	3	not out	0
Haseeb Ahsan	not out	1		
Extras	(b 4, lb 5)	9	(b 19, lb 7, nb 7)	33
		106	(8 wickets declared)	**657**

PAKISTAN	O	M	R	W	O	M	R	W
Fazal	62	21	145	3	2	1	3	0
Mahmood Hussain	41.2	4	153	4				
Kardar	32	4	107	1	3	1	13	0
Haseeb	21	0	84	0				
Nasim	14	1	51	0				
Alimuddin	2	0	17	1				
Hanif					3	1	10	0
Saeed					2	2	0	0
Wazir					1	0	2	0

FALL OF WICKETS
First innings: 122, 209, 266, 356, 541, 551, 556, 570, 579

WEST INDIES	O	M	R	W	O	M	R	W
Gilchrist	15	4	32	4	41	5	121	1
E. St E. Atkinson	8	0	27	1	49	5	136	2
Smith	13	4	23	3	61	30	93	1
Valentine	6.2	1	15	1	39	8	109	2
D. St E. Atkinson					62	35	61	1
Sobers					57	25	94	1
Walcott					10	5	10	0

FALL OF WICKETS
First innings: 35, 39, 44, 53, 81, 84, 91, 93, 96, 106
Second innings: 152, 264, 418, 539, 598, 626, 649, 649

GEORGE HEADLEY
West Indies v England, Kingston, 14, 15, 16, 18 March 1935

WEST INDIES

I. Barrow	b Farnes	3
†C. M. Christiani	b Paine	27
G. A. Headley	not out	270
J. E. D. Sealy	b Paine	91
L. N. Constantine	lbw b Paine	34
G. H. Mudie	c Townsend b Paine	5
R. L. Fuller	lbw b Hollies	1
R. S. Grant	c Wyatt b Paine	77
L. G. Hylton	not out	5
*G. C. Grant		
E. A. Martindale		
Extras	(b 8, lb 13, nb 1)	22
	(7 wickets declared)	**535**

ENGLAND

*R. E. S. Wyatt	retired hurt	1		absent hurt	
D. C. H. Townsend	c Christiani b Martindale	8		b Martindale	11
W. R. Hammond	c Hylton b Constantine	11		b Martindale	34
G. A. E. Paine	lbw b Martindale	0	(7)	not out	10
E. R. T. Holmes	b Martindale	0	(6)	lbw b Sealy	3
†L. E. G. Ames	c Constantine b Mudie	126	(5)	c R. S. Grant b Constantine	17
E. H. Hendren	c Barrow b R. S. Grant	40	(4)	c Constantine b Mudie	11
J. Iddon	lbw b Mudie	54	(1)	lbw b Constantine	0
C. I. J. Smith	b Constantine	10	(8)	b Martindale	4
K. Farnes	b Constantine	5	(9)	c Christiani b Martindale	0
W. E. Hollies	not out	1	(10)	c Martindale b Constantine	6
Extras	(b 4, lb 6, nb 5)	15		(b 4, lb 1, w 2)	7
		271			**103**

ENGLAND	O	M	R	W
Smith	22	2	83	0
Farnes	24	4	72	1
Wyatt	5	1	12	0
Hollies	46	11	114	1
Holmes	8	0	40	0
Paine	56	12	168	5
Iddon	7	1	24	0

FALL OF WICKETS
First innings: 5, 92, 294, 352, 376, 381, 528

WEST INDIES	O	M	R	W	O	M	R	W
Martindale	17	1	56	3	16	5	28	4
Hylton	19	1	59	0	4	1	11	0
Constantine	23.2	4	55	3	9	3	13	3
Fuller	6	2	10	0	2	0	2	0
R. S. Grant	16	1	48	1	9	2	19	0
Mudie	17	7	23	2	12	5	17	1
G. C. Grant	1	0	5	0				
Sealy					2	0	6	1

FALL OF WICKETS
First innings: 23, 26, 26, 26, 95, 252, 265, 267, 271
Second innings: 14, 18, 45, 68, 83, 83, 89, 93, 103

---

* Captain   † Wicket-keeper

CLEM HILL
Australia v England, Sheffield, 3, 4, 5 July 1902

AUSTRALIA

V. T. Trumper	b Braund	1	c Lilley b Jackson	62
R. A. Duff	c Lilley b Barnes	25	c Hirst b Rhodes	1
C. Hill	c Rhodes b Barnes	18	c MacLaren b Jackson	119
*J. Darling	c Braund b Barnes	0	c Braund b Barnes	0
S. E. Gregory	c Abel b Barnes	11	run out	29
M. A. Noble	c Braund b Rhodes	47	b Jackson	8
A. J. Y. Hopkins	c Braund b Barnes	27	not out	40
W. W. Armstrong	c and b Braund	25	b Rhodes	26
†J. J. Kelly	b Barnes	0	c Hirst b Rhodes	0
H. Trumble	c and b Jackson	32	b Rhodes	0
J. V. Saunders	not out	0	b Rhodes	1
Extras	(b 3, lb 5)	8	(lb 3)	3
		194		**289**

ENGLAND	O	M	R	W	O	M	R	W
Hirst	15	1	59	0	10	1	40	0
Braund	13	4	34	2	12	0	58	0
Barnes	20	9	49	6	12	4	50	1
Jackson	5.1	1	11	1	17	2	60	3
Rhodes	13	3	33	1	17.1	3	63	5
Jessop					4	0	15	0

FALL OF WICKETS
First innings: 3, 39, 39, 52, 73, 127, 137, 137, 194, 194
Second innings: 20, 80, 80, 187, 214, 225, 277, 287, 287, 289

ENGLAND

*A. C. MacLaren	b Noble	31	(4) c Trumper b Noble	63
R. Abel	b Noble	38	c Hill b Noble	8
J. T. Tyldesley	c Armstrong b Noble	22	b Trumble	14
Hon. F. S. Jackson	c Gregory b Saunders	3	(6) b Noble	14
C. B. Fry	st Kelly b Saunders	1	lbw b Trumble	4
†A. F. A. Lilley	b Noble	8	(7) b Noble	9
L. C. Braund	st Kelly b Saunders	0	(8) c Armstrong b Noble	9
G. H. Hirst	c Trumble b Saunders	8	(9) b Noble	0
G. L. Jessop	c Saunders b Noble	12	(1) lbw b Trumble	55
W. Rhodes	not out	7	not out	7
S. F. Barnes	c Darling b Saunders	7	b Trumble	5
Extras	(b 4, lb 3, nb 1)	8	(b 4, lb 1, w 1, nb 1)	7
		145		**195**

AUSTRALIA	O	M	R	W	O	M	R	W
Trumble	18	10	21	0	21.5	3	49	4
Saunders	15.3	4	50	5	12	0	68	0
Trumper	4	1	8	0	6	0	19	0
Noble	19	6	51	5	21	4	52	6
Armstrong	5	2	7	0				

FALL OF WICKETS
First innings: 61, 86, 101, 101, 102, 106, 110, 130, 131, 145
Second innings: 14, 75, 84, 98, 162, 165, 174, 174, 186, 195

LEN HUTTON
England v Australia, The Oval, 20, 22, 23, 24 August 1938

ENGLAND

L. Hutton	c Hassett b O'Reilly	364
W. J. Edrich	lbw b O'Reilly	12
M. Leyland	run out	187
*W. R. Hammond	lbw b Fleetwood-Smith	59
E. Paynter	lbw b O'Reilly	0
D. C. S. Compton	b Waite	1
J. Hardstaff, jr	not out	169
†A. Wood	c and b Barnes	53
H. Verity	not out	8
K. Farnes		
W. E. Bowes		
Extras	(b 22, lb 19, w 1, nb 8)	50
	(7 wickets declared)	**903**

AUSTRALIA	O	M	R	W
Waite	72	16	150	1
McCabe	38	8	85	0
O'Reilly	85	26	178	3
Fleetwood-Smith	87	11	298	1
Barnes	38	3	84	1
Hassett	13	2	52	0
Bradman	2.2	1	6	0

FALL OF WICKETS
First innings: 29, 411, 546, 547, 555, 770, 876

AUSTRALIA

W. A. Brown	c Hammond b Leyland	69	c Edrich b Farnes	15
C. L. Badcock	c Hardstaff b Bowes	0	b Bowes	9
S. J. McCabe	c Edrich b Farnes	14	c Wood b Farnes	2
A. L. Hassett	c Compton b Edrich	42	lbw b Bowes	10
S. G. Barnes	b Bowes	41	lbw b Verity	33
†B. A. Barnett	c Wood b Bowes	2	b Farnes	46
M. G. Waite	b Bowes	8	c Edrich b Verity	0
W. J. O'Reilly	c Wood b Bowes	0	not out	7
L. O'B. Fleetwood-Smith	not out	16	c Leyland b Farnes	0
*D. G. Bradman	absent hurt	–	absent hurt	–
J. H. W. Fingleton	absent hurt	–	absent hurt	–
Extras	(b 4, lb 2, nb 3)	9	(b 1)	1
		201		**123**

ENGLAND	O	M	R	W	O	M	R	W
Farnes	13	2	54	1	12.1	1	63	4
Bowes	19	3	49	5	10	3	25	2
Edrich	10	2	55	1				
Verity	5	1	15	0	7	3	15	2
Leyland	3.1	0	11	1	5	0	19	0
Hammond	2	0	8	0				

FALL OF WICKETS
First innings: 0, 19, 70, 145, 147, 160, 160, 201
Second innings: 15, 18, 35, 41, 115, 115, 117, 123

* Captain   † Wicket-keeper

CHARLES MACARTNEY
The Australians v Nottinghamshire, 25, 27 June 1921

AUSTRALIANS

W. Bardsley	b Richmond	0
T. J. E. Andrews	c Oates b Barratt	29
C. G. Macartney	lbw b Hardstaff	345
J. M. Taylor	c Whysall b Barratt	50
C. E. Pellow	c Oates b Staples	100
J. M. Gregory	c G. Gunn b Hardstaff	19
J. Ryder	b Hardstaff	20
H. L. Hendry	st Oates b Hardstaff	51
W. A. Oldfield	b Staples	40
E. A. McDonald	b Hardstaff	1
A. A. Mailey	not out	0
Extras	(b 8, lb 10, w 1, nb 1)	20
		675

NOTTINGHAMSHIRE

G. Gunn	b McDonald	4	c Oldfield b Mailey	20
G. M. Lee	c Pellew b Gregory	1	run out	9
J. Gunn	c McDonald b Gregory	0	b Gregory	1
J. Hardstaff	b Gregory	16	b McDonald	6
A. W. Carr	b McDonald	15	c Oldfield b Mailey	31
W. Payton	lbw b McDonald	2	lbw b Gregory	14
W. Whysall	b Gregory	15	b Gregory	9
S. J. Staples	b Mailey	2	c Andrews b Mailey	3
F. Barratt	not out	2	c Gregory b Mailey	4
L. Richmond	st Oldfield b Mailey	0	not out	1
T. Oates	absent hurt	–	absent hurt	–
Extras	(lb 1)	1	(b 1, nb 1)	2
		58		**100**

NOTTINGHAMSHIRE

	O	M	R	W
Barratt	23	4	89	2
Richmond	36	1	193	1
Staples	27	3	131	2
J. Gunn	9	1	71	0
Lee	2	0	14	0
Carr	1	0	24	0
Hardstaff	28.2	3	133	5
Whysall	1	1	0	0

AUSTRALIANS

	O	M	R	W	O	M	R	W
Gregory	8	1	23	4	11	1	26	3
McDonald	10	0	24	3	13	6	25	1
Ryder	7	2	9	0	1	1	0	0
Mailey	1.4	1	1	2	13.5	1	36	4
Hendry					3	0	11	0

PETER MAY
England v West Indies, Edgbaston, 30, 31 May, 1, 3, 4 June 1957

ENGLAND

P. E. Richardson	c Walcott b Ramadhin	47	c sub b Ramadhin	34
D. B. Close	c Kanhai b Gilchrist	15	c Weekes b Gilchrist	42
D. J. Insole	b Ramadhin	20	b Ramadhin	0
*P. B. H. May	c Weekes b Ramadhin	30	not out	285
M. C. Cowdrey	c Gilchrist b Ramadhin	4	c sub b Smith	154
T. E. Bailey	b Ramadhin	1		
G. A. R. Lock	b Ramadhin	0		
†T. G. Evans	b Gilchrist	14	(6) not out	29
J. C. Laker	b Ramadhin	7		
F. S. Trueman	not out	29		
J. B. Statham	b Atkinson	13		
Extras	(b 3, lb 3)	6	(b 23, lb 16)	39
		186	(4 wickets declared)	**583**

WEST INDIES

B. H. Pairaudeau	b Trueman	1	b Trueman	7
†R. B. Kanhai	lbw b Statham	42	c Close b Trueman	1
C. L. Walcott	c Evans b Laker	90	(6) c Lock b Laker	1
E. de C. Weekes	b Trueman	9	c Trueman b Lock	33
G. St. A. Sobers	c Bailey b Statham	53	(3) c Cowdrey b Lock	14
O. G. Smith	lbw b Laker	161	(7) lbw b Laker	5
F. M. M. Worrell	b Statham	81	(5) c May b Lock	0
*J. D. C. Goddard	c Lock b Laker	24	not not	0
D. St E. Atkinson	c Statham b Laker	1	not out	4
S. Ramadhin	not out	5		
R. Gilchrist	run out	0		
Extras	(b 1, lb 6)	7	(b 7)	7
		474	(7 wickets)	**72**

WEST INDIES

	O	M	R	W	O	M	R	W
Worrell	9	1	27	0				
Gilchrist	27	4	74	2	26	2	67	1
Ramadhin	31	16	49	7	98	35	179	2
Atkinson	12.4	3	30	1	72	29	137	0
Sobers					30	4	77	0
Smith					26	4	72	1
Goddard					6	2	12	0

FALL OF WICKETS
First innings: 32, 61, 104, 115, 116, 118, 121, 130, 150, 186
Second innings: 63, 65, 113, 524

ENGLAND

	O	M	R	W	O	M	R	W
Statham	39	4	114	3	2	0	6	0
Trueman	30	4	99	2	5	3	7	2
Bailey	34	11	80	0				
Laker	54	17	119	4	24	20	13	2
Lock	34.4	15	55	0	27	19	31	3
Close					2	1	8	0

FALL OF WICKETS
First innings: 4, 83, 120, 183, 197, 387, 466, 469, 474, 474
Second innings: 1, 9, 25, 27, 43, 66, 68

BARRY RICHARDS
South Australia v Western Australia, Perth, 20, 21, 22, 23 November 1970

SOUTH AUSTRALIA

B. A. Richards	lbw b Mann	356
J. J. Causby	c Chadwick b Lock	38
*I. M. Chappell	st Marsh b Lock	129
G. S. Chappell	c Marsh b McKenzie	11
K. G. Cunningham	c Inverarity b Lock	13
K. Langley	run out	7
E. W. Freeman	c Irvine b Lock	6
†R. P. Blundell	b Mann	0
A. A. Mallett	not out	6
T. J. Jenner	c McKenzie b Mann	5
J. R. Hammond		
Extras	(nb 4)	4
	(9 wickets declared)	**575**

W. AUSTRALIA	O	M	R	W
McKenzie	19	2	101	1
Lillee	18	1	117	0
Brayshaw	12	1	69	0
Mann	20.6	1	120	3
Lock	16	1	108	4
Inverarity	8	0	56	0

FALL OF WICKETS

First innings: 109, 417, 447, 551, 553, 563, 564, 575

WESTERN AUSTRALIA

D. Chadwick	c Blundell b Jenner	49	c and b Hammond	2
C Scarff	c Blundell b Hammond	11	b Cunningham	7
J. T. Irvine	b Jenner	33	c and b G. S. Chappell	57
R. J. Inverarity	c G. S. Chappell b Hammond	85	c and b G. S. Chappell	35
R. D. Meuleman	retired hurt	28	absent hurt	–
I. J. Brayshaw	lbw b Freeman	22	c Richards b Mallett	13
†R. W. Marsh	c I. M. Chappell b Hammond	9	c I. M. Chappell b Richards	19
A. L. Mann	c Blundell b Hammond	2	c I. M. Chappell b Hammond	1
D. K. Lillee	c Cunningham b Hammond	12	b Hammond	6
G. D. McKenzie	b Hammond	10	not out	18
*G. A. R. Lock	not out	2	c Hammond b Mallett	8
Extras	(lb 7, w 2, nb 17)	26	(b 1, nb 8)	9
		289		**175**

S. AUSTRALIA	O	M	R	W	O	M	R	W
Freeman	15	1	53	1	4	0	16	0
Hammond	12.3	1	54	6	9	2	25	3
G. S. Chappell	8	1	23	0	12	1	41	2
Jenner	22	4	78	2	8	0	25	0
Mallett	18	5	37	0	12.5	2	43	2
Cunningham	9	2	18	0	4	0	12	1
Richards					1	0	4	1

FALL OF WICKETS

First innings: 33, 88, 110, 239, 256, 261, 270, 285, 289
Second innings: 3, 15, 102, 110, 137, 141, 142, 161, 175

LAWRENCE ROWE
West Indies v England, Bridgetown, 6, 7, 9, 10, 11 March, 1974

ENGLAND

*M. H Denness	c Murray b Sobers	24	lbw b Holder	0
D. L. Amiss	b Julien	12	c Julien b Roberts	4
J. A. Jameson	c Fredericks b Julien	3	lbw b Roberts	9
G. Boycott	c Murray b Julien	10	c Kanhai b Sobers	13
K. W. R. Fletcher	c Murray b Julien	37	not out	129
A. W. Greig	c Sobers b Julien	148	c Roberts b Gibbs	25
†A. P. E. Knott	b Gibbs	87	lbw b Lloyd	67
C. M. Old	c Murray b Roberts	1	b Lloyd	0
G. G. Arnold	b Holder	12	not out	2
P. J. Pocock	c Lloyd b Gibbs	18		
R. G. D. Willis	not out	10		
Extras	(lb 5, nb 28)	33	(b 7, lb 5, nb 16)	28
		395	(7 wickets)	**277**

WEST INDIES	O	M	R	W	O	M	R	W
Holder	27	6	68	1	15	6	37	1
Roberts	33	8	75	1	17	4	49	2
Julien	26	9	57	5	11	4	21	0
Sobers	18	4	57	1	35	21	55	1
Gibbs	33.4	10	91	2	28.3	15	40	1
Lloyd	4	2	9	0	12	4	13	2
Fredericks	3	0	5	0	6	2	24	0
Rowe					1	0	5	0
Kallicharran					1	0	5	0

FALL OF WICKETS

First innings: 28, 34, 53, 68, 130, 293, 306, 344, 371, 395
Second innings: 4, 8, 29, 40, 106, 248, 248

WEST INDIES

R. C. Fredericks	b Greig	32
L. G. Rowe	c Arnold b Greig	302
A. I. Kallicharran	c Greig	119
C. H. Lloyd	c Fletcher b Greig	8
V. A. Holder	c and b Greig	8
*R. B. Kanhai	b Arnold	18
G. St A. Sobers	c Greig b Willis	0
†D. L. Murray	not out	53
B. D. Julien	c Willis b Greig	1
A. M. E. Roberts	not out	9
L. R. Gibbs		
Extras	(b 3, lb 8, nb 35)	46
	(8 wickets declared)	**596**

ENGLAND	O	M	R	W
Arnold	26	5	91	1
Willis	26	4	100	1
Greig	46	2	164	6
Old	28	4	102	0
Pocock	28	4	93	0

FALL OF WICKETS

First innings: 126, 375, 390, 420, 465, 466, 551, 556

Walter Hammond, until usurped by Bradman the greatest batsman in the world. His cover-drive, as shown here, is acknowledged as one of the great shots of cricket.

Allan Border
Australia v West Indies, Port-of-Spain, 16, 17, 18, 20, 21 March 1984

AUSTRALIA

K. C. Wessels	c Gomes b Garner	4		lbw b Garner	8
†W. B. Phillips	c Dujon b Garner	4		run out	0
G. M. Ritchie	b Garner	1		b Small	26
*K. J. Hughes	c Dujon b Garner	24		lbw b Marshall	33
A. R. Border	not out	98	(6)	not out	100
D. W. Hookes	b Garner	23	(7)	c Richardson b Gomes	21
D. M. Jones	c and b Richards	48	(8)	b Richards	5
G. F. Lawson	c and b Daniel	14	(9)	b Marshall	20
T. G. Hogan	c Greenidge b Daniel	0	(5)	c Logie b Daniel	38
R. M. Hogg	c Marshall b Daniel	11		c Garner b Richards	9
T. M. Alderman	c Richardson b Garner	1		not out	21
Extras	(b 6, lb 4, nb 17)	27		(b 6, lb 1, w 1, nb 14)	22
		255		(9 wickets)	**299**

WEST INDIES

C. G. Greenidge	c Phillips b Hogg	24
D. L. Haynes	run out	53
R. B. Richardson	c Wessels b Alderman	23
*I. V. A. Richards	c Phillips b Alderman	76
H. A. Gomes	b Lawson	3
A. L. Logie	lbw b Hogan	97
†P. J. L. Dujon	b Hogan	130
M. D. Marshall	lbw b Lawson	10
J. Garner	not out	24
W. W. Daniel	not out	6
M. A. Small		
Extras	(b 7, lb 12, w 2, nb 1)	22
	(8 wickets declared)	**468**

WEST INDIES

	O	M	R	W	O	M	R	W
Garner	28.1	9	60	6	15	4	35	1
Marshall	19	4	73	0	22	3	73	2
Daniel	15	2	40	3	9	3	11	1
Small	10	3	24	0	14	2	51	1
Gomes	10	0	33	0	27	5	53	1
Richards	10	4	15	1	25	5	65	2
Logie					0.1	0	4	0

FALL OF WICKETS
First innings: 4, 7, 16, 50, 85, 185, 233, 233, 253, 255
Second innings: 1, 35, 41, 114, 115, 153, 162, 196, 238

AUSTRALIA

	O	M	R	W
Lawson	32	3	132	2
Hogg	31	2	103	1
Alderman	35	9	91	2
Hogan	28	3	123	2

FALL OF WICKETS
First innings: 35, 93, 124, 129, 229, 387, 430, 462

Denis Compton
England v Australia, Old Trafford, 8, 9, 10, 12, 13 July 1948

ENGLAND

C. Washbrook	b Johnston	11		not out	85
G. M. Emmett	c Barnes b Lindwall	10		c Tallon b Lindwall	0
W. J. Edrich	c Tallon b Lindwall	32		run out	53
D. C. S. Compton	not out	145		c Miller b Toshack	0
J. F. Crapp	lbw b Lindwall	37		not out	19
H. E. Dollery	b Johnston	1			
*N. W. D. Yardley	c Johnson b Toshack	22			
†T. G. Evans	c Johnson b Lindwall	34			
A. V. Bedser	run out	37			
R. Pollard	b Toshack	3			
J. A. Young	c Bradman b Johnson	4			
Extras	(b 7, lb 17, nb 3)	27		(b 9, lb 7, w 1)	17
		363		(3 wickets declared)	**174**

AUSTRALIA

A. R. Morris	c Compton b Bedser	51		not out	54
I. W. Johnson	c Evans b Bedser	1		c Crapp b Young	6
*D. G. Bradman	lbw b Pollard	7		not out	30
A. L. Hassett	c Washbrook b Young	38			
K. R. Miller	lbw b Pollard	31			
S. G. Barnes	retired hurt	1			
S. J. E. Loxton	b Pollard	36			
†D. Tallon	c Evans b Edrich	18			
R. R. Lindwall	c Washbrook b Bedser	23			
W. A. Johnston	c Crapp b Bedser	3			
E. R. H. Toshack	run out	0			
Extras	(b 5, lb 4, nb 3)	12		(nb 2)	2
		221		(1 wicket)	**92**

AUSTRALIA

	O	M	R	W	O	M	R	W
Lindwall	40	8	99	4	14	4	37	1
Johnston	45.5	13	67	3	14	3	34	0
Loxton	7	0	18	0	8	2	29	0
Toshack	41	20	75	2	12	5	26	1
Johnson	38	16	77	0	7	3	16	0
Miller					14	7	15	0

FALL OF WICKETS
First innings: 22, 28, 96, 97, 119, 141, 216, 337, 352, 363
Second innings: 1, 125, 129

ENGLAND

	O	M	R	W	O	M	R	W
Bedser	36	12	81	4	19	12	27	0
Pollard	32	9	53	3	10	8	6	0
Edrich	7	3	27	1	2	0	8	0
Yardley	4	0	12	0				
Young	14	5	36	1	21	12	31	1
Compton					9	3	18	0

FALL OF WICKETS
First innings: 3, 13, 82, 135, 139, 172, 208, 219, 221
Second innings: 10

Bev Congdon
New Zealand v England, Trent Bridge, 7, 8, 9, 11, 12 June 1973

ENGLAND

G. Boycott	lbw b Taylor	51	run out		1
D. L. Amiss	c Wadsworth b Taylor	42	not out		138
G. R. J. Roope	lbw b D. R. Hadlee	28	c Wadsworth b Collinge		2
A. R. Lewis	c Wadsworth b Taylor	2	c Wadsworth b Taylor		2
K. W. R. Fletcher	lbw b D. R. Hadlee	17	b D. R. Hadlee		8
A. W. Greig	c Parker b Collinge	2	lbw b Collinge		139
*R. Illingworth	b D. R. Hadlee	8	c Parker b Pollard		3
†A. P. E. Knott	b Congdon	49	c Hastings b Pollard		2
J. A. Snow	b D. R. Hadlee	8	b R. J. Hadlee		7
G. G. Arnold	c Wadsworth b Taylor	1	not out		10
N. Gifford	not out	25			
Extras	(lb 10, nb 7)	17	(b 4, lb 6, nb 3)		13
		250	(8 wickets declared)		**325**

NEW ZEALAND

G. M. Turner	c Roope b Greig	11	c Roope b Arnold		9
J. M. Parker	c Knott b Greig	2	c Illingworth b Snow		6
*B. E. Congdon	run out	9	b Arnold		176
B. F. Hastings	c Roope b Arnold	3	lbw b Arnold		11
M. G. Burgess	c Knott b Arnold	0	c Knott b Arnold		26
V. Pollard	not out	16	lbw b Greig		116
†K. J. Wadsworth	c Knott b Greig	0	c Roope b Arnold		46
B. R. Taylor	c Knott b Snow	19	lbw b Snow		11
D. R. Hadlee	b Snow	0	hit wkt b Greig		14
R. J. Hadlee	b Snow	0	not out		4
R. O. Collinge	b Greig	17	b Greig		0
Extras	(b 8, lb 6, nb 6)	20	(lb 13, w 1, nb 7)		21
		97			**440**

NEW ZEALAND	O	M	R	W	O	M	R	W
Collinge	27	6	62	1	24	7	43	2
R. J. Hadlee	26	5	64	0	19	3	79	1
Taylor	29	7	53	4	23	3	87	1
D.R. Hadlee	19	6	42	4	13	2	51	1
Congdon	6.4	1	12	1	9	1	28	0
Pollard					9	3	24	2

FALL OF WICKETS
First innings: 92, 106, 108, 140, 147, 161, 162, 184, 191, 250
Second innings: 2, 8, 11, 24, 234, 241, 263, 311

ENGLAND	O	M	R	W	O	M	R	W
Snow	13	5	21	3	43	10	104	2
Arnold	18	8	23	2	53	15	131	5
Greig	10.4	0	33	4	45.1	10	101	3
Roope					9	2	17	0
Gifford					17	7	35	0
Illingworth					21	7	31	0

FALL OF WICKETS
First innings: 24, 31, 34, 34, 45, 45, 71, 72, 72, 97
Second innings: 16, 16, 68, 130, 307, 402, 414, 431, 440, 440

Basil D'Oliveira
England v Australia, The Oval, 22, 23, 24, 26, 27 August 1968

ENGLAND

J. H. Edrich	b Chappell	164	c Lawry b Mallett		17
C. Milburn	b Connolly	8	c Lawry b Connolly		18
E. R. Dexter	b Gleeson	21	b Connolly		28
*M. C. Cowdrey	lbw b Mallett	16	b Mallett		35
T. W. Graveney	c Redpath b McKenzie	63	run out		12
B. L. D'Oliveira	c Inverarity b Mallett	158	c Gleeson b Connolly		9
†A. P. E. Knott	c Jarman b Mallett	28	run out		34
R. Illingworth	lbw b Connolly	8	b Gleeson		10
J. A. Snow	run out	4	c Sheahan b Gleeson		13
D. L. Underwood	not out	9	not out		1
D. J. Brown	c Sheahan b Gleeson	2	b Connolly		1
Extras	(b 1, lb 11, w 1)	13	(lb 3)		3
		494			**181**

AUSTRALIA

*W. M. Lawry	c Knott b Snow	135	c Millburn b Brown		4
R. J. Inverarity	c Milburn b Snow	1	lbw b Underwood		56
I. R. Redpath	c Cowdrey b Snow	67	lbw b Underwood		8
I. M. Chappell	c Knott b Brown	10	lbw b Underwood		2
K. D. Walters	c Knott b Brown	5	c Knott b Underwood		1
A. P. Sheahan	b Illingworth	14	c Snow b Illingworth		24
†B. N. Jarman	st Knott b Illingworth	0	b D'Oliveira		21
G. D. McKenzie	b Brown	12	(9) c Brown b Underwood		0
A. A. Mallett	not out	43	(8) c Brown b Underwood		0
J. W. Gleeson	c Dexter b Underwood	19	b Underwood		5
A. N. Connolly	b Underwood	3	not out		0
Extras	(b 4, lb 7, nb 4)	15	(lb 4)		4
		324			**125**

AUSTRALIA	O	M	R	W	O	M	R	W
McKenzie	40	8	87	1	4	0	14	0
Connolly	57	12	127	2	22.4	2	65	4
Walters	6	2	17	0				
Gleeson	41.2	8	109	2	7	2	22	2
Mallett	36	11	87	3	25	4	77	2
Chappell	21	5	54	1				

FALL OF WICKETS
First innings: 28, 84, 113, 238, 359, 421, 458, 468, 489, 494
Second innings: 23, 53, 67, 90, 114, 126, 149, 179, 179, 181

ENGLAND	O	M	R	W	O	M	R	W
Snow	35	12	67	3	11	5	22	0
Brown	22	5	63	3	8	3	19	1
Illingworth	48	15	87	2	28	18	29	1
Underwood	54.3	21	89	2	31.3	19	50	7
D'Oliveira	4	2	3	0	5	4	1	1

FALL OF WICKETS
First innings: 7, 136, 151, 161, 185, 188, 237, 269, 302, 324
Second innings: 4, 13, 19, 29, 65, 110, 110, 110, 120, 125

* Captain   † Wicket-keeper

GRAHAM GOOCH
England v West Indies, Bridgetown, 13, 14, 15, 17, 18 March 1981

WEST INDIES

C. G. Greenidge	c Gooch b Jackman	14		lbw b Dilley	0
D. L. Haynes	c. Bairstow b Jackman	25		lbw b Botham	25
I. V. A. Richards	c Botham b Dilley	0	(4)	not out	182
E. H. Mattis	lbw b Botham	16	(5)	c Butcher b Jackman	24
*C. H. Lloyd	c Gooch b Jackman	100	(7)	lbw b Botham	66
H. A. Gomes	c Botham b Dilley	58		run out	34
†D. A. Murray	c Bairstow b Dilley	9	(9)	not out	5
A. M. E. Roberts	c Bairstow b Botham	14		c Bairstow b Botham	0
J. Garner	c Bairstow b Botham	15			
M. A. Holding	c Gatting b Botham	0	(3)	c Boycott b Jackman	33
C. E. H. Croft	not out	0			
Extras	(b 4, lb 6, w 2, nb 2)	14		(b 3, lb 7)	10
		265		(7 wickets declared)	**379**

ENGLAND

G. A. Gooch	b Garner	26		c Garner b Croft	116
G. Boycott	b Holding	0		c Garner b Holding	1
M. W. Gatting	c Greenidge b Roberts	2		b Holding	0
D. I. Gower	c Mattis b Croft	17		b Richards	54
R. O. Butcher	c Richards b Croft	17		lbw b Richards	2
*I. T. Botham	c Murray b Holding	26		c Lloyd b Roberts	1
P. Willey	not out	19		lbw b Croft	17
†D. L. Bairstow	c Mattis b Holding	0		c Murray b Croft	2
J. E. Emburey	c Lloyd b Roberts	0		b Garner	9
R. D. Jackman	c Roberts b Croft	7		b Garner	7
G. R. Dilley	c Gomes b Croft	0		not out	7
Extras	(b 1, lb 1, nb 6)	8		(b 1, lb 3, nb 4)	8
		122			**224**

ENGLAND	O	M	R	W	O	M	R	W
Dilley	23	7	51	3	25	3	111	1
Botham	25.1	5	77	4	29	5	102	3
Jackman	22	4	65	3	25	5	76	2
Emburey	18	4	45	0	24	7	57	0
Gooch	2	0	13	0				
Willey					6	0	23	0

FALL OF WICKETS
First innings: 24, 25, 47, 65, 219, 224, 236, 258, 258, 265
Second innings: 0, 57, 71, 130, 212, 365, 365

WEST INDIES	O	M	R	W	O	M	R	W
Roberts	11	3	29	2	20	6	42	1
Holding	11	7	16	3	19	6	46	2
Croft	13.5	2	39	4	19	1	65	3
Garner	12	5	30	1	16.2	6	39	2
Richards					17	6	24	2

FALL OF WICKETS
First innings: 6, 11, 40, 55, 72, 94, 94, 97, 122, 122
Second innings: 2, 2, 122, 134, 139, 196, 198, 201, 213, 224

DOUGLAS JARDINE
England v West Indies, Old Trafford, 22, 24, 25 July 1933

WEST INDIES

C. A. Roach	b Clark	13		lbw b Langridge	64
†I. Barrow	b Wyatt	105		c Langridge b Clark	0
G. A. Headley	not out	169		c and b Langridge	24
E. L. G. Hoad	b Clark	1		c Hammond b Langridge	14
*G. C. Grant	c Ames b Robins	16		c Hammond b Langridge	14
L. N. Constantine	c Robins b Clark	31	(7)	b Langridge	64
C. A. Wiles	c Hammond b Verity	0	(6)	st Ames b Langridge	2
O. C. Da Costa	b Clark	20		c Sutcliffe b Clark	0
E. E. Achong	b Verity	6		c Ames b Langridge	10
V. A. Valentine	b Robins	6		not out	19
E. A. Martindale	b Robins	2		c Verity b Robins	1
Extras	(lb 6)	6		(b 8, lb 4, nb 1)	13
		375			**225**

ENGLAND

C. F. Walters	lbw b Martindale	46
H. Sutcliffe	run out	20
W. R. Hammond	c Martindale b Constantine	34
R. E. S. Wyatt	c Constantine b Martindale	18
*D. R. Jardine	c Constantine b Martindale	127
†L. E. G. Ames	c Headley b Martindale	47
J. Langridge	c Grant b Achong	9
R. W. V. Robins	st Barrow b Achong	55
H. Verity	not out	0
E. W. Clark	b Martindale	0
G. G. Macaulay	absent hurt	–
Extras	(b 7, lb 6, w 1, nb 4)	18
		374

ENGLAND	O	M	R	W	O	M	R	W
Clark	40	8	99	4	15	1	64	2
Macaulay	14	2	48	0				
Robins	28.4	2	111	3	11.1	0	41	1
Verity	32	14	47	2	13	2	40	0
Hammond	5	0	27	0				
Langridge	9	1	23	0	17	4	56	7
Wyatt	7	1	14	1	4	1	11	0

FALL OF WICKETS
First innings: 26, 226, 227, 266, 302, 306, 341, 354, 363, 375
Second innings: 5, 86, 95, 112, 118, 131, 132, 191, 214, 225

WEST INDIES	O	M	R	W
Martindale	23.4	4	73	5
Constantine	25	5	55	1
Valentine	28	8	49	0
Achong	37	9	90	2
Headley	15	1	65	0
Grant	2	0	12	0
Da Costa	10	6	12	0

FALL OF WICKETS
First innings: 63, 83, 118, 134, 217, 234, 374, 374, 374

JAVED MIANDAD
Glamorgan v Essex, Colchester, 29, 31 August, 1 September 1981

ESSEX

G. A. Gooch	lbw b Nash	16	c A. L. Jones b Lloyd	113
B. R. Hardie	c Daniels b Ontong	37	not out	114
*K. W. R. Fletcher	lbw b Daniels	6	b Ontong	6
K. S. McEwan	c E. W. Jones b Daniels	0	c Javed b Ontong	2
A. W. Lilley	c Featherstone b Ontong	14	c E. W. Jones b Hobbs	88
N. Phillip	c Javed b Daniels	21	lbw b Hobbs	4
S. Turner	lbw b Nash	36	c Daniels b Ontong	31
R. E. East	c Daniels b Ontong	19	(9) c and b Hobbs	4
†D. E. East	c Featherstone b Nash	5	(8) st E. W. Jones b Hobbes	4
J. K. Lever	not out	14	st E. W. Jones b Hobbs	9
D. L. Acfield	c Javed b Ontong	0		
Extras	(b 4, lb 6, w 6, nb 3)	19	(b 16, lb 15, w 4, nb 1)	36
		187	(9 wickets declared)	**411**

GLAMORGAN

A. Jones	b Lever	31	c D. E. East b Lever	0
J. A. Hopkins	c Gooch b Lever	46	c Fletcher b Lever	16
R. C. Ontong	lbw b Turner	5	c R. E. East b Turner	4
Javed Miandad	st D. E. East b Acfield	81	not out	200
N. G. Featherstone	st D. E. East b R. E. East	59	c Fletcher b Lever	0
A. L. Jones	c Gooch b Acfield	15	lbw b Acfield	36
†E. W. Jones	c Fletcher b Acfield	1	st D. E. East b R. E. East	24
*M. A. Nash	c Lever b Acfield	10	(10) c Turner b Lever	1
B. J. Lloyd	lbw b Acfield	4	(8) b Acfield	0
S. A. B. Daniels	c Fletcher b Acfield	2	(11) lbw b Lever	8
R. N. S. Hobbs	not out	6	(9) c Fletcher b Acfield	0
Extras	(b 2, lb 10, w 1, nb 1)	14	(b 12, lb 8, nb 2)	22
		274		**311**

GLAMORGAN	O	M	R	W	O	M	R	W
Nash	19	4	76	3	6	0	33	0
Daniels	11	3	33	3	7	0	45	0
Ontong	13.4	2	37	4	21	3	102	3
Lloyd	6	0	22	0	31	4	110	1
Hobbs					21.5	3	85	5

FALL OF WICKETS

First innings: 20, 29, 29, 69, 93, 132, 152, 167, 174, 187
Second innings: 169, 186, 188, 332, 341, 388, 398, 402, 411

ESSEX	O	M	R	W	O	M	R	W
Lever	19	3	59	2	17	2	62	5
Phillip	15	1	51	0	3	0	12	0
Turner	9	1	30	1	8	0	34	1
R. E. East	28	7	56	1	30	8	97	1
Acfield	24.5	8	64	6	33	7	84	3

FALL OF WICKETS

First innings: 56, 61, 99, 229, 229, 232, 245, 262, 265, 274
Second innings: 0, 7, 44, 44, 155, 224, 227, 270, 291, 311

DEAN JONES
Australia v India, Madras, 18, 19, 20, 21, 22 September 1986

AUSTRALIA

D. C. Boon	c Kapil Dev b Sharma	122	(2) lbw b Maninder	49
G. R. Marsh	c Kapil Dev b Yadav	22	(1) b Shastri	11
D. M. Jones	b Yadav	210	c Azharuddin b Maninder	24
R. J. Bright	c Shastri b Yadav	30		
*A. R. Border	c Gavaskar b Shastri	106	(4) b Maninder	27
G. M. Ritchie	run out	13	(5) c Pandit b Shastri	28
G. R. J. Matthews	c Pandit b Yadav	44	(6) not out	27
S. R. Waugh	not out	12	(7) not out	2
†T. J. Zoehrer				
C. J. McDermott				
B. A. Reid				
Extras	(b 1, lb 7, w 1, nb 6)	15	(lb 1, nb 1)	2
	(7 wkts dec)	**574**	(5 wkts dec)	**170**

INDIA

S. M. Gavaskar	c & b Matthews	8	c Jones b Bright	90
K. Srikkanth	c Ritchie b Matthews	53	c Waugh b Matthews	39
M. B. Amarnath	run out	1	c Boon b Matthews	51
M. Azharuddin	c & b Bright	50	c Ritchie b Bright	42
R. J. Shastri	c Zoehrer b Matthews	62	(7) not out	48
C. S. Pandit	c Waugh b Matthews	35	(5) b Matthews	39
*Kapil Dev	c Border b Matthews	119	(6) c Bright b Matthews	1
†K. S. Moré	c Zoehrer b Waugh	4	(9) lbw b Bright	0
Chetan Sharma	c Zoehrer b Reid	30	(8) c McDermott b Bright	23
N. S. Yadav	c Border b Bright	19	b Bright	8
Maninder Singh	not out	0	lbw b Matthews	0
Extras	(b 1, lb 9, nb 6)	16	(b 1, lb 3, nb 2)	6
		397		**347**

INDIA	O	M	R	W	O	M	R	W
Kapil Dev	18	5	52	0	1	0	5	0
Chetan Sharma	16	1	70	1	6	0	19	0
Maninder	39	8	135	0	19	2	60	0
Yadav	49.5	9	142	4	9	0	35	0
Shastri	47	8	161	1	14	2	50	2
Srikkanth	1	0	6	0				

FALL OF WICKETS

First innings: 48, 206, 282, 460, 481, 544, 574.
Second innings: 31, 81, 94, 125, 165.

AUSTRALIA	O	M	R	W	O	M	R	W
McDermott	14	2	59	0	5	0	27	0
Reid	18	4	93	1	10	2	48	0
Matthews	28.2	3	103	5	39.5	7	146	5
Bright	23	3	88	2	25	3	94	5
Waugh	11	2	44	1	4	1	16	0
Border					3	0	12	0

FALL OF WICKETS

First innings: 62, 65, 65, 142, 206, 220, 245, 330, 387.
Second innings: 55, 158, 204, 251, 253, 291, 331, 334, 344.

---

* Captain   † Wicket-keeper

Stan McCabe
Australia v England, Sydney 2, 3, 5, 6, 7 December 1932

AUSTRALIA

*W. M. Woodfall	c Ames b Voce	7		b Larwood	0
W. H. Ponsford	b Larwood	32		b Voce	2
J. H. W. Fingleton	c Allen b Larwood	26		c Voce b Larwood	40
A. F. Kippax	lbw b Larwood	8	(6)	b Larwood	19
S. J. McCabe	not out	187	(4)	lbw b Hammond	32
V. Y. Richardson	c Hammond b Voce	49	(5)	c Voce b Hammond	0
†W. A. S. Oldfield	c Ames b Larwood	4		c Leyland b Larwood	1
C. V. Grimmett	c Ames b Voce	19		c Allen b Larwood	5
L. E. Nagel	b Larwood	0		not out	21
W. J. O'Reilly	b Voce	4	(11)	b Voce	7
T. W. Wall	c Allen b Hammond	4	(10)	c Ames b Allen	20
Extras	(b 12, lb 4, nb 4)	20		(b 12, lb 2, w 1, nb 2)	17
		360			**164**

ENGLAND

	O	M	R	W	O	M	R	W
Larwood	31	5	96	5	18	4	28	5
Voce	29	4	110	4	17.3	5	54	2
Allen	15	1	65	0	9	5	13	1
Hammond	14.2	0	34	1	15	6	37	2
Verity	13	4	35	0	4	1	15	0

FALL OF WICKETS
First innings: 22, 65, 82, 87, 216, 231, 299, 300, 305, 360
Second innings: 2, 10, 61, 61, 100, 104, 105, 113, 151, 164

ENGLAND

H. Sutcliffe	lbw b Wall	194		not out	1
R. E. S. Wyatt	lbw b Grimmett	38		not out	0
W. R. Hammond	c Grimmett b Nagel	112			
Nawab of Pataudi, sr	b Nagel	102			
M. Leyland	c Oldfield b Wall	0			
*D. R. Jardine	c Oldfield b McCabe	27			
H. Verity	lbw b Wall	2			
G. O. B. Allen	c and b O'Reilly	19			
†L. E. G. Ames	c McCabe b O'Reilly	0			
H. Larwood	lbw b O'Reilly	0			
W. Voce	not out	0			
Extras	(b 7, lb 17, nb 6)	30			
		524		(0 wickets)	**1**

AUSTRALIA

	O	M	R	W
Wall	38	4	104	3
Nagel	43.4	9	110	2
O'Reilly	67	32	117	3
Grimmett	64	22	118	1
McCabe	15	2	42	1
Kippax	2	1	3	0

FALL OF WICKETS
First innings: 112, 300, 423, 423, 470, 479, 519, 522, 522, 524

Nawab of Pataudi
India v England, Headingley, 8, 9, 10, 12, 13 June 1967

ENGLAND

J. H. Edrich	c Engineer b Surti	1		c Wadekar b Chandrasekhar	22
G. Boycott	not out	246			
K. F. Barrington	run out	93	(2)	c Engineer b Chandrasekhar	46
T. W. Graveney	c sub b Chandrasekhar	59	(3)	b Chandrasekhar	14
B. L. D'Oliveira	c sub b Chandrasekhar	109	(4)	not out	24
*D. B. Close	not out	22			
†J. T. Murray			(5)	c sub b Prasanna	4
R. Illingworth			(6)	not out	12
K. Higgs					
J. A. Snow					
R. N. S. Hobbs					
Extras	(b 8, lb 12)	20		(b 3, lb 1)	4
	(4 wickets declared)	**550**		(4 wickets)	**126**

INDIA

	O	M	R	W	O	M	R	W
Guha	43	10	105	0	5	0	10	0
Surti	11	2	25	1				
Chandrasekhar	45	9	121	2	19	8	50	3
Bedi	15	8	32	0				
Prasanna	59	8	187	0	21.3	5	54	1
Pataudi	4	1	13	0				
Wadekar	1	0	9	0	2	0	8	0
Hanument Singh	3	0	27	0				
Saxena	2	0	11	0				

FALL OF WICKETS
First innings: 7, 146, 253, 505
Second innings: 58, 78, 87, 92

INDIA

†F. M. Engineer	c and b Illingworth	42		c and b Close	87
R. C. Saxena	b D'Oliveira	9	(7)	b Snow	16
A. L. Wadekar	run out	0		c Close b Illingworth	91
C. G. Borde	b Snow	8		b Illingworth	33
Hanumant Singh	c D'Oliveira b Illingworth	9		c D'Oliveira b Illingworth	73
*Nawab of Pataudi, jr	c Barrington b Hobbs	64		b Illingworth	148
E. A. S. Prasanna	c Murray b Illingworth	0	(8)	lbw b Close	19
S. Guha	b Snow	4	(9)	b Higgs	1
R. F. Surti	c and b Hobbs	22	(2)	c Murray b Snow	5
B. S. Bedi	lbw b Hobbs	0		c Snow b Hobbs	14
B. S. Chandrasekhar	not out	0		not out	0
Extras	(lb 6)	6		(b 10, lb 13)	23
		164			**510**

ENGLAND

	O	M	R	W	O	M	R	W
Snow	17	7	34	2	41	11	108	2
Higgs	14	8	19	0	24	3	71	1
D'Oliveira	9	4	29	1	11	5	22	0
Hobbs	22.2	9	45	3	45.2	13	100	1
Illingworth	22	11	31	3	58	26	100	4
Close	3	3	0	0	21	5	48	2
Barrington					9	1	38	0

FALL OF WICKETS
First innings: 39, 40. 59, 59, 81, 81, 92, 151, 151, 164
Second innings: 5, 173, 217, 228, 362, 388, 448, 469, 506, 510

Hanif Mohammad, who played
the longest innings in Tests.

EDDIE PAYNTER
England v Australia, Brisbane, 10, 11, 13, 14, 15, 16 February 1933

AUSTRALIA

Batsman	First innings		Second innings	
V. Y. Richardson	st Ames b Hammond	83	c Jardine v Verity	32
*W. M. Woodfull	b Mitchell	67	c Hammond b Mitchell	19
D. G. Bradman	b Larwood	76	c Mitchell b Larwood	24
S. J. McCabe	c Jardine b Allen	20	(5) b Verity	22
W. H. Ponsford	b Larwood	19	(4) c Larwood b Allen	0
L. S. Darling	c Ames b Allen	17	run out	39
E. H. Bromley	c Verity b Larwood	26	c Hammond b Allen	7
†H. S. B. Love	lbw b Mitchell	5	lbw b Larwood	3
T. W. Wall	not out	6	c Jardine b Allen	2
W. J. O'Reilly	c Hammond b Larwood	6	b Larwood	4
H. Ironmonger	st Ames b Hammond	8	not out	0
Extras	(b 5, lb 1, nb 1)	7	(b 13, lb 9, nb 1)	23
		340		**175**

ENGLAND

Batsman	First innings		Second innings	
*D. R. Jardine	c Love b O'Reilly	46	lbw b Ironmonger	24
H. Sutcliffe	lbw b O'Reilly	86	c Darling b Wall	2
W. R. Hammond	b McCabe	20	(4) c Bromley b Ironmonger	14
R. E. S. Wyatt	c Love b Ironmonger	12		
M. Leyland	c Bradman b O'Reilly	12	(3) c McCabe b O'Reilly	86
†L. E. G. Ames	c Darling b Ironmonger	17	(5) not out	14
G. O. B. Allen	c Love b Wall	13		
E. Paynter	c Richardson b Ironmonger	83	(6) not out	14
H. Larwood	b McCabe	23		
H. Verity	not out	23		
T. B. Mitchell	lbw b O'Reilly	0		
Extras	(b 6, lb 12, nb 3)	21	(b 2, lb 4, nb 2)	8
		356		**162**

ENGLAND	O	M	R	W	O	M	R	W
Larwood	31	7	101	4	17.3	3	49	3
Allen	24	4	83	2	17	3	44	3
Hammond	23	5	61	2	10	4	18	0
Mitchell	16	5	49	2	5	0	11	1
Verity	27	12	39	0	19	6	30	2

FALL OF WICKETS
First innings: 133, 200, 233, 264, 267, 292, 315, 317, 329, 340
Second innings: 46, 79, 81, 91, 136, 163, 169, 169, 171, 175

AUSTRALIA	O	M	R	W	O	M	R	W
Wall	33	6	66	1	7	1	17	1
O'Reilly	67.4	27	120	4	30	11	65	1
Ironmonger	43	19	69	3	35	13	47	2
McCabe	23	7	40	2	7.4	2	25	0
Bromley	10	4	19	0				
Bradman	7	1	17	0				
Darling	2	0	4	0				

FALL OF WICKETS
First innings: 114, 157, 165, 188, 198, 216, 225, 264, 356, 356
Second innings: 5, 78, 118, 138

BERT SUTCLIFFE
New Zealand v South Africa, Johannesburg, 24, 26, 28, 29 December 1953

SOUTH AFRICA

Batsman	First innings		Second innings	
D. J. McGlew	c Reid b MacGibbon	13	b MacGibbon	8
A. R. A. Murray	c Chapple b Blair	7	(9) c Blair b Overton	13
W. R. Endean	c Sutcliffe b Reid	93	c sub b Reid	1
K. J. Funston	lbw b Overton	0	c Overton b MacGibbon	11
R. A. McLean	c Blair b Overton	27	(7) lbw b Reid	36
C. B. van Ryneveld	b Blair	65	(8) c Reid b MacGibbon	17
*J. E. Cheetham	c Mooney b MacGibbon	20	(6) c Sutcliffe b Reid	1
H. J. Tayfield	not out	20	(5) b Reid	34
†J. H. B. Waite	c Mooney b MacGibbon	0	(2) c Reid b MacGibbon	5
D. E. J. Ironside	b Reid	13	not out	11
N. A. T. Adcock	run out	0	c Poore b Overton	6
Extras	(b 3, lb 2, nb 8)	13	(lb 3, nb 2)	5
		271		**148**

NEW ZEALAND	O	M	R	W	O	M	R	W
Blair	17	4	50	2	5	0	14	0
Reid	18	3	63	2	16	5	34	4
Overton	20	4	68	2	12.1	1	33	2
MacGibbon	22	5	61	3	20	2	62	4
Rabone	3	0	16	0				

FALL OF WICKETS
First innings: 13, 37, 43, 100, 168, 226, 244, 244, 271, 271
Second innings: 11, 13, 24, 37, 44, 67, 112, 122, 138, 148

NEW ZEALAND

Batsman	First innings		Second innings	
*G. O. Rabone	c Endean b Ironside	1	c Van Ryneveld b Adcock	22
M. E. Chapple	b Adcock	8	c Waite b Ironside	22
M. B. Poore	b Adcock	15	b Adcock	1
B. Sutcliffe	not out	80	c Endean b Murray	10
J. R. Reid	c Endean b Adcock	3	(6) c Funston b Ironside	1
L. S. M. Miller	b Ironside	14	(7) c Waite b Adcock	0
J. E. F. Beck	c Waite b Murray	16	(8) c Endean b Ironside	7
†F. L. H. Mooney	b Ironside	35	(5) c Funston b Adcock	10
A. R. MacGibbon	c Endean b Ironside	0	not out	11
G. W. F. Overton	c Murray b Ironside	0	(11) run out	2
R. W. Blair	st Waite b Tayfield	6	(10) b Adcock	4
Extras	(b 3, lb 4, nb 2)	9	(b 3, lb 5, nb 2)	10
		187		**100**

SOUTH AFRICA	O	M	R	W	O	M	R	W
Adcock	14	2	44	3	19	4	43	5
Ironside	19	4	51	5	20.5	10	37	3
Murray	12	3	30	1	8	3	10	1
Tayfield	8.2	2	53	1				

FALL OF WICKETS
First innings: 5, 9, 23, 35, 57, 81, 138, 146, 154, 187
Second innings: 35, 38, 58, 75, 75, 76, 76, 84, 89, 100

* Captain   † Wicket-keeper

JACK HOBBS
England v Australia, The Oval, 14, 16, 17, 18 August 1926

ENGLAND

J. B. Hobbs	b Mailey	37	b Gregory	100
H. Sutcliffe	b Mailey	76	b Mailey	161
F. E. Woolley	b Mailey	18	lbw b Richardson	27
E. H. Hendren	b Gregory	8	c Oldfield b Grimmett	15
*A. P. F. Chapman	st Oldfield b Mailey	49	b Richardson	19
G. T. S. Stevens	c Andrews b Mailey	17	c Mailey b Grimmett	22
W. Rhodes	c Oldfield b Mailey	28	lbw b Grimmett	14
G. Geary	run out	9	c Oldfield b Gregory	1
M. W. Tate	b Grimmett	23	not out	33
H. Larwood	c Andrews b Grimmett	0	b Mailey	5
†H. Strudwick	not out	4	c Andrews b Mailey	2
Extras	(b 6, lb 5)	11	(b 19, lb 18)	37
		280		**436**

AUSTRALIA

W. M. Woodfull	b Rhodes	35		c Geary b Larwood	0
W. Bardsley	c Strudwick b Larwood	2	(4)	c Woolley b Rhodes	21
C. G. Macartney	b Stevens	25		c Geary b Larwood	16
W. H. Ponsford	run out	2	(2)	c Larwood b Rhodes	12
T. J. E. Andrews	b Larwood	3	(6)	Tate b Larwood	15
*R. L. Collins	c Stevens b Larwood	61	(5)	c Woolley b Rhodes	4
A. J. Richardson	c Geary b Rhodes	16	(8)	b Rhodes	4
J. M. Gregory	c Stevens b Tate	73	(7)	c Sutcliffe b Tate	9
†W. A. S. Oldfield	not out	33		b Stevens	23
C. V. Grimmett	b Tate	35		not out	8
A. M. Mailey	c Strudwick b Tate	0		b Geary	6
Extras	(b 5, lb 12)	17		(lb 7)	7
		302			**125**

AUSTRALIA	O	M	R	W	O	M	R	W
Gregory	15	4	31	1	18	1	58	2
Grimmett	33	12	74	2	55	17	108	3
Mailey	33.5	3	138	6	42.5	6	128	3
Macartney	7	4	16	0	26	16	24	0
Richardson	7	2	10	0	41	21	81	2

FALL OF WICKETS

First innings: 53, 91, 108, 189, 213, 214, 231, 266, 266, 280
Second innings: 172, 220, 277, 316, 373, 375, 382, 425, 430, 436

ENGLAND	O	M	R	W	O	M	R	W
Tate	37.1	17	40	3	9	4	12	1
Larwood	34	11	82	3	14	3	34	3
Geary	27	8	43	0	6.3	2	15	1
Stevens	29	3	85	1	3	1	13	1
Rhodes	25	15	35	2	20	9	44	4

FALL OF WICKETS

First innings: 9, 44, 51, 59, 90, 122, 229, 231, 298, 302
Second innings: 1, 31, 31, 35, 63, 83, 83, 87, 114, 125

GILBERT JESSOP
England v Australia, The Oval, 11, 12, 13 August 1902

AUSTRALIA

V. T. Trumper	b Hirst	42		run out	2
R. A. Duff	c Lilley b Hirst	23		b Lockwood	6
C. Hill	b Hirst	11		c MacLaren b Hirst	34
*J. Darling	c Lilley b Hirst	3		c MacLaren b Lockwood	15
M. A. Noble	c and b Jackson	52		b Braund	13
S. E. Gregory	b Hirst	23		b Braund	9
W. W. Armstrong	b Jackson	17		b Lockwood	21
A. J. Y. Hopkins	c MacLaren b Lockwood	40		c Lilley b Lockwood	3
H. Trumble	not out	64	(10)	not out	7
†J. J. Kelly	c Rhodes b Braund	39	(11)	lbw b Lockwood	0
J. V. Saunders	lbw b Braund	0	(9)	c Tyldesley b Rhodes	2
Extras	(b 5, lb 3, nb 2)	10		(b 7, lb 2)	9
		324			**121**

ENGLAND

*A. C. MacLaren	c Armstrong b Trumble	10	b Saunders	2
L. C. H. Palairet	b Trumble	20	b Saunders	6
J. T. Tyldesley	b Trumble	33	b Saunders	0
T. W. Hayward	b Trumble	0	c Kelly b Saunders	7
Hon. F. S. Jackson	c Armstrong b Saunders	2	c and b Trumble	49
L. C. Braund	c Hill b Trumble	22	c Kelly b Trumble	2
G. L. Jessop	b Trumble	13	c Noble b Armstrong	104
G. H. Hirst	c and b Trumble	43	not out	58
W. H. Lockwood	c Noble b Saunders	25	lbw b Trumble	2
†A. F. A. Lilley	c Trumper b Trumble	0	c Darling b Trumble	16
W. Rhodes	not out	0	not out	6
Extras	(b 13, LB 2)	15	(b 5, lb 6)	11
		183	(9 wickets)	**263**

ENGLAND	O	M	R	W	O	M	R	W
Lockwood	24	2	85	1	20	6	45	5
Rhodes	28	9	46	0	22	7	38	1
Hirst	29	5	77	5	5	1	7	1
Braund	16.5	5	29	2	9	1	15	2
Jackson	20	4	66	2	4	3	7	0
Jessop	6	2	11	0				

FALL OF WICKETS

First innings: 47, 63, 69, 82, 126, 174, 175, 256, 324, 324
Second innings: 6, 9, 31, 71, 75, 91, 99, 114, 115, 121

AUSTRALIA	O	M	R	W	O	M	R	W
Trumble	31	13	65	8	33.5	4	108	4
Saunders	23	7	79	2	24	3	105	4
Noble	7	3	24	0	5	0	11	0
Armstrong					4	0	28	1

FALL OF WICKETS

First innings: 31, 36, 62, 67, 67, 83, 137, 179, 183, 183
Second innings: 5, 5, 10, 31, 48, 157, 182, 214, 248

---

* Captain   † Wicket-keeper

ARTHUR SHREWSBURY
England v Australia, Lord's, 19, 20, 21 July 1886

ENGLAND

W. G. Grace	c Jarvis b Palmer	18
W. H. Scotton	b Garrett	19
A. Shrewsbury	c Bonnor b Trumble	164
W. W. Read	c Spofforth b Giffen	22
*A. G. Steel	lbw b Spofforth	5
W. Barnes	c Palmer b Garrett	58
R. G. Barlow	c Palmer b Spofforth	12
G. Ulyett	b Spofforth	19
†E. F. S. Tylecote	b Spofforth	0
J. Briggs	c Jones b Trumble	0
G. A. Lohmann	not out	7
Extras	(b 24, lb 4, nb 1)	29
		353

AUSTRALIA	O	M	R	W
Garrett	72	40	77	2
Evans	36	20	37	0
Palmer	38	15	45	1
Spofforth	56	26	73	4
Trumble	14	4	27	2
Giffen	40	18	63	1
Jones	3	1	2	0

FALL OF WICKETS

First innings: 27, 77, 112, 119, 280, 303, 333, 333, 340, 353

AUSTRALIA

S. P. Jones	c Grace b Briggs	25	(4) b Briggs	17
*H. J. H. Scott	lbw b Briggs	30	(5) b Briggs	2
G. Giffen	b Steel	3	(6) b Barlow	1
†A. H. Jarvis	b Briggs	3	(7) not out	13
G. J. Bonnor	c Grace b Steel	0	(8) b Briggs	3
J. W. Trumble	c Tylecote b Briggs	0	(3) c Tylecote b Barnes	20
G. E. Palmer	c Shrewsbury b Barnes	20	(1) c Lohmann b Barlow	48
J. M. Blackham	b Briggs	23	(9) b Briggs	5
T. W. Garrett	not out	7	(2) b Briggs	4
F. R. Spofforth	b Barnes	5	(11) c and b Briggs	0
E. Evans	c Ulyett b Barnes	0	(10) run out	0
Extras	(b 4, lb 1)	5	(b 13)	13
		121		**126**

ENGLAND	O	M	R	W	O	M	R	W
Barnes	14.3	7	25	3	10	5	18	1
Lohmann	7	3	21	0	14	9	11	0
Briggs	34	22	29	5	38.1	17	45	6
Steel	21	8	34	2	16	9	14	0
Barlow	6	3	7	0	25	20	12	2
Ulyett					8	3	13	0

FALL OF WICKETS

First innings: 45, 52, 59, 60, 62, 67, 99, 109, 121, 121
Second innings: 6, 56, 91, 95, 98, 105, 120, 126, 126, 126

GARY SOBERS
West Indies v England, 8, 9, 10, 12, 13, 14 February 1968

ENGLAND

G. Boycott	b Hall	17	b Sobers	0
J. H. Edrich	c Kanhai b Sobers	96	b Hall	6
*M. C. Cowdrey	c Murray b Gibbs	101	lbw b Sobers	0
K. F. Barrington	c and b Holford	63	lbw b Griffith	13
T. W. Graveney	b Hall	30	c Griffith b Gibbs	21
†J. M. Parks	c Sobers b Holford	3	lbw b Gibbs	3
B. L. D'Oliveira	st Murray b Holford	0	not out	13
F. J. Titmus	lbw b Hall	19	c Camacho b Gibbs	4
D. J. Brown	c Murray b Hall	14	b Sobers	0
J. A. Snow	b Griffiths	10		
I. J. Jones	not out	0		
Extras	(b 12, lb 7, nb 4)	23	(b 8)	8
		376	(8 wickets)	**68**

WEST INDIES	O	M	R	W	O	M	R	W
Hall	27	5	63	4	3	2	3	1
Griffith	31.2	7	72	1	5	2	13	1
Sobers	31	11	56	1	16.5	7	33	3
Gibbs	47	18	91	1	14	11	11	3
Holford	33	10	71	3				

FALL OF WICKETS

First innings: 49, 178, 279, 310, 318, 318, 351, 352, 376, 376
Second innings: 0, 0, 19, 19, 38, 51, 61, 68

WEST INDIES

G. S. Camacho	b Snow	5	b D'Oliveira	25
†D. L. Murray	c D'Oliveira b Brown	0	(8) lbw b Brown	14
R. B. Kanhai	c Graveney b Snow	26	c Edrich b Jones	36
S. M. Nurse	b Jones	22	(2) b Snow	73
C. H. Lloyd	not out	34	b Brown	7
*G. St. A. Sobers	lbw b Snow	0	not out	113
B. F. Butcher	c Parks b Snow	21	(4) c Parks b D'Oliveira	25
D. A. J. Holford	c Parks b Snow	6	(7) lbw b Titmus	35
C. C. Griffith	c D'Oliveira b Snow	8	lbw b Jones	14
W. W. Hall	b Snow	0	c Parks b Jones	0
L. R. Gibbs	c Parks b Jones	0	not out	1
Extras	(b 12, lb 5, w 1, nb 3)	21	(b 33, lb 10, nb 5)	48
		143	(9 wickets declared)	**391**

ENGLAND	O	M	R	W	O	M	R	W
Brown	13	1	34	1	33	9	65	2
Snow	21	7	49	7	27	4	91	1
Jones	14.1	4	39	2	30	4	90	3
D'Oliveira					32	12	51	2
Titmus					7	2	32	1
Barrington					6	1	14	0

FALL OF WICKETS

First innings: 5, 5, 51, 80, 80, 120, 126, 142, 142, 143
Second innings: 102, 122, 164, 174, 204, 314, 351, 388, 388

Herbert Sutcliffe
England v Australia, Melbourne, 29, 31 December, 1, 2, 3, 4, 5 January 1928–29

AUSTRALIA

W. M. Woodfall	c Jardine b Tate	7	c Duckworth b Tate		107
V. Y. Richardson	c Duckworth b Larwood	3	b Larwood		5
H. S. T. L. Hendry	c Jardine b Larwood	23	st Duckworth b White		12
A. F. Kippax	c Jardine b Larwood	100	b Tate		41
*J. Ryder	c Hendren b Tate	112	b Geary		5
D. G. Bradman	b Hammond	79	c Duckworth b Geary		112
†W. A. S. Oldfield	b Geary	3	b White		7
E. L. A'Beckett	c Duckworth b White	41	b White		6
R. K. Oxenham	b Geary	15	b White		39
C. V. Grimmett	c Duckworth b Geary	5	not out		4
D. D. Blakie	not out	2	b White		0
Extras	(b 4, lb 3)	7	(b 6, lb 7)		13
		397			**351**

ENGLAND

J. B. Hobbs	c Oldfield b A'Beckett	20	lbw b Blackie		49
H. Sutcliffe	b Blackie	58	lbw b Grimmett		135
W. R. Hammond	c A'Beckett b Blackie	200	(4) run out		32
*A. P. F. Chapman	b Blackie	24	(6) c Woodfall b Ryder		5
E. H. Hendren	c A'Beckett b Hendry	19	b Oxenham		45
D. R. Jardine	c and b Blackie	62	(3) b Grimmett		33
H. Larwood	c and b Blackie	0			
G. Geary	lbw b Grimmett	1	not out		4
M. W. Tate	c Kippax b Grimmett	21	(7) run out		0
†G. Duckworth	b Blackie	3	(9) not out		0
J. C. White	not out	8			
Extras	(b 1)	1	(b 15, lb 14)		29
		417	(7 wickets)		**332**

ENGLAND

	O	M	R	W	O	M	R	W
Larwood	37	3	127	3	16	3	37	1
Tate	46	17	87	2	47	15	70	2
Geary	31.5	4	83	3	30	4	94	2
Hammond	8	4	19	1	16	6	30	0
White	57	30	64	1	56.5	20	107	5
Jardine	1	0	10	0				

FALL OF WICKETS

First innings: 5, 15, 57, 218, 282, 287, 373, 383, 394, 397
Second innings: 7, 60. 138. 143. 201, 226, 252, 345, 351, 351

AUSTRALIA

	O	M	R	W	O	M	R	W
A'Beckett	37	7	92	1	22	5	39	0
Hendry	20	8	35	1	23	5	33	0
Grimmett	55	14	114	2	42	12	96	2
Oxenham	35	11	67	0	28	10	44	1
Blackie	44	13	94	6	39	11	75	1
Ryder	4	0	14	0	5.5	1	16	1

FALL OF WICKETS

First innings: 28, 161, 201, 238, 364, 364, 381, 385, 391, 417
Second innings: 105, 199, 257, 318, 326, 328, 328

Victor Trumper
Australia v England, Old Trafford, 24, 25, 26 July 1902

AUSTRALIA

V. T. Trumper	c Lilly b Rhodes	104	c Braund b Lockwood		4
R. A. Duff	c Lilley b Lockwood	54	b Lockwood		3
C. Hill	c Rhodes b Lockwood	65	b Lockwood		0
M. A. Noble	c and b Rhodes	2	(6) c Lilley b Lockwood		4
S. F. Gregory	c Lilley b Rhodes	3	lbw b Tate		24
*J. Darling	c MacLaren b Rhodes	51	(4) c Palairet b Rhodes		37
A. J. Y. Hopkins	c Palairet b Lockwood	0	c Tate b Lockwood		2
W. W. Armstrong	b Lockwood	5	b Rhodes		3
†J. J. Kelly	not out	4	not out		2
H. Trumble	c Tate b Lockwood	0	lbw b Tate		4
J. V. Saunders	b Lockwood	3	c Tyldesley b Rhodes		0
Extras	(b 5, lb 2, w 1)	8	(b 1, lb 1, nb 1)		3
		299			**86**

ENGLAND

L. C. H. Palairet	c Noble b Saunders	6	b Saunders		17
R. Abel	c Armstrong b Saunders	6	(5) b Trumble		21
J. T. Tyldesley	c Hopkins b Saunders	22	c Armstrong b Saunders		16
*A. C. MacLaren	b Trumble	1	(2) c Duff b Trumble		35
K. S. Ranjitsinhji	lbw b Trumble	2	(4) lbw b Trumble		4
Hon F. S. Jackson	c Duff b Trumble	128	c Gregory b Saunders		7
L. C. Braund	b Noble	65	st Kelly b Trumble		3
†A. F. A. Lilley	b Noble	7	c Hill b Trumble		4
W. H. Lockwood	not out	7	b Trumble		0
W. Rhodes	c and b Trumble	5	not out		4
F. W. Tate	not out	5	b Saunders		4
Extras	(b 6, lb 2)	8	(b 5)		5
		262			**120**

ENGLAND

	O	M	R	W	O	M	R	W
Rhodes	25	3	104	4	14.4	5	26	3
Jackson	11	0	58	0				
Tate	11	1	44	0	5	3	7	2
Braund	9	0	37	0	11	3	22	0
Lockwood	20.1	5	48	6	17	5	28	5

FALL OF WICKETS

First innings: 135, 175, 179, 183, 256, 256, 288, 292, 292, 299
Second innings: 7, 9, 10, 64, 74, 76, 77, 79, 85, 86

AUSTRALIA

	O	M	R	W	O	M	R	W
Trumble	43	16	75	4	25	9	53	6
Saunders	34	5	104	3	19.4	4	52	4
Noble	24	8	47	2	5	3	10	0
Trumper	6	4	6	0				
Armstrong	5	2	19	0				
Hopkins	2	0	3	0				

FALL OF WICKETS

First innings: 12, 13, 14, 30, 44, 185, 203, 214, 235, 262
Second innings: 44, 68, 72, 92, 97, 107, 109, 109, 116, 120

---

* Captain † Wicket-keeper

ACKNOWLEDGEMENTS

The publishers would like to thank the following for providing photographs:

All Sport 2, 7, 9, 15, 17T, 23, 24, 25, 26, 27, 28, 37, 38, 39, 44, 46, 54, 56, 58T, 88, 90, 92, 93, 95, 96, 111, 112, 113L & R, 120, 136

Associated Press 18, 35, 61, 91, 138

Patrick Eagar 10–11, 11, 12, 16, 19, 20, 21T & B, 22, 29, 30, 31, 32, 33, 34L & R, 42, 43, 49, 50, 51, 59, 60, 65, 66, 86, 87, 94, 97, 100, 101, 104, 106, 107, 127, 137

Essex County Newspapers 116

John Frost Historical Newspaper Service 129

Hulton-Deutsch Collection 17B, 57, 62, 63, 74, 80, 83, 85, 102, 103, 122, 123, 128, 130T

Roger Mann 13, 14, 36, 40, 53, 68, 69, 71, 72, 73, 75, 76, 78, 79, 81, 84, 98, 108, 109, 110, 114, 117, 118, 121T & B, 125, 126, 130B, 134, 135, 139, 140T & B, 142, 143, 165, 171

Mansell Collection 52, 67, 131, 133, 157

Mirror Australian Telegraph Publications 41, 45, 47, 58B

Graham Morris 55

Nottinghamshire County Cricket Club 77, 132R, 141, 147

S&G Press Agency Limited 99, 115

Bob Thomas Sports Photograpy 105

Gerry Wright 82, 132L